'An interesting, well-written and colourful history of the variety form, which will appeal to students, researchers and general readers. It is chockfull of material which is well organised and referenced – the content is terrific.' Jason Price, Lecturer in Drama and Performance Studies, University of Sussex.

Variety theatre dominated British cultural life during the first half of the twentieth century. Vast, ornate theatres entertained audiences twice nightly with an array of acts such as singers, comics, dancers, ventriloquists, magicians, strongwomen, performing animals and nude acts. Variety was the birthplace of both stand-up comedy and the live rock show, and was an important influence on everything from the Futurist movement to Joan Littlewood's Theatre Workshop, to the punk singer Ian Dury.

Oliver Double provides a detailed history of variety theatre examining the techniques used by performers and the key ways in which they appealed to audiences. This book also draws on a series of new, unpublished interviews with variety veterans including Vera Lynn, the Beverley Sisters and Roy Hudd.

OLIVER DOUBLE is Senior Lecturer in Drama at the University of Kent. Once a stand-up comedian himself, his teaching in this area is highly acclaimed and has received national media attention. He is the author of *Getting the Joke: The Inner Workings of Stand-Up Comedy* (2005) and *Stand Up! On Being a Comedian* (1997).

D0995691

Also by Oliver Double:

Stand Up! On Being a Comedian
Getting the Joke: The Inner Workings of Stand-Up Comedy

Britain Had Talent

A History of Variety Theatre

OLIVER DOUBLE

First published 2012 by
PALGRAVE MACMILLAN

Palgrave Macmillan in the UK is an imprint of Macmillan Publishers Limited,
registered in England, company number 785998, of Houndmills, Basingstoke,
Hampshire RG21 6XS.

Palgrave Macmillan in the US is a division of St Martin's Press LLC,
175 Fifth Avenue, New York, NY 10010.

Palgrave Macmillan is the global academic imprint of the above companies
and has companies and representatives throughout the world.

Palgrave® and Macmillan® are registered trademarks in the United States,
the United Kingdom, Europe and other countries

ISBN: 978–0–230–28459–3 hardback
ISBN: 978–0–230–28460–9 paperback

This book is printed on paper suitable for recycling and made from fully
managed and sustained forest sources. Logging, pulping and manufacturing
processes are expected to conform to the environmental regulations of the
country of origin.

A catalogue record for this book is available from the British Library.

A catalog record for this book is available from the Library of Congress.

10 9 8 7 6 5 4 3 2 1
21 20 19 18 17 16 15 14 13 12

Printed in China

For Joan Rhodes

Contents

List of Illustrations

Acknowledgements

The author and publishers wish to thank the following for permission to reproduce copyright material:

> Babs, Joy and Teddie Beverley for an extract from the Beverley Sisters' song 'We Have to Be So Careful', originally issued as a 78rpm single, Columbia (DB3212), 1953.

Every effort has been made to trace rights holders, but if any have been inadvertently overlooked the publishers would be pleased to make the necessary arrangements at the first opportunity.

I'd also like to thank everybody who helped me with this book in any way, shape or form, starting with those veterans of variety and others with some connection to it who were kind enough to let me interview them: Morris Aza; Teddie Beverley; Wyn Calvin; Barry Cryer; Michael Grade; Roy Hudd; Ken Joy; Warren Lakin; Vera Lynn; Chas McDevitt; Roland Muldoon; Peter Prentice; Joan Rhodes; Ronnie Ronalde; Jack Seaton; Arthur Smith; and Don Smoothey. Additional thanks to Chas McDevitt and Roy Hudd – as well as Michael Harradine and Ian Baird – for helping me to set up some of these interviews.

Thanks are also due to the British Music Hall Society, and in particular their excellent historian Max Tyler, who took me to see their magnificent archive, his own amazing collection of music hall stuff, and lent me some of it. I also want to thank Rachel Hann for sending me the Edward Gordon Craig article from *The Mask*; Ken Pickering for helping me with publication advice; and Brian Wren for showing me around the Hackney Empire. Max Tyler, Richard Anthony Baker, Nick Charlesworth, Chris Woodward, Andrew Gatherer, Gerry Mawdsley (president of the George Formby Society), David Bret, and John at JSP Records all deserve thanks for helpful advice about the copyright status of various variety-related materials.

I'm grateful to the University of Kent for giving me a term of study leave which allowed me to get a lot of the work done – and indeed to any student who has worked with me on one of the variety projects for the popular performance module. Thanks also to everybody at

Palgrave Macmillan, particularly Jenni Burnell, my editor, who has been helpful, encouraging and downright cheery throughout.

Finally, a massive thank you to my wife Jacqui, as ever, who has offered interest and moral support, as well as agreeing to read through the whole bloody thing, looking for mistakes and offering advice on prose style and all that. And a final, final thank you to my sons Joe and Tom for taking an interest in some of this stuff and generally being nice to have around the house.

Introduction

I first became interested in variety because I used to be a stand-up comedian, and I have long been fascinated by types of performance which lack a narrative or obvious characters, where performers ostensibly appear onstage as 'themselves', and address the audience directly. I have written about variety before in my books on stand-up, and initially I was ambivalent towards it, put off by the old-fashioned prejudices it sometimes contained, and the fact that some of it is so difficult to understand after all these decades. Listening to theatre recordings of Max Miller from the late 1930s can be perplexing. Why exactly are the audience exploding into gales of laughter after that apparently innocuous word or sentence?

Researching this book has meant tracking down as much of this kind of material as possible – audio recordings, rare film footage, trade journals, newspaper reviews, biographies, theatre programmes, posters (or 'bills' as they were known in variety) and other ephemera. In the course of going through all of this, any reservations I might have had about variety have melted away, and my excitement about it has grown. I have developed a deep respect for the creativity, skill and sheer hard work of the hundreds or even thousands of performers who plied their trade up and down the country.

Variety theatre was an energetic, important and extremely popular phenomenon that ran through the centre of British cultural life like the lettering in seaside rock. The offspring of the Victorian music halls, variety was one of the most important forms of entertainment of the first half of the twentieth century. It took place in big theatres with names like 'Hippodrome', 'Palace' or 'Empire', putting on shows twice nightly, six nights a week. In its heyday, hundreds of thousands of people would flock to see it, watching shows made up of a string of acts which might include singers, big bands, comics, dancers, ventriloquists, magicians, jugglers, acrobats, paper-tearers, impressionists, quick-change artists, performing animals and nude acts.

It is now fifty years since the last of the variety theatres were starting to disappear, but variety's memory persists in the national consciousness. Stand-up comedy evolved in the variety theatres, and they were also the birthplace of the live rock show in Britain. Variety's influence can be seen in anything from the Futurist movement to Joan Littlewood's Theatre Workshop, from the way television is scheduled to the work of the punk singer Ian Dury.

Yet in spite of all of this, few people have attempted to take variety seriously, or even paid it any attention at all. Books about nineteenth-century music hall are many and varied, and have been published for over a hundred years. Variety, on the other hand, has inspired a mere handful, many of them published by tiny, specialized publishers or only concentrating on one particular aspect of the form. There has been almost no academic writing on variety whatsoever.

My aim in writing this book is to help to fill this gap in the literature by putting something together which I hope is closely researched and analytical enough to be useful in a university context. It should be suitable for academics at all levels – undergraduates, postgraduates, lecturers, researchers and professors. However, it is also aimed at the general reader. I hope it will be enjoyed by variety enthusiasts, amateur theatre historians, people who once saw – or maybe even performed in – variety (in the theatre or on television), or just anyone who has a casual curiosity about the way entertainment works.

Structure of the book

Part One starts by explaining the format of a variety show, and examining how the business was organized. The chapters which follow provide a detailed history of variety – looking at how it evolved out of music hall, how it was saved from a potentially fatal slump in the 1920s, its revival and reinvention in the 1930s, the dominance of imported American stars after the Second World War, and the reasons for its final decline in the 1950s and 1960s.

Part Two analyses how variety worked as performance and entertainment. It looks at what I consider to be the defining features of variety performance – personality, participation, skill and novelty – explaining such issues as how performers presented versions of themselves to the audience, how audiences were manipulated into giving the correct response, and how tricks and stunts were structured to get the maximum laughter and applause.

Part Three shows what happened to variety after the theatres had closed down, what it grew into, and the legacy it left behind in stand-up comedy, pop music and elsewhere.

The most magical aspect of doing the book was that I have been lucky enough to interview a number of veterans of variety and others who were connected to the business in some way. Some were big names (Vera Lynn, Ronnie Ronalde, the Beverley Sisters), others have become well known since those times (Barry Cryer, Roy Hudd, Michael Grade), and still others were successful acts from further down the bill (Ken Joy, Jack Seaton, Peter Prentice of El Granadas & Peter). On a professional level, it was fascinating to be able to ask them about how they approached their job, the nuts and bolts of performance, and to share my emerging theories with them to see what they could add to them. On a personal level, it was delightful to be able to talk to such a fascinating bunch of people, some of them in their nineties.

In particular, I will never forget the afternoon I spent in the basement flat of the former variety strongwoman Joan Rhodes, who described her age as 'somewhere between 80 and death'. She was actually 89 years old at the time, and sadly would die shortly afterwards. She was extremely frail, but still had something of her former glamour in her well-spoken, almost haughty manner. After a fascinating conversation – in the course of which she showed me one of the 6-inch nails she bent onstage – I sensed she was getting tired and even thought my questions might be grating a bit. However, I had misread her. She looked me in the eye and calmly said, 'I like you – do you play Scrabble?' I admitted that I did, and agreed to stay and play a game with her, which she won, as the light of the spring afternoon faded. Before I left, she said, 'You may kiss me' – I did so, very formally, on the cheek – and she shook my hand. In spite of her age and frailness, there was still a touch of steel in her grip.

Part One

History of Variety Performance

1

Britain's Got Talent

It's Sunday 21 June 2009, and I'm going to Wembley Arena with my wife and two sons for the 1.30 p.m. performance of the *Britain's Got Talent* live show. As we leave the station, we quickly become aware that we're not the only ones who are making our way there through the hot summer air. The crowds are positively thronging as we reach the concourse in front of the venue, which is filled with stalls selling unofficial merchandise – scarves emblazoned with the names of the acts, little Unions Jacks, even light-up bunny ears. Inside the venue, the official merchandising stalls will sell you a more tasteful array of mugs, posters, keyrings, bags, T-shirts and programmes. We take our seats and listen to a non-stop barrage of high-energy pop hits. Finally the house music stops, the lighting changes, and instantly the air is rent by ear-splitting screams of excitement from all around us.

We are perplexed and amused by the hysteria the rest of the audience is unashamedly unleashing, but perhaps we shouldn't be. Since it started broadcasting in June 2007, *Britain's Got Talent* has become one of ITV1's most popular programmes, regularly attracting around half of the total peak-time audience.[1] The 2009 final of this top-rated talent show attracted an extraordinary 19.2 million viewers, and in the course of the series the public cast over 4 million votes.[2] Since 2008, the programme has produced annual spin-off live tours, and the performance we are at is just one of a run of 26 shows at big theatres and arenas around the UK.

While it is first and foremost a talent show, *Britain's Got Talent* is essentially variety entertainment. Piers Morgan, a member of the show's judging panel, has described it as 'the ultimate variety show', and newspaper critics have called it 'the closest thing we've got to a mainstream variety show' and admitted, 'We're watching variety and we love it.'[3] In addition to a large cash sum, the prize for winning the series is to appear at the Royal Variety Performance.

Having said this, there's plenty in the live show which differentiates it from variety theatre as it used to exist. To start with, the promoters have wisely employed a professional compère – the impressively efficient Stephen Mulhern – whereas traditionally, variety theatre managed without one. Then there is the use of film footage, which is so heavy that this barely qualifies as a live show. At the beginning, a lengthy montage of clips from the 2009 series is projected onto a giant screen at the back of the stage, and each individual act is prefaced by their own individual montage of TV highlights. As if that weren't enough, many of the audience are filming the show on cameras or phones. We're on the thirteenth row, and the bottom of my field of vision is filled with lots of little glowing screens, each showing its own view of what's happening onstage.

On the other hand, there's plenty here to connect it with variety theatre, starting with the staging. Oblong-shaped LED bars flank the stage forming a kind of proscenium, and traditional red-velvet tabs twice make an appearance – Stephen Mulhern stands in front of a large red curtain while introducing the show, and later, CGI red tabs are projected behind the singer Susan Boyle, in what must be a conscious reference to variety's past. Even the projected footage at the back of the stage has an echo in variety, recalling the 'bioscope' of the music hall – films shown between the live acts.

However, the most powerful echoes of variety are in the performance itself. There's no narrative, fictional setting or any other kind of overarching conceptual structure, just a series of unconnected individual acts. As in variety, the performers work directly to the audience, making eye contact and speaking and singing directly to them. The audience play an active role in the show, the applause they give at the end of each number or routine validating the efforts of the performers onstage. They also applaud any conspicuous show of skill, particularly when a singer hits a loud sustained note.

The skills of street-dance team Diversity unknowingly echo the daring throw-and-catch moves of adagio acts like the Ganjou Brothers & Juanita, and even the long lean-forward of the music hall comedian Little Tich's Big Boot Dance. There's also novelty in the show, in the spoof dancing of the rotund father-and-son act Stavros

Flatley, and the cheerfully awful gold-clad, middle-aged rapper DJ Talent.

Above all, each act is built around the identity of the performer, and the clips which introduce them show not just moments of performance but also film of them talking about their offstage life and the 'journey' they have been on to get here. The effect of this becomes particularly obvious when Susan Boyle hits the stage.

Boyle has become instantly famous thanks to her first appearance on the TV show on 11 April 2009. It's a supremely manipulative piece of television. The pre-performance interview sets her up as a rather pathetic figure. We see an image of her stuffing a large piece of food into her mouth, and her looks are such that a journalist would subsequently describe her as 'small and rather chubby, with a squashed face, unruly teeth and unkempt hair'.[4] She reveals to Ant and Dec that she is nearly 48 years old, unemployed, single ('Never been married – never been kissed!'), and lives with her cat, Pebbles.

She takes to the stage, and the editing leads us to believe we are about to see a cruelly enjoyable train wreck of a performance. As she chats with the judges, stumbling over her words and announcing that she hopes to become a professional singer, we see cynical reaction shots from both them and the audience – brows knit, and derisive giggles are shared. Then when she sings the first line of her song with power and control, the reaction is transformed – eyes widen, jaws drop, and the audience burst into spontaneous applause. She finishes to a standing ovation, and the judges heap praise on her, each alluding to the fact that they were completely surprised by her talent.

Following the show, the clip was posted on YouTube, where it was watched over 26 million times within a week, spawning international media coverage.[5] Boyle was immediately tipped to win the series, but ended being beaten to second place to the street-dance troupe, Diversity. Following her defeat, the stress of the experience became overwhelming and she was admitted to a private clinic. *The Guardian* commented, 'Boyle has…suffered a more accelerated version of a common musical journey: from unknown to Priory in seven weeks rather than the months it takes hardened professionals.'[6] Even Gordon Brown, the Prime Minister, expressed his concern for her well-being.[7]

All of this is reflected in the audience's reaction at the Wembley Arena. Boyle gets a standing ovation even as she steps onto the stage, and each of her numbers is greeted in the same way. In an important essay about popular entertainment written in the late 1970s, Clive

Barker argued that 'the private life of the performer forms an important part of the performer's persona', giving the example of Judy
Garland, whose well-publicized offstage struggles 'helped to invest
the singer with an aura of pathos'.[8] In the same way, Boyle's exces-
sively accelerated trip from 'unknown to Priory' gives the audience
the pleasure of seeing the little woman struggling with adversity and
triumphing through her talent. It is this as much as the performance
she gives onstage that wins her the unusually extravagant audience
response.

It strikes me that there is a certain irony here. It has often been
argued that television killed variety theatre, but now a TV show –
Britain's Got Talent – has engendered a series of live tours which
represent the biggest resurgence of live variety since the theatre
circuits collapsed in the late 1950s. I'd guess that there are around
8,000 people here this afternoon, and this is one of two shows at this
venue on this day alone. Most variety theatres would be pleased with
a total weekly attendance of 16,000.

However, what the *Britain's Got Talent* live show lacks is the
true depth and power of variety theatre. There are no Max Millers
or Gracie Fields here, nobody whose persona is expertly crafted
through their performance onstage rather than their trials and tribu-
lations offstage. There is none of the expertise with which variety
performers built their relationship with an audience. As one TV
critic has pointed out, *Britain's Got Talent* is 'the variety show with
no variety'.[9] Almost all of the acts at the Wembley Arena are singers or street dancers. There are no comedians, magicians, acrobats,
jugglers, ventriloquists or any of the other weird and wonderful acts
which appeared in variety theatres. The extent and range of skill on
offer here this afternoon is far more limited. Nor is there anything to
approach the sheer bizarreness of the more outlandish speciality acts
which variety produced.

This is not surprising. The *Britain's Got Talent* live show got its
acts from a flavour-of-the-month TV programme which has been
around for only a few years, whereas the top acts of the variety were
the product of a large circuit of big theatre chains running large venues which put on two shows a night, six nights a week in towns and
cities up and down the country throughout the first six decades of the
twentieth century.

2

The Variety Bill

Although it is now half a century since the vast majority of the variety theatres were closing their doors for the last time, an image of what variety was still lingers on in the public imagination. Thanks to television programmes like *Sunday Night at the London Palladium*, we understand that a variety show involved a compère like Tommy Trinder or Bruce Forsyth introducing a series of individual acts, which would perform straight out to the audience with the hope of entertaining them as much as possible. The show would start with a chorus line of high-kicking showgirls, and at the end all of the acts would come back onto the stage and wave to the audience over the closing credits.

Perhaps unsurprisingly, this image of variety is only partly accurate. The televised version took some of the most essential elements of variety theatre but also added its own touches. The compère is an obvious example. In the majority of shows which took place in variety theatres, there was nobody to introduce the acts onto the stage. Instead, the audience would know which act was on the stage by consulting their programme, where each item on the bill would have a number printed next to it. This number would be shown while the act was performing, either on painted wooden number boards built into the proscenium, or later by similar boards which picked out the number by illuminating a series of miniature light bulbs. If the running order of the show was changed, the numbers on the number board would not run sequentially, because they had to match the number printed next to the name of the act on the programme.[1]

Having said this, what television took from variety theatre was its very heart – the direct, immediate relationship between performer and audience, and crucially, the separateness of the individual acts. Unlike legitimate theatre, or even more popular forms like panto-mime and revue, a variety show was not bound together by a nar-rative or even a theme. Each act stood for itself, and there was, as Brooks McNamara put it, 'no transfer of information from one act to another'.[2] However, there were certain conventions about the way that the individual acts were put together to create a coherent show, and attempts to explain these usually work by describing a hypotheti-cal 'typical' bill.[3] I am going to take a different approach – looking at a show which actually happened.

The Lewisham Hippodrome

I have on the desk in front of me the programme for the show that was seen at the Lewisham Hippodrome in the week commencing Monday 8 April 1946 (see Illustration 2.1). The first thing to notice is that it runs twice a night, with performances starting at 6 p.m. and

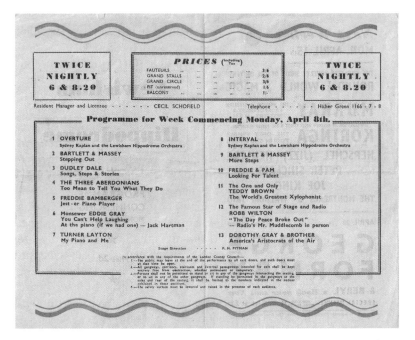

Figure 2.1 The inside pages of the programme for the Lewisham Hippodrome, week commencing Monday 8 April 1946.

8.20 p.m., from Monday to Saturday. This is important, as the intro-duction of the twice nightly system was one of the key changes in the evolution of nineteenth-century music hall into twentieth-century variety theatre.

The Lewisham Empire stood on Rushey Green, Catford. Built in 1911 and designed by the celebrated theatre architect Frank Matcham, it was a typical suburban variety theatre – a large stone building decorated with domes, arches, columns and curlicues, the name 'Hippodrome' proudly inscribed on the walls. Michael Grade, who was taken to see shows there as a child, remembers it as 'a classic variety theatre' on a 'wonderful site ... Right on the corner ... it was *the* landmark building really, in Lewisham, Catford.'[4] Inside, the auditorium was vast, capable of seating up to 2,428 in its three tiers of seating, plus an extra 20 in the boxes. With standing room, as many as 3,222 people could watch one of the twelve shows it staged every week.[5] This was one of the first bills to be presented in this theatre since it had been taken over by Phil and Syd Hyams of SA Varieties, who had previously based their business on super cinemas and cine-variety shows. As such it is a strong bill, described by a local newspaper as 'a bunch of stars, all of whom are famous'.[6]

1. OVERTURE
Sydney Kaplan and the Lewisham Hippodrome Orchestra

The first item on the bill is not an act as such, but a piece of music played by the theatre's resident orchestra. The conductor, Sydney Kaplan, is a reasonably well-known figure, having broadcast on the BBC. The choice of tune is something light and popular like Tolchard Evans' 'Lady of Spain', or John Philip Sousa's 'Semper Fidelis'.[7]

2. BARTLETT & MASSEY
Stepping Out

As the audience greet the end of the overture with perhaps a gen-tle ripple of applause and the number boards on the proscenium arch change from '1' to '2', the first proper act to take the stage on most variety bills is a dance act. The troupes of high-kicking dancing girls as seen on television would only normally feature in the biggest variety theatres like the Palladium, where resident troupes like the Sherman Fisher Girls or the John Tiller Girls would present kick-lines of perhaps 16 dancers.

Most variety shows start off with a more modest touring dance act, usually a duo or perhaps a trio. These acts work hard to entertain the audience, presenting a series of fast routines involving flashy, spectacular moves and fast tap steps. As well as well-coordinated group numbers, each member of the act might do a solo routine to allow his or her partner to go off for a costume change. Many dance acts are boy–girl duos, but Bartlett & Massey are 'two pert girls' who are 'well appreciated for their precise and peppy dance offering above average in skill and production'.[8]

Being 'well appreciated' is a relative term for the opening act of a variety bill. Their thankless task is to hit the audience with as much energy and pizzazz as possible in order to take the chill off them and warm them up for the more important acts to follow. Often latecomers are still taking their seats while they perform, and although they might well win some applause for their efforts, it is quieter and more restrained than the reception granted to acts that will appear later in the show.

3. DUDLEY DALE
Songs, Steps & Stories

As the applause for the end of Bartlett & Massey's act starts to fade, the orchestra play a few bars of music, the number boards change from '2' to '3', and without a moment's pause which might allow the audience's energy to drop, the Liverpudlian comic Dudley Dale appears on the stage. He is what we would now refer to as a stand-up comedian, although in the variety era he is known as a 'front cloth comic'. This is because he appears not in front of the very first pair of tabs (or curtains) but in front of a cloth hung just behind them, painted with a cartoonish street scene often featuring the names of real local businesses which pay the theatre for the advertising value of being seen by audiences every week.[9]

The second spot comic is often a young and inexperienced act hoping to build a bigger career by working his or her way up the bill, but Dudley Dale has been working for over thirty years, having first appeared in variety at the Argyle Theatre, Birkenhead in 1914. As the bill matter printed under his name in the programme suggests, his act includes dancing and singing as well as comic patter, and although he is doing a solo act in this show, he is also known to present another act with his 'Gang', a group of boy singers and dancers.[10]

4. THE THREE ABERDONIANS
Too Mean to Tell You What They Do

Dudley Dale is followed by another comedy act, the Three Aberdonians. Although slightly less experienced than Dale, having been formed in 1930 by Tom and Charlie Barr and Roza Louise Thompson, they are better known, having appeared in the 1938 Royal Variety Performance and been given their deliciously memorable bill matter – 'Too Mean to Tell You What They Do' – by the legendary variety impresario Val Parnell.[11] They are a fast-paced slapstick act, with Roza providing most of the 'distinction' in acrobatic skill.[12] A publicity photo shows her wearing a tartan dress and beaming delightfully as she leans straight out towards the camera, balancing on her right leg while her left sticks straight up behind her. She is grabbing the noses of her male partners, who kneel down either side of her, besuited and Brylcreemed, a silly-arse grin on each of their faces.[13] The physical stunts and gags are supplemented by comic patter, some of which is directed between the three of them and some delivered straight out to the audience.[14] Like their bill matter, some of the gags exploit the Scottishness of the performers by playing on the stereotype of meanness.[15]

5. FREDDIE BAMBERGER
Jest-er Piano Player

Next on is Freddie Bamberger, a dark-haired, big-nosed, beetle-browed comedy pianist. His comic patter, delivered with overbrimming nonchalance, includes gags along the lines of this gem about the digs he is staying in:

> They're not cheap. Sixpence and ninepence per night. Of course, I'm paying ninepence, I – I get a mattress as well.[16]

The main attraction is his piano playing, which is geared less to songs and more to a series of stunts which show off his skill in a way that is both ostentatious and tongue-in-cheek. He plays 'Trees' using just his left hand, providing both the melody and an extremely showy accompaniment in which his fingers spider up and down the keyboard with remarkable speed and dexterity.[17] In another routine, he announces, 'Now here's a very, very difficult trick. It took me three years to learn this trick – one night.' He then proceeds to cover the keyboard with a piece of black cloth and play the tune *through* it, despite not being able to see the keys.[18]

6. Monsewer EDDIE GRAY
You Can't Help Laughing
At the piano (if we had one) – Jack Hartman

It is only a few acts into the show that we start to get the really big names, and 'Monsewer' Eddie Gray is certainly one of these, having made his reputation as both a solo act and a member of the legendary Crazy Gang. A raucous Cockney, with round spectacles and a thick, black, curly moustache, he talks to the audience in a crackpot mixture of English and French:

> *Mesdames et monsewers* – 'ow are you, all right? [laughter] Now *ce soir, ce soir*, that's foreign for '*ce soir*'. [laughter][19]

To musical accompaniment, he juggles three clubs, dropping one every now and then and catching it on his foot, before booting it back into the air and juggling it once more. Then he hops from leg to leg in a funny little dance, passing the clubs underneath each leg as he does so. He shows how easy it all is by casually humming along with the tune as he accomplishes his feats.[20] At one point, his stooge wanders on eating fish and chips, plucks one of the clubs out of the air, pretends to use it as a salt cellar, then throws it over his shoulder.[21]

7. TURNER LAYTON
My Piano and Me

The first half of the show closes with another big name. Turner Layton became famous as half of the singing duo Layton & Johnstone, before going solo in 1935. A chubby-faced but handsome African-American, he sings romantic songs like 'My SOS to You' and 'East of the Sun', his rich voice laden with vibrato as he carefully elocutes the lyrics in an English-sounding accent. The act overflows with sentiment and sophistication. He wears an elegant black dinner suit as he plays the grand piano, his attitude radiating urbanity and refinement, a wistful smile on his face as he sings.[22]

8. INTERVAL
Sydney Kaplan and the Lewisham Hippodrome Orchestra

To modern eyes it might look a bit odd to list the interval music as an actual item on the bill, but this was a standard convention. The theatre orchestra would play a piece of music during the interval for the benefit of customers who chose to stay in their seats rather than go out to the bar or the toilet, and in some cases, the particular piece of music to be played was listed in the programme. At the Lewisham Hippodrome, Sydney Kaplan conducts a medley called something like 'Parisiana' or 'Tunes of the Times'.[23]

9. BARTLETT & MASSEY
More Steps

It was a standard convention of variety theatre that the opening dance act would also open the second half of the show. Generally speaking, each act in the first half of the show is slightly better known than the previous one, and each is allowed a little more time to spend with the audience. The second half of the show goes back to the beginning, restarting with the most obscure act on the bill. Bartlett & Massey come back with an even shorter routine than their first one, warming the audience up again after the interval and covering the time when the last stragglers are making their way back from the bar or toilets.

10. FREDDIE & PAM
Looking for Talent

As the number boards change from '9' to '10', a short musical cue welcomes Freddie Bamberger back on with a different routine. This time he appears in a double act with his wife Pam, an attractive woman in an off-the-shoulder evening dress with flowing gauze skirt.[24] They exchange a bit of crosstalk, a kind of fast-intercut comic patter which was common in variety. It was not a standard convention for anybody other than the opening dance act to do two spots on the same bill, but it started to happen more often towards the end of the variety era, when budgets were getting tighter.

11. The One and Only
TEDDY BROWN
The World's Greatest Xylophonist

This far through the bill, it is time for another really big act, and Teddy Brown is certainly that. An enormously fat man, he plays on his colossal size in various ways. His bill matter punningly alludes to it – exploiting both meanings of the word 'Greatest' – and he some-times appears in front of a backdrop painted with a giant cartoon of his rotund figure.[25] He plays a six-octave xylophone, which boasts two octaves more than the standard instrument, and his virtuosity is much admired, one reviewer calling it 'truly surprising'.[26] He also throws in some comic patter, and invites the audience to join in some of his numbers, gravely intoning the instruction, 'Sing!' In one of his sig-nature stunts, he quickly plays a continuous series of notes down the length of his xylophone, turning his whole body through 360 degrees

without missing a beat and completing the move by jerking his right
mallet into the air in triumph.[27]

12. The Famous Star of Stage and Radio
ROBB WILTON
'The Day Peace Broke Out'
– Radio's Mr Muddlecomb in person

As the number boards change from '11' to '12', the orchestra plays
a burst of music and the top of the bill takes to the stage. Each act
has been introduced in this way, but the more famous acts become
associated with their signature tunes, and when they are played, the
audience know exactly who is coming on and applaud in anticipation.
The top of the bill is expected to draw audiences into the theatre to see
the show, and entertains them for longer than anybody else, usually
staying on for twenty minutes. Robb Wilton is a strong bill topper at
the Lewisham Hippodrome, not just a star but a national institution.

At this point he has been working in variety for decades, making his
first London appearance in 1909 and appearing in the Royal Variety
Performance as early as 1926.[28] His long career has seen him doing
anything from monologues ('He said, "I'll punch your head", I said,
"Whose?" He said, "Yours", I said, "Mine", He said, "Yes", I said,
"Oh" ')[29] to sketches, like the one in which he remains inappropriately
cheery and upbeat ('Turned out nice again today, hasn't it?'),[30] while
taking the confession of a hysterical, wobble-voiced murderess played
by his wife, Florence Palmer. He is possibly even more famous on the
airwaves than on the stage, appearing regularly on BBC radio in the
guise of Mr Muddlecombe JP (as misspelled in the programme), and
his solo comedy routines as a loveably work-shy, pub-obsessed member of the Home Guard – always starting with the catchphrase, 'The
Day War Broke Out...' – were universally popular during the war,
playing as important a part in lifting the nation's morale as Tommy
Handley's *ITMA*. On stage and radio, he always plays the part of the
amiable bumbler, cheerfully stammering his way through life however
befuddling it might be.

Topping the bill at the Lewisham Hippodrome, Wilton plays on
his wartime radio success, with a routine which fills the audience in
on how his reluctant Home Guard member is adjusting to peacetime.
His delivery is exquisitely detailed, with a rich northern accent and a
rhythm punctuated with a series of perfectly timed tuts, pauses and
'er's. His hands are constantly involved in a carefully choreographed
ballet of fidgeting, pushing back through his hair, rubbing his eyes,

or coming to rest on his cheek with his little finger slipped into the corner of his mouth. As usual, we see him explaining his plans to his wife, most of them involving spending his time with Charlie Evans, the old drinking pal who featured so heavily in his wartime radio monologues:

> I said, 'I'll do something.' She said, 'What?' I said, 'How do I kn- I – I don't know till I see Charlie Evans tonight.' [laughter] She said, 'What's Charlie Evans going to do?' I said, "E doesn't know till 'e sees me! [laughter] We've got to talk it over.' She said, 'Talk what over?' I said, 'Post war plans.' She said, 'What's them?' I said, 'That means future plans. We – we'll meet tonight at the local at eight o'clock. And by closing time – [laughter] we might have a very good idea of how we stand.' [laughter] 'Well', she said, 'neither of you had any idea of how you stood at closing time last night'. [laughter] And she said, 'On Peace Night, you got mixed up in a fight.' I said, 'Well, blimey, if you can't 'ave a fight on Peace Night, when can you have one?' [laughter][31]

13. DOROTHY GRAY & BROTHER
America's Aristocrats of the Air

Logically, the show should finish as Robb Wilton takes his final applause, the loudest and most enthusiastic of the night. However, it does not end there, but instead the number boards change from '12' to '13', and a short burst of music welcomes onto the stage Dorothy Gray & Brother, who present a skilful, dangerous-looking act, in which they do 'some teetotum work on trapezes that ought to tear their teeth out by the roots'.[32] Despite hanging by their teeth at a great height and spinning spectacularly, they do not get a great reception. In fact, as they are risking their lives for the entertainment of the audience, some patrons get up from their seats and start to make their way to the exits.

It was common to follow the star act with a comparatively obscure speciality act, and although the convention started to disappear towards the end of the variety era, some theatres continued to do it right into the mid-1950s.[33] The task facing the final act was as functional as that of the opening dance act. They were there simply to stop the customers getting up and leaving during the bill topper's act, and they had to be exciting enough to keep as many of the audience as possible in their seats. At around this time, *The Stage* noted that, 'It is too often the custom of music-hall audiences to stream out steadily throughout the last act in order to avoid the general rush at the end. It takes a good last turn to prevent this general exodus.'[34]

It might seem odd that people would want to leave before the end of the show, but in the days before mass car ownership, it was vital that they could leave in time to catch the public transport home.[35] Peter Prentice, who was part of a whip-cracking, rope-swinging family act called El Granadas & Peter which often appeared in thankless final spot on the bill, remembers: 'No matter how much they were enjoying it, they had to go for their buses, and the buses stopped at ten or ten thirty. The last bus home was at ten thirty and they'd start melting away.'[36]

A nicely balanced bill

The show staged at the Lewisham Hippodrome in the week commencing 8 April 1946 gives a good idea of what it was like to see a night of variety in the middle of the twentieth century. A series of dancers, comedians, singers, musicians and speciality acts would follow each other onto the stage in a show filled with comedy, sentiment, skills, thrills, glamour and grotesquerie. After just twelve performances, this particular collection of acts in this particular order would almost certainly never be seen again. Peter Prentice recalls, 'You can often arrive on a Monday and not know anybody on the programme. On the other hand, you meet up with old friends and you're friends again for a week, then you all go your separate ways again.'[37]

Unlike most other theatre of the time, the show is not a single production, but a series of individual productions stuck together to make a whole. If conventional narrative theatre is a painting, variety is a collage. Collages are not entirely random, and the juxtapositions involve composition and aesthetic judgement. In much the same way, variety shows were carefully composed to make the maximum impact, each act playing its part to build the show to a climax at the top of the bill.

The conventions seen in the Lewisham bill were more or less standard. The show would start with a dance act (or sometimes a speciality act), followed by a comic, and the first half would build to the second top, leading into the interval. The opening act would come back to start the second half, which would build to the top of the bill – almost always a comedian, singer or band – often followed by a quick speciality act. Working within these conventions required skill and aesthetic judgement. In 1936, Bertie Adams, the manager of the Holborn Empire told *The Observer*:

> The essence of making variety a success resides in the 'booking committee' – those responsible at headquarters for engaging the turns. It is not

always essential merely to book 'stars' – though that is also essential in its time. The essence of the thing is to get together a nicely balanced bill – with 'variety' in the true sense in it. Something that shall keep people laughing all the time – but at different things and in different ways. It's quite possible that an artist who's good in one bill might not be good in another. He wants contrast – he wants change – to set him off. It's how you place an artist in a bill that helps him.[38]

This sense of careful composition meant that there was a different feel to shows put together by different bookers. An article in *The Times* in 1951 explained how Moss Empires' Managing Director Val Parnell composed the bills at the Palladium:

Week by week, out of whatever materials are to hand, he has the chance of creating a programme and an atmosphere which may express, and certainly does reflect, his own personality ... Glad as he will be of full houses, he will also want to vary and experiment, to add or subtract this or that colour until each programme as a whole corresponds with his conception of what a real music-hall show should be.[39]

Artistes booking control

Responsibility for booking the acts in the rest of the Moss Empires chain fell to Cissie Williams, who was one of the most powerful figures in variety theatre with a suitably fearsome reputation. Character comedian Beryl Reid described her as 'much feared and sought after' with 'the awe-inspiring quality of a Second Coming'.[40] Jack Seaton worked as an errand boy at the London Palladium during the Second World War and saw her in action:

She wasn't terrifying, but she was rather direct, you know. Another one who wouldn't suffer fools ... And if anybody was called into the office and she was going to tell them off, she had a little dog – and her assistant was a lovely man called Ted Gollop – and anybody who was called into the office, she'd say, 'Ted, take the dog for a walk.' And you knew very well whoever it was, was going to get a rollicking.[41]

Williams's power lay in her position as Artistes Booking Control for the Moss Empires chain. Moss was not only the biggest chain of theatres but also the most important and prestigious. There was an established hierarchy among variety theatres, which were known as number ones, number twos or number threes depending on their importance. Definitions of what constituted a number one, two or three seem to differ depending on who you ask, with different acts claiming different statuses for different theatre chains. Ken Joy, who appeared in variety with his parents' musical comedy act as a child even claims that some theatres, like Sheffield's Attercliffe Palace, were known as 'number fours'.[42]

Generally speaking, number three theatres would be independents or belong to one of the smaller chains. A number two might be a theatre belonging to Syndicate Halls, booked by Florence Leddington. Moss Empires were universally acknowledged as number one theatres, with their flagship venue the Palladium the very top of the tree. Cissie Williams was not in sole charge of Moss Empires – she worked under the Managing Director George Black and his successor Val Parnell – but whereas Black and Parnell only arranged the bills for the Palladium, she booked the acts for the rest of the entire chain.

Being in charge of the top theatre chain meant rigorously maintaining standards, which she did by regularly watching the shows at the Finsbury Park Empire, Moss's second most important theatre. Here she would hold court every Monday, armed with sandwiches and a flask of tea, passing judgement on the acts to the agents who nervously surrounded her. She might insist on an act being tightened up, or demand that a line be cut. Famously, she hated acts with dirty shoes, and would refuse to book them again.[43] Standards were also monitored by the report cards which theatre managers would complete for each act and send back to Moss's head office every week. These contained factual information like the name of the act, the date and venue, and the fee paid, as well as a space for general remarks.

Barring clauses

Given that each show was made up of perhaps eight or ten acts, booking for an entire chain of theatres was an awesome task. Louis Benjamin, who worked for Moss as an office boy in 1937, recalled: 'Contracts department was a very large department in those days, servicing about thirty-six theatres on a twice-nightly basis with up to twelve acts a bill; so you can imagine how many contracts went out per week.'[44] This process was vital, because the standard Moss Empires contract played a vital part in the complex task of keeping their theatres peopled with acts.

Cancellations would have been a real headache, and the Moss contract demanded that acts which cancelled due to illness not only

notify the management immediately, but also provide them with a
medical certificate. It also allowed them to shift acts to other venues in order to fill any unforeseen gaps, stating, 'The Artiste may be
transferred during the whole or any part of the agreement (not less
than one week) to any other Theatre owned or controlled by or associated with the Management by consent of the Artiste such consent
not to be unreasonably withheld.'[45]

Probably the most important part of the contract was the 'barring
clause', which prevented acts from appearing in theatres belonging to
rivals chains within a given distance and time period. For example, an
act appearing in one of Moss's West End theatres was not allowed to
appear in any rival venue within one mile within sixteen weeks before
the engagement or two weeks after it. For suburban theatres, it was
two miles and thirty two weeks, and for provincial halls six miles and
forty weeks. The point of this was, as comic Ted Ray put it, 'neither
management felt like helping the other in presenting the most attractive bills available'.[46] Moss kept records of where all of its acts were
appearing in what it called an Opposition Book.[47]

Barring clauses were introduced by the big chains in the early
years of the twentieth century, and they were one of the methods that
helped them to put smaller independent music halls out of business.[48]
In the early days of the barring clause, some performers found ways
of getting around it. The Beverley Sisters' father, for example, worked
under several different names, as Teddie Beverley recalls: 'Why a lot
of artists had different names is because … there was a barring clause,
obviously … So they changed their name. So that when they were billed
at another theatre nearby, it wasn't their name. So you'll see my father
under George E. Coram and George Rymer.'[49]

Stage waits

Having booked the acts, another difficult task was to get each show
to run smoothly. The theatres provided the lighting, orchestra, tabs,
basic backdrops like the street scene front cloth, and front of house
staff, and all of these worked together to make the show run as it
should. As at the Lewisham Hippodrome, each act had to build on
the success of the last, and for this to work there had to be no pause
whatsoever between them. According to the speciality act Valantyne
Napier, the ideal was that, 'Everything must follow quickly one after
the other. As one act finished and took their call the other was ready
to open.'[50] A gap between acts was known as a 'stage wait', and Napier

described this as an 'unforgivable sin in any performance ... In a No 1 theatre heads would roll!'[51]

One way of avoiding stage waits was the music which the orchestra played to welcome each act onto the stage. More importantly, the staging of each act allowed the show to run without gaps. The reason the second spot comic performed before the front cloth was to allow the stagehands to set the stage behind it for the next act. While Dudley Dale was getting laughs with his songs, steps and stories, the stage could be set for the Three Aberdonians. An act which could 'close in one' – in other words, finish the act right downstage by the footlights – was an asset to a booker looking to avoid stage waits.[52]

It was also vital that the entire show should run to time. The first house had to finish on time to allow one audience to get out of the theatre and another to fill it up for the second house. Given the size of most variety theatres, this was another awesome task. At the London Palladium, there was a gap of just fifteen minutes between the end of the last act in the first house and the beginning of the overture in the second, as Ian Bevan recalled in 1952:

> The dapper manager, Barry Stori, directs operations as the theatre disgorges some three thousand people and takes in another three thousand. The foyer is more densely packed than Piccadilly station at the rush hour, but the station has escalators and concrete floors. Here there are carpeted stairs, yet all evidence of crowd movement – mud, cigarette butts, litter – is removed almost as the people pass by.[53]

The second house had to run to time because of the pressures of public transport. It would have been acceptable for people to start leaving to catch the last bus home while Dorothy Gray & Brother were on, much less so while a big star like Robb Wilton was doing his act.

All of this meant that acts were given fixed timeslots, and these were rigidly enforced. Peter Prentice recalls that the first time El Granadas & Peter appeared at the London Palladium, the act was cut from ten minutes to five: 'And instead of cutting things out, my father said, "Right, we'll do them quicker." And I think we did six minutes, and the stage manager Harry Black kept saying, "You're doing six minutes, you're only down for five!" '[54] More seriously, a manager's report card might inform head office about any act doing a minute over or under their allotted time, leading to a stiff telling off, either in writing or in person from the formidable Cissie Williams.[55]

Having said this, there were one or two acts who would rebel against such restrictions, like the bizarre musical comedian Herschel Henlere, as fellow comic Wyn Calvin recalls: 'They would drop the house tabs on him, and he would go through and take his call, but he'd go through the tabs, and ... he would have taken on a piano-accordion with him in front of the house tabs. He would do another number on the piano-accordion.'[56]

The need for strict time discipline might help to explain the fact that most shows in variety theatres did not use a compère to link the acts together. Having run and compèred stand-up comedy shows through much of the 1990s, the lack of a compère in variety the-atre has long been a complete mystery to me. The advantages of having somebody to host the show seem obvious. A compère can take the chill off the audience at the beginning, and help to regu-late the mood of the audience throughout the show. Arthur Smith, who has compèred on the London stand-up circuit from the alter-native comedy days of the 1980s to the present, explains that, 'As a compère ... if an act's gone down the pan, you know, you've got to whip them back into a bit of a jolly state. If someone's completely stormed it, you've almost got to, like, bring them down a bit, for the next acts.'[57]

The Victorian music halls had the chairman to do all of this, but when the twice nightly system came in at the beginning of the variety era, he was replaced by the impersonal number boards and musical cues. What this suggests is that it was the time discipline necessary to put on two shows a night that led the theatre chains to largely avoid using compères. Whereas it is perfectly possible for a single act to keep to a rigid timeslot, it is much harder for an act that has to come on a number of times throughout the evening. As present-day compère Arthur Smith explains, 'You're gonna be fairly upbeat and convivial and talking to people and able to improvise and react.'[58] Inevitably, a spontaneous, improvising compère is going to find it hard to stick to precise timings. Occasionally, though, theatres might use one of the acts on the bill to do a little compèring between acts in order to avoid stage waits, as Wyn Calvin remembers:

> It was unusual, but if you were for instance the second spot comic, then you might be asked to introduce, where necessary, acts later on in the bill ... If somebody had used a full stage, a speciality act, and then you got the top of the bill coming on, who was accompanied by a pianist on the grand piano, etc., then you may be asked, 'Would you do two minutes to introduce him or her?'[59]

When in doubt – Send for Trout

Selling a variety show was as complicated as booking and managing it. With plays, musicals, opera and revue, the production can be given a clear identity before it even opens, through choice of title, poster and programme design, press releases and so on. The hope is that it will enjoy a long run, and in that time its identity will grow as it acquires press reviews and generates word-of-mouth reputation. Variety shows, on the other hand, were a collage of individual acts with no overall theme of identity to market them under. Because the particular combination of acts only appeared together for a week, the opportunities for the show's reputation to build were strictly limited.

This meant that the shows had to be sold on the strength of the individual acts, and that responsibility fell to men like Lawson Trout, the Advertising and Publicity Representative for Moss Empires in Birmingham, whose calling card read, 'When in doubt – Send for Trout.' Trout kept a series of 5-inch x 3-inch record cards for each act that appeared at theatres like the Birmingham Empire and the Hippodromes in Birmingham and Dudley. These were rather like the theatre managers' report cards sent back the head office at the end of each week, but the information they contain is slightly different.

Each of Trout's cards records the name of the act, the date of appearance at each theatre, and a bit of text describing the act that could be used for marketing purposes. In some cases, this is simply the act's bill matter, to be listed under their name on posters and programmes. For example:

Jenny McAndrew – Schoolgirl ventriloquist
The Oxford Five – Football and fun on bicycles
Handy – The Egyptian Sphinx mystery wrestler

Intriguing as these might look to modern eyes, shows were not really sold on the strength of the speciality acts which appeared early in the show, but more on the fame of the big names brought in to top the bills. As a result, Trout wrote much longer comments for bill toppers, presumably to provide copy for the local press. The card for George Formby, who appeared at the Birmingham Empire in April 1934 and at the Hippodrome six times between August 1934 and November 1943, gives a potted biography for the comic singer, mentioning his most successful records and films, as well as an appearance in the Royal Variety Performance in 1937. It also notes that his final appearance at the Birmingham Hippodrome followed 'a flying tour of the battlefields of Italy where he has been entertaining the troops', and includes a general description of the act: 'His success has been due to his native Lancastrian grit and humour linked with an entirely natural and sympathetic personality. His mastery of the Banjulele has also helped considerably in establishing him as one of our merriest entertainers.'[60]

A very big billing

The most important cog in the variety publicity machine was the bill (i.e. poster), with its distinctive typography picking out the names of each act in blocky, sans-serif fonts, letters stretched and elongated for maximum visual impact. Each name would be boxed off with its own bill matter, and this was such an important part of the marketing that the theatre chains would punish acts who did not supply it in time for printing deadlines. In November 1938, variety trade paper *The Performer* noted that, 'The announcement in our columns last week that a well-known management had informed the [Variety Artistes'] Federation that it had had to cancel the contracts of two acts who had failed to send in their bill matter in good time merits repetition.'[61] Bills were printed in various sizes and posted up outside theatres and around the town. They were important enough for theatre managers to send out a junior employee to go around and check that they had gone up on all the hoardings they had paid for.[62]

Responsibility for graphic design fell to men like Norman Hoskins, who worked as an assistant advertising manager for Moss Empires, producing the small cards used in box offices, the slides projected in the theatres during the interval advertising next week's acts, and the 40-inch x 60-inch quad posters which would be displayed outside newsagents and similar shops. He recalled:

> The secret was to make lots of 'tops of the bill'. My 'piece de resistance' was a box office card...for the Finsbury Park Empire, on which I had managed to place six well-known variety acts side by side...The poor printers were often forced to shave the wooden letters to make them fit into such restricted spaces.[63]

Taking such care with layout was important because in order to pull the public in, the star act had to be the most visible name on the bill. They would appear at the top, just under the name of the theatre, with the biggest, blockiest lettering and perhaps a photo or cartoon of their face.

Acts were very aware of the value of typography. Vera Lynn (born Vera Welch) chose her stage surname partly because it would 'stand out on a bill' because it 'would allow for plenty of space round each letter'.[64] Similarly, singer and whistler Ronnie Ronalde (born Ronald Charles Waldron), carefully adapted his stage name for maximum impact when printed up on bills:

> My name became Ronnie Ronalde. But when I used to draw up the bills at the age of 16, I realized that a single name, you get a bigger billing. You know – so I chopped off the 'Ronnie' and just had 'Ronalde'. So I always had very big billing... if you looked at the bill, you saw 'Ronalde'.[65]

The size of the lettering was important because of its publicity value, but also because it indicated an act's position in the backstage hierarchy. Ted Ray recalled that 'furious arguments and long-standing feuds have been caused by a mere quarter of an inch more or less on the heights of the lettering accorded to a star. I have actually seen artistes take out a ruler and measure their names!'[66]

Another indicator of status was position on the bill, top of the bill and second top being the most coveted spots. In variety, upward mobility was limited by convention. Comics, singers and bands tended to be the only acts allowed to rise to the top of the bill, whereas dancers and speciality acts almost always occupied the less prestigious positions. Acts would also want to move up from the number three theatres to the number ones, and being regularly booked by Moss would have been a source of pride. Teddie Beverley is still proud of the fact that the Beverley Sisters only played 'the number one theatres in the number one cities. The principal theatres. Now we only did those. We never, never even went to number two theatres. Or number three.'[67]

Backstage, hierarchy would have been marked out by the allocation of dressing rooms, the biggest acts getting the ones nearest to the stage, the smallest acts getting the ones that were furthest away. Although small acts like Bartlett & Massey might have shared a bill with stars like Robb Wilton, their ability to mingle was often limited. Peter Prentice recalls that as a member of a speciality act, he rarely spent much time talking to the bill toppers: 'See, people think... you're working in a theatre and you can go and you can talk to the stars. You can't. They've often got a gang round them that protects them.'[68]

The value of the agency

Hierarchy was important partly because being a variety artiste could be such a difficult and precarious profession, and having reached the top of the bill, acts would be keen for their position to be properly recognized. Most performers had to put hard effort into becoming established by selling themselves to the booking managers of the big chains. This often started with a 'show date' – a week's engagement at a theatre like the Metropolitan, Edgware Road, the Brixton Empress, the Chelsea Palace or the East Ham Palace, for expenses only.[69] Here, an act might get seen by an agent.

It was possible to get directly booked by a theatre booking manager, but agents increasingly became the intermediaries who sold the acts to the theatres. Big agencies were run by the likes of Harry Foster, Jack Payne, Julius Darewski, and Bert and Lillian Aza. In exchange for a standard 10 per cent slice of the act's fee, an agent would not only get them as many bookings as possible, but also send sets of their photos to the theatres, check that they got the proper billing in programmes and posters, and get them publicity by placing stories in newspapers and trade journals.[70] Agents could be powerful and important figures, and Morris Aza decided to set up his own agency towards the end of the variety era because he could see the influence his parents Bert and Lillian wielded:

> I saw the value of the agency because what I realized was my name was very important to me...everybody was saying, 'Oh yeah, is your father so-and-so, is your mother so-and-so?' and everybody in the business knew them...I began to get favours out of people without even knowing or noticing it because that name meant so much to them.[71]

After the Second World War, the Grades became some of the most influential agents in variety. The sons of Russian-Jewish immigrants, brothers Lew Grade, Bernard Delfont and Leslie Grade – Michael Grade's father – were involved in various businesses, including Collins and Grade and West End Varieties, as well as their own solo agencies.[72] Their power was such that their names were printed in programmes next to the star acts that they represented. A 1958 programme from the Regal Theatre, Hull, for example, lists the top of the bill as, 'Bernard Delfont presents THE BEVERLEY SISTERS'.[73]

Agents were licensed by the London County Council, and such strict regulation was needed because some of them could be less than honest. There were rumours that unscrupulous agents would profiteer off their acts by lying to them about the amount of money a theatre was willing to pay them.[74] Sometimes these were more than rumours, and big name acts found themselves having to go to court over exploitative contracts.

Frankie Howerd, for example, signed with the Jack Payne Organisation in 1947, under a deal which made Payne his personal manager. This allowed Payne to claim more from Howerd's earnings than the standard 10 per cent share which agents normally took. As time went on, Payne's slice got bigger, so that by 1950, he was taking nearly half of the £600 per week which Howerd was being paid for a show at the Palladium, in addition to claiming a separate fee of £300 for setting up the deal in the first place. Howerd took him to court, where Payne was ordered to pay him £5,216.[75]

No one produced them!

The main reason why variety was such a precarious profession was that each act was effectively an independent production. Vera Lynn explains:

> You did your own thing. Like a singer like myself, I used to carry my own pianist always... and you told them where you wanted the piano and the microphone and my husband used to keep an eye on the lights and things, amber for this or a pink for that, you know. So you were your own company – just within yourself or your family.[76]

Such independence was a source of pride, as Valantyne Napier pointed out: 'Variety performers still felt quite distinct from other branches of the theatrical profession. Rightly so. They were independent performers. No one produced them! Their weekly salaries were four or five times as much as a ballet dancer or "legit" actor.'[77]

Because the performers produced their own acts, this gave them enormous artistic control. Speciality act Joan Rhodes proudly explained, 'I didn't take advice from anybody. I thought I knew it all when I was young. No, nobody ever told me what to do or how to do it.'[78] Similarly, Teddie Beverley recalls that, 'Everything we said, did, wore, every word, every syllable, every harmony, every note of orchestration, every movement was ours.'[79] However, with that control came the responsibility of providing almost every element of the act, from material to lighting plots. The cost of this could be intimidating, particularly for acts that were just starting out, and Joan Rhodes provided a detailed account of what she had to do to run her glamorous strongwoman act:

> I made my own costumes then. It cost me half a crown to make a costume, a black costume ... What happened was, there was a shop ... near Piccadilly ... and I used to call it 'the naughty knicker shop' and it was obviously, you know what it was for. And they had these basque things which are still fashionable now. So I bought one of those, and then I just made a black skirt from elastic, and one leg coming through so I could use it. I did everything – until I got fairly well known. And in the first show, I got £17 a week – for twelve shows. And I grumbled a little bit about it, because I had to pay my digs, and I had to buy my props. I used to have to buy telephone books, I used to buy great big ones ... They cost 4 pence each at the time, I used to go to a waste paper place ... And then I used to get the steel bars at a place near the Angel ... they must have thought I was quite mad, this place where they sold girders and things, and I would go in and say, 'Can I have some mild steel, three feet long?' And they would do it, you know, they'd cut it for me, and they'd laugh about it.[80]

Comedians had the additional cost of providing themselves with material, as they rarely wrote the jokes they told onstage themselves. Instead, they might buy jokes on spec from casual scriptwriters. A very young Bob Monkhouse, for example, once sold Max Miller a page of gags for 5 shillings at the stage door of the Lewisham Hippodrome.[81] They might also enter into a more formal arrangement with a scriptwriter like Bill McDonnell, a Scots maths teacher who supplemented his income by an average of £150 per year by writing songs, sketches and monologues for variety comics. His terms were precisely laid out in a letter to the popular radio and variety comedian Suzette Tarri, written in 1943. For example, sole rights for a complete routine for use in variety and radio for one year (with renewal option) cost £10.10.0, whereas you could get a set of 'domestic gags for ad lib use' for a comparatively modest £2.2/–. Another cheaper option was to buy the 'part rights' for a routine, which the writer could also sell to other acts.[82]

An even cheaper way of getting gags was to simply take them from a commercially published joke book, perhaps one of Robert Orben's slim pamphlets like *One-Liners* or *The Encyclopedia of Patter*, or Lewis and Faye Copeland's improbably vast tome, *10,000 Jokes, Toasts and Stories*.[83] Published in 1939, this contains 10,065 numbered gags and comic verses – 65 more than advertised in the title! – sorted into broad themes like 'Love, Courtship and Marriage' and 'Races and Nations', and listed under such subheadings as

'Drunks', 'Boarding Houses' and 'Mothers-in-Law'. Max Wall was one comic who admitting to culling gags from joke books, explaining that he would think of the general format for a routine into which he would pop gags from one of Orben's pamphlets which he described as 'excellent books so long as you pick a joke to fit the situation and also to suit yourself'.[84]

Singers and bandleaders had to provide their own music, buying songs from one of the many music publishers in London's Denmark Street (known as 'London's Tin Pan Alley'). Vera Lynn remembers how this used to work:

> [W]e used to visit all the music publishing houses and everybody got to know everybody...they would get used to the kind of songs that you were choosing when you went, and they would recommend certain songs, say, 'Oo, we've got a good song that might suit you'...so that's really how you found your songs – going around listening to them and, 'Yes, I like that', or 'No, that doesn't suit me'.[85]

Some acts might even be able to get a song for free from a song plugger, as Teddie Beverley explains: 'When you were on the radio, the music publishers would beg you to sing their songs. They would even pay you. That was illegal...We never took money but they used to pay people to sing their songs'.[86] Vera Lynn claims that 'a lot of people' would take bribes from the song pluggers, but she 'wouldn't have any of that' because, 'It was more important to me to find the right song and to sing that.'[87]

In the smaller theatres, acts could get away with providing one copy of the music and getting the pit orchestra to busk the rest, but the number ones insisted that the music should be fully arranged, with band parts for each instrument. As an article in *The Times* pointed out, some of these would have been redundant for most of the time, as only the biggest theatres would have a full range of instruments : 'Parts for oboe, horns and bassoons can be carried round for years without ever having the pleasure of finding players for these instruments.'[88]

Band call

Monday mornings were when the acts – as independent producers – worked with the backstage staff to arrange the few elements which the theatre itself provided. They would go through the cues and the basic staging of the act with the stage manager, and discuss the lighting plot with the electrician. Then there was the ritual of the band call, in which each act would rehearse with the orchestra. An article in *The Times* from 1961 vividly described this:

> As the various artists arrive their band books are placed in a tidy row along the footlights – each act with its own particular pile – top of the bill or opening act, it makes no difference, first to put his books down will be first to rehearse with the conductor and orchestra … At these rehearsals one could be surprised at the care, musical taste, and understanding of those who gather on the stage explaining their wants to the conductor.[89]

The first-come-first-served principle was an important part of the band call. It was the one point in the week when the normal hierarchy was suspended and the star acts could not pull rank, as Barry Cryer – who started his career as a comic in the final years of variety as well as working backstage at the Leeds Empire – recalls: '[T]here was a courtesy thing, a protocol – the band call on a Monday morning when people … rehearsed their songs and whatever, the stars did not get priority. It's the order in which you put your music down on the stage. If the star wasn't first, tough, you know.'[90]

Cryer also remembers annoying the orchestras when he worked as a comic in variety: 'I wasn't very popular with the pit orchestras … because I had a pre-recorded musical intro to come on to. So the Musicians' Union members weren't thrilled, because they couldn't play. Mind you, they got some time off, I don't suppose they were that worried.'[91]

Some musical directors would exploit the power they wielded over acts during band calls. Sydney Kaplan, who conducted the orchestra in the 1946 Lewisham Hippodrome show was notorious for a scam which involved shaming acts with tatty band parts into allowing him to produce new ones for them. He would then present them with gold-embossed red leather copies of their band parts, together with an extortionate bill for his services.[92]

Digs

In 1952, Ian Bevan wrote:

> Each week the variety shows break up and scatter, and come together again in different units … For us, Sunday is a day of rest; for the performers, it is a day of trains. Each Saturday night they say 'goodbye' to the acts who have been on the bill with them that week; each Monday morning they say 'hello' to those who will be with them for the week to come.[93]

On Sunday 14 April 1946, all those acts that had spent the previous six nights entertaining audiences at the Lewisham Hippodrome would have moved on to their next engagement in another town, and as individual producers they would have borne the cost of travelling there themselves. Most would have gone by train, and some would have probably belonged to the Music Hall Artistes' Railway Association, which gave its members a third off rail fares and a special baggage allowance – particularly handy for speciality acts with a lot of props to lug about.[94] Peter Prentice remembers:

> You travelled by train. There used to be a thing called a baggage man. And he was the theatre baggage man and you left the props for him to take to the station for you to collect to put on the train to go to your next place. And we got off the train there, you put the props and your cases and bikes and things in the left luggage, and then the baggage man would come on the Monday morning and pick it up and take it to the theatre.[95]

The itinerant performers who peopled the variety stage had certain key locations where they could meet up with their fellow acts. The Express Dairy on Charing Cross Road was one place where performers could rub shoulders over a snack or a cup of tea, perhaps finding a friendly agent or songwriter who might be able to do business with them. Another was Crewe railway station, where acts who were moving from one engagement to the next on a Sunday might run into one another while changing trains.

Then there were the digs – the theatrical lodgings where they would live for the week while appearing in the local variety theatre. Like transport, accommodation was another cost and another organizational task that fell to the performers themselves. As they arrived in a new town on a Sunday afternoon, they would be greeted at the station by landladies touting for trade, although many would have arranged their accommodation in advance.

Digs were usually fairly ordinary working-class homes with some spare rooms which they let out to performers, hot meals provided, for a modest fee. In some cases, the accommodation they offered was equally modest, as impressionist Florence Desmond recalled: 'Some of the digs we lived in had no baths and no indoor sanitation. The lavatory was usually at the end of the garden next to the toolshed.'[96] Ken Joy describes in some detail how the quality of digs might vary:

> You had a little list of ... the best digs, the best landladies. And it was always a fight to get back to the same one that you'd been to on previous tours.

And they were great, they were great. But some were bloody awful, you know. Many's the time I've been into digs where you come back from the theatre for your supper and you get beans on toast and the following night it's toast on beans ... I've been to places where it was so cold ... I used to heat up an iron to put it in the bed just to warm it up – or iron the sheets, you know, to warm the sheets up. Many's the time I've gone into digs where the wallpaper was curling off, it was stuck on with drawing pins and all sorts of things.[97]

Staying in digs – good or bad – could be a colourful experience, and a rich folklore grew up around them. There were tales of land-ladies who served rice pudding out of chamber pots or acts getting their revenge for poor accommodation by hiding a kipper in the chest of drawers before they left.[98] There was also a code among performers that if they wrote 'And I shall certainly tell my friends' in the visitors' book it was a warning that the digs were awful.[99] These kinds of gags and stories were normally reserved for offstage chat, but they could sometimes creep into the actual act for the amusement of the audi-ence, as in Freddie Bamberger's gag about paying an extra threepence because he wanted a mattress as well as the room.

The complexity of variety

There was warmth and camaraderie among the community of vari-ety performers, but also fierce competition. Each act was a separate business, competing with all the others for the best engagements and always trying to move up the hierarchy perhaps to top billing, with the tallest lettering, the best dressing rooms and the biggest fee. This undoubtedly drove up standards. The top acts were the ones who drew the most people to the theatres and entertained them the most while they were there, so to get to the top meant working hard to make the act as good as it could possibly be. This meant buying the best material, costumes, props and set, and maintaining them to the highest standard, so as to avoid missing out on repeat bookings sim-ply because of having dirty shoes. It also meant rehearsing the hard-est so that the gags, songs and stunts would be the best on offer. It was the fact that so many acts were competing with each other that made the best of them so much more brilliant and diverse than the performers seen on present day revivals, like the *Britain's Got Talent* live show.

However, if the fact that each act was an individual production made variety strong, it also made it complex. Putting together a show like the one at the Lewisham Hippodrome was a very complicated business, with booking managers negotiating with agents and issuing separate contracts to each act, and performers collaborating with musical directors, stage managers and electricians. The variety world was a web of interwoven business interests, with theatre chains, booking managers, agents, performers, song publishers, gag writers, railway companies, and theatrical landladies all trading with each other and trying to get themselves the best deal possible.

This complexity must have made the product strong, and the shows seen in the number one theatres would have been extraordinarily entertaining. However, it also made variety vulnerable to changes in public taste and shifting market forces, and when these started to happen in the mid-1950s, the web would be pulled apart with remarkable speed.

3

Music Hall Becomes Variety, 1890–1927

Music hall is much more interesting

Read the *Encyclopaedia Britannica*'s entry on music hall and variety, and you could be forgiven for thinking that variety theatre was pretty much extinct by the end of the 1920s. 'The advent of the talking motion picture in the late 1920s caused variety theatres throughout Great Britain to be converted into cinemas', it declares, adding that, 'The Windmill Theatre near Piccadilly Circus, London, was notable among a few survivors that remained after World War II from what had been hundreds of music halls.'[1]

This is misleading in more ways than one. For a start, the Windmill Theatre was never a music hall in the first place. Built as a cinema, it was converted to a theatre in 1931, and it presented not variety but nude revue. With an audience capacity of only 326, it was a very different beast from the huge variety halls, the largest of which seated ten times that number. More importantly, though, it is extraordinary that as authoritative a source as the *Encyclopaedia Britannica* could get the date of variety's demise so wrong. There certainly was a slump in the 1920s, but variety survived it, thrived again, and would not truly fall apart until the end of the 1950s. Somehow, thirty odd years of variety theatre has been airbrushed out of history.

This is par for the course. Since the late nineteenth century, there have been numerous books about music hall, initially produced by upper-class bohemians who frequented the halls, like W. R. Titterton,

Maurice Willson Disher and W. Macqueen Pope, and more recently by academics like J. S. Bratton, Peter Bailey and Dagmar Kift. Variety, on the other hand, has inspired just a measly handful of writing. As Dave Russell has noted, 'Almost no serious research has been undertaken into the variety industry beyond [1914] and the existing literature is thus full of very loose generalizations concerning the "death" of variety.'[2]

The origin of the problem might lie in the fact that the later variety tradition has often been portrayed as a sadly diminished rump of the earlier, more vital music hall. The early histories of music hall all tended to take this view. In 1912, W. R. Titterton argued that 'interesting as is the variety theatre and its myriad developments, the music hall is much more interesting and a thousand times more vital',[3] and misty-eyed nostalgia for the Victorian music hall was so popular that in 1938, Maurice Willson Disher parodied it, imagining how people in the future would reminisce about the stars of his own time:

> In time you will feel irritable towards young people. They will deafen you with their zest for life. Out of a desire for self-preservation you will belittle all that they are up to. 'Going to a music-hall?' you will ask in a quaveringly benevolent voice. And you will add, 'Music-halls aren't what they were in my young days. Stars were stars then. There's nobody now to compare with Will Fyffe or Gracie Fields. Enjoy yourself – if you can'... I mention this merely to show how we have always regarded the music-hall and always shall... We speak of it wistfully with a stifled sob in our voice.

Crucially he went on to add, 'That is why we pretend not to know that the music-hall still exists.'[4]

The difference in the way that music hall and variety have been viewed is written into the very terminology used to differentiate them. By the early 1900s, the term 'variety' was being used to differentiate the then-current scene from the earlier music hall, and it had taken on a pejorative edge.[5] 'Music hall' was seen as authentic, vital and democratic, whereas 'variety' was refined, efficient and soullessly respectable. Pejorative or not, the terms have been used since then to distinguish between the earlier and later halves of a continuous tradition, but confusingly, 'music hall' was still being used to describe the current scene when the last theatres closed in the early 1960s. To make things even more terminologically tangled, variety was also sometimes known as 'vaudeville', a word which is normally used to refer its American equivalent.

The rise of the Empires

Variety's ancestor, the music hall, emerged from a primeval swamp of tavern singing, broadside ballads and catch-and-glee clubs in the mid-nineteenth century. The immediate precursors of the music hall were song and supper rooms like the Coal Hole, the Cyder Cellars and Evans's Supper Rooms.[6] At such venues, customers could eat and drink until the early hours of the morning while listening to entertainers singing songs which were sometimes extremely bawdy.

On 17 May 1852, Charles Morton opened the Canterbury Music Hall in Lambeth, which accommodated 700 people, and unlike the song and supper rooms, admitted women.[7] This was a key moment, as it is normally recognized as the first bona fide music hall, thus giving Morton his nickname, 'The Father of the Halls'.[8] The success of the Canterbury was such that music halls quickly started springing up all over London and in provincial towns and cities. The entertainment they housed was dominated by singers who usually performed in character, singing songs which were frequently comic, parodying current trends or social types, and often boasting choruses which begged to be joined in with. Eating and drinking were still important, and audiences in the early halls would sit around tables or wander about rather than being restricted by fixed theatre seating.

The evolution from music hall to variety began towards the end of the nineteenth century, as big theatre chains began to emerge. Ambitious entrepreneurs such as H. E. Moss, Oswald Stoll, Walter De Frece, Richard Thornton, Frank McNaghten, Tom Barrasford and William Henry Broadhead set their sights above owning just one or two successful halls. Sometimes collaborating in complicatedly interwoven combines, and sometimes competing ruthlessly against each other, they built up their chains of theatres, usually starting in Scotland or the North of England and moving inexorably southwards towards London like conquering armies. The new theatres they built were called Empires, Palaces and Hippodromes.

To look at one example in detail, the powerful Moss Empires chain was started by H. E. Moss, who started running music halls in Edinburgh in the 1870s at the age of 25. He collaborated with Richard Thornton in building up his chain in Scotland and the North of England. Oswald Stoll was made managing director of Moss Empires which was formed when the ten different companies Moss had established were formally merged. Moss's theatres were built on a grand scale, and the volume of bookings he could offer to performers gave him the power to put rivals out of business. For example, the 3,000-seat Sheffield Empire, was built at a cost of £65,000 and opened on 4 November 1895, and several smaller music halls found they could not exist in its shadow. Moss reached London in 1899, when he opened Empires at Holloway, New Cross and Stratford. Richard Thornton went on to withdraw from Moss's circuit, building up an allied chain in the North-East, and in 1910, Stoll left to establish his own chain of Empires.[9]

Oswald Stoll was the archetypal variety magnate, as he was seen as a businessman more than a theatre man. Frederick Willis wrote that he 'looked like the last person in the world to have anything to do with music halls. He might have been a respectable, small business man, with a little suburban house and an interest in the local nonconformist church.'[10] With the rise of men like Stoll, music hall was becoming an early example of hard-edged consumer capitalism. Asa Briggs argued that by the 1920s, 'enormous concentrations of power were becoming almost as common in the entertainment world as they were in heavy industry'.[11]

As well as being an ultra hard-nosed businessman, Stoll was also a reformer, who saw it as his mission to turn disreputable music hall into respectable variety. As Fred Russell put it in trade magazine *The Performer* when Stoll died in 1942, 'one appreciates more and more what a powerful influence Sir Oswald exercised on our industry, and how much the raising of the standard of public entertainment was due to his unremitting effort'.[12]

Stoll was not the only one who wanted music halls to become more respectable. In the 1890s, a woman called Ormiston Chant ran a purity campaign against them, motivated by a desire to stop the prostitutes who plied their trade in the promenades at the back of the halls. She was successful enough to be ridiculed in the lyrics of more than one music hall song, and in 1894, the licensing committee of the London County Council (LCC) forced the Empire in Leicester Square to erect canvas screens shielding the area used by the prostitutes from the rest of the auditorium. The crowd that tore down the screens in protest contained a young Winston Churchill, who made his first public speech in what he described as the 'somewhat unvirginal surroundings' of the wreckage left behind.[13]

Unlike Chant, Stoll's reforming zeal was probably motivated as much by profit as by morality, because as the big chains grew up, the business of music hall was changing. From the days of semi-formalized tavern singing, sales of alcohol were a central plank of profitability, and admission to music halls often came in the form of 'wet money', whereby the customer paid for a token at the entrance which could be cashed in for drinks at the bar.[14]

However, the LCC, which shared Chant's view of music halls as places of drunkenness and immorality, started to use its ability to deny drinks licences as a way of restricting their growth. In the 1890s, the halls were making as much as 15–20 per cent of their takings from drinks sales, so the LCC's actions had a serious impact, forcing the halls to increase the profitability of the entertainment on the stage, partly by increasing attendances.[15]

This meant bringing in respectable family audiences, and the owners of the theatre chains were quite explicit about it. In 1907, Frank McNaghten explained, 'I am often asked why I call my halls "Palaces" and "Hippodromes". This is to draw a distinction between the old "music hall" of the past, frequented by men only, and the new Vaudeville entertainment of the present day, to be patronised by women and children.'[16] This was a crucial shift, as the respectable family audience would become the mainstay of variety theatre throughout its life, but the change was not welcomed by everyone. In 1912, the early music hall historian W. R. Titterton noted disdainfully that, 'The music-hall public is changing. A deliberate attempt is being made to capture the Halls for the well-to-do. The programme of entertainment is being altered to suit the new *clientèle*.'[17]

Entertaining the new *clientèle*

In order to entice husbands, wives and children, managers such as Moss and Stoll made various changes to make the entertainment they offered more temptingly respectable. These changes were built into the very fabric of the buildings where the shows took place. The early music halls had evolved from taverns, and still bore some of their features, with a drinking audience sitting around tables. The palatial new variety theatres, designed by architects like Frank Matcham, were a very different kettle of caviar. They were essentially conventional proscenium arch auditoriums, with rows of fixed seating, balconies and boxes, and were lavishly decorated with a riot of columns and curlicues, gilded plasterwork and plush carpets. According to a contemporary account, when the Matcham-designed Edinburgh Empire opened in 1892, the audience were impressionable enough to actually applaud the auditorium itself:

> To a packed auditorium when all the electric lights were put full on, just before the performance, the effect was magical. The Theatre, with its

stately proportions and beautiful decorations, stood revealed in all its grandeur, and the audience, charmed with the brilliant spectacle, broke out into a loud and hearty cheer.[18]

As variety performer Valantyne Napier pointed out, 'Compared to the general living conditions of that time', the new variety theatres 'were indeed palatial to the vast working class audiences who filled the auditoriums'.[19]

To befit such grand environments, the entertainment began to include more highbrow elements. The Empire, Leicester Square became famous for its ballet, and the Palladium played host to both the Thomas Beecham Opera Company and the actor Lewis Waller, performing a Mark Antony speech from Shakespeare's *Julius Caesar*.[20] Whether such elements raised or lowered the artistic standards of the variety theatres was a matter of debate, but W. R. Titterton described the presence on the bill of opera singers and Russian ballerinas like Diaghilev in emotive terms, claiming that 'the music-hall stage has been invaded by hordes of marauding savages'.[21]

The first Royal Variety Performance, which took place in the Palace Theatre, Shaftesbury Avenue on 1 July 1912, was widely seen as a pivotal moment, when variety was finally stamped with the indelible mark of respectability. As the *Manchester Guardian* put it, 'A Royal box has now been created for ever in the music-hall.'[22] A few decades later, when there had been numerous similar shows at theatres like the Coliseum, the Victoria Palace and the Palladium, music hall historian W. Macqueen-Pope wrote: 'Music Hall, the entertainment of the people by the people for the people had been granted – or, rather, had won – Royal recognition. It could go no higher.'[23]

The transition from music hall to variety met with some severe disgruntlement among more traditional audience members. In November 1913, Charles E Hands complained in the *Daily Mail* that, 'the conquering hordes of the upper and middle classes...have taken away our music-halls from us'. He argued that the so-called 'wonderful improvement' over the previous twenty years amounted to 'no more than the exclusion from the auditorium of the vulgar working-class population'. Increased ticket prices meant that, 'The only place left for us was a gallery two miles high, and that at a price that made a hole in the week's spending money', and to add insult to injury, 'they won't let us have any beer. So that if we want an occasional evening's complete enjoyment we have to spend half of it in a palace and half of it in a public house, and neither of them quite satisfies us.'[24]

Early music hall historian W. R. Titterton shared this sense of outrage, taking a comically strident approach:

> The worst is so terrible that I hardly dare to mention it. *They have taken away our beer!* In some halls they have banished him to the bar. From some they have banished him altogether and have inscribed over the portals this accursed motto: 'Abandon hops all ye that enter here.'[25]

The performers who worked for the growing chains of theatres had more serious problems, because the new barons of variety, the Mosses and the Stolls, enjoyed fearsome levels of power and exercised strict control over them. Frank McNaghten, for example, made a speech at the opening of the Burnley Palace in 1907 in which he told the audience: 'Anything noticed of an objectionable nature should be reported immediately to the manager. It will receive my immediate attention in Sheffield.'[26]

Twice nightly

In 1916, the music hall comedian George Formby senior recorded the song 'Twice Nightly', sending up the new format which had come to dominate the variety circuit in the previous two decades. In the same kind of weedy-but-cheery Lancashire accent which his ukulele-playing son is still remembered for, he sang:

> It seems a daring thing to dash upon the stage and hum – twice nightly,
> Sometimes you run the risk of being kicked into the drum – twice nightly,
> When first I joined the music halls a long, long time ago,
> I used to be an acrobat and only did one show,
> But now I'm sorry for myself, they make you work you know,
> Twice nightly.[27]

As the song implies, the system of putting the same show on twice a night increased the efficiency of the entertainment by making the performers work twice as hard, without necessarily doubling the money they were paid. The origins of the system are contested, but the earliest claim is probably that of Louis Leglere, who ran two houses a night at the Ridgen's Alhambra in Sandgate in 1860.[28] The system was pioneered by Tom Barrasford, who created a chain of 14 halls in four years in the 1890s.[29] The first Moss theatre to run shows twice nightly was the Nottingham Empire, which opened in February 1898, and this was such a success that it was quickly adopted by the whole chain.[30]

Presenting the same show twice in a night changed the nature of the entertainment, not least in that it meant a smaller number of acts being booked. A classic music hall bill might go on for three or four hours. For example, an 1897 programme for the Oxford Music Hall advertises a massive bill of 26 items, including big names like James Fawn, T. E. Dunville and Marie Loftus, alongside other attractions such as Barnard's Marionettes, the Eight Eldorado Girls, and a ventriloquist called Lieutenant Travis. One notable turn is an early appearance by the sketch comedian Harry Tate, who was presenting a quick-change sketch in which he impersonated seven famous music hall comedians.[31]

A 1904 programme from the New Cross Empire – the stern faces of Moss and Stoll staring out from the front cover – suggests a very different kind of show. The twice nightly system was clearly new enough at this point to have to be explained to the customers, in a rather excited tone: 'Two Complete and Distinct Performances Nightly! All Artistes appear at each Performance, and Both Performances are alike.' Performances began at 6.50 p.m. and 9.10 p.m., and each lasted two hours. The bill itself contained just 12 items, fewer than half the number at the Oxford, including G. H. Chirgwin, Alec Hurley and List's Performing Bears.[32] Clearly, this must have been a far more tightly controlled show than the one at the Oxford seven years earlier.

The rigours of the twice nightly system and the barring clauses used by the big chains to avoid losing their best acts to the opposition left the performers feeling aggrieved and exploited, and this had repercussions more serious than the light joshing heard in Formby's song. Harsher working conditions led to the music hall strike of 1907, which saw the improbable spectacle of the extremely famous comic singer Marie Lloyd picketing outside the theatres, and allegedly shouting abuse at Lockhart's Elephants as they crossed a picket line. The strike led to an agreed labour contract for performers, which placed some limits on the power of the barring clause.[33]

Another victim of the rise of the Empires and the introduction of the twice nightly system was the chairman. Since the pre-music hall days of tavern singing, the entertainment had been presided over by a chairman, who would introduce the acts and try and impose some kind of order on the audience. Knowles of the Cambridge Music Hall, for example, had a ritual exchange with the audience in the Gods who would shout, 'Who?' as he announced the next act. He would respond by assuming a dignified attitude and declaring, 'You heard!'.[34] Initially, the number boards which replaced the chairman in variety consisted of a golden easel on either side of the proscenium, with elaborately dressed and bewigged footman changing the numbers. According to Frederick Willis, they were mercilessly ridiculed by the audience: 'Every time this grand figure appeared to change the number the house rocked with ironical cheers.'[35]

The virus of variety

The introduction of the twice nightly system and the general drive towards respectability were not the only things that distinguished twentieth-century variety from Victorian music hall. There were other important changes to the entertainment. Most importantly, whereas music hall was dominated by comic songs and chorus songs, variety was, as the name implies, much more varied. As early as 1889, George Bernard Shaw saw the change coming with remarkable prescience: 'If left to develop freely, our best music halls would in course of time present a combination of promenade concert, theatre, and circus... that is, you would have a good band, decent concert singers, acrobats, jugglers, ballets, and dramatic sketches, all in the same evening.'[36] Half a century later, Max Beerbohm argued that 'the virus of "Variety"' had stopped him going to the music hall because, rather perversely, he had preferred the 'monotony... of song after song, good, bad, and indifferent'.[37]

Songs remained an important part of variety – along with the front cloth comics, dancers, speciality acts and performing animals – but in the early years of the twentieth century, the musical style radically changed. In 1912 Moss Empires booker Albert de Courville brought over the Ragtime Octette, and by 1913, there were at least 130 American ragtime bands touring Britain.[38] Hot on the heels of ragtime came jazz, with de Courville bringing over the Original Dixieland Jazz Band (ODJB) in 1919 to play in the revue *Joy Bells*. At the insistence of their co-star – the jazz-hating music hall comedian George Robey – the ODJB were dropped from the show, but went on to appear at the Palladium.[39]

Like Robey, the early music hall historians also disliked the new styles of syncopated American music. W. Macqueen-Pope referred to ragtime as 'a good joke, not an accepted medium', while Maurice Willson Disher wrote of 'the whole plague of pianos that stunned the ears of peace-loving souls'.[40]

Although music hall songs varied in rhythm, tone and tempo, they shared a recognizable style which was glaringly different from the hot new American sounds. The music hall style never completely disappeared from the variety stages, partly because music hall veterans continued to perform on variety stages until the last theatres disappeared, but younger performers were more enthusiastic about the new American styles. Ted Ray, for example, went to America in 1926 while playing in a dance band, and recalled: 'We looked to the States for those fascinating records and for the band numbers that could take the British fans by storm.'[41]

This throws up another key reason for the mutation of music hall into variety. Music hall songs were almost always the exclusive property of the singer who sung them, and would be absolutely associated with that singer. If you heard 'Down at the Old Bull and Bush' sung in a music hall, you could be sure it was Florrie Forde singing it, and even if it were not, hearing it would make you think of her. With jazz and ragtime, this exclusivity disappeared. All of the singers were looking to America for the latest hot tune, and when it was found, multiple covers of it would be heard in variety.[42]

Boom and bust

Ironically, at the very time that music hall was – according to the Dishers and the Macqueen-Popes – losing its way artistically, it was also enjoying its greatest commercial success. In 1912, the LCC licensed 51 variety theatres with a total capacity of 76,370, each of putting on shows twice nightly, and it has been estimated that annual attendances in London could have been 25 million or more.[43] During the First World War, the Palladium alone was selling three million tickets a year.[44]

However, by the 1920s the boom was followed by a devastating slump which endangered variety's very existence. Performers found their livelihoods severely under threat. Max Wall's stepfather Harry Wallace had to give up a career as half of the song-and-dance double act Burns & Bentley, and start working as a market trader instead.[45] Florence Desmond started her career in around 1920, and in her autobiography she wrote that the 'terrible slump' meant that she 'couldn't have picked a worse time to start doing an act on the "Halls"'.[46]

Theatres began to close or to be converted to accommodate other types of entertainment. As if to symbolize the death of music hall, many of its most iconic venues disappeared. The Tivoli closed on 7 February 1914, having to be demolished as part of a scheme to widen the Strand, but when it eventually reopened in 1923, it was as a cinema.[47] Oswald Stoll closed the Middlesex in November 1918, as he found it 'impossible to compile a sufficiently attractive programme'.[48] The Oxford was rebuilt as the New Oxford Theatre in 1920 in order to host not variety but spectacular revue, finally closing with heavy losses in 1923.[49] The Empire, where Churchill had spoken to the screen-smashing mob, closed in January 1927.[50] The Alhambra and the Pavilion were both demolished to make way for cinemas in the 1930s.[51]

The slump might have been precipitated by overexpansion, but probably the biggest threat to variety's existence was the emergence of various rival forms of popular entertainment. One of these was revue, which became so popular that, as Ian Bevan put it, 'the word "revue" almost ousted "variety" in the lexicon of the halls'.[52] Unlike variety, a revue was a show with a title, an actual production rather than just a collection of acts. It was written and directed, and cast members would appear in more than one item. There would be song and dance numbers performed by a chorus, sketches, and usually some sort of finale.

Revues staged in variety theatres were extremely diverse. In big theatres like the Palladium they could be big-budget spectaculars, but in the 1920s the number two and three theatres in the provinces were dominated by cut-price revues with shabby scenery and no big stars. The structure of the shows also differed. At one end of the scale, there were heavily themed shows like the 1936 London Palladium revue *O-Kay for Sound*, in which the Crazy Gang and other variety acts were contained within a loose narrative, even if this stopped short of becoming a fully-fledged stage musical. According to the critic James Agate:

> Our genial management has put a frame round the new production by suggesting that what we are watching is the making of that extraordinary thing which the film trade calls a musical. The show is neither the better nor the worse for this, just as boiled mutton remains the same whether you eat it off gold, silver, or tin; it all depends on the caper sauce.[53]

At the other end, there were revues which were little more than straight variety bills tarted up with a production number or two. A typical example is *Swing It*, which toured in 1936–37, with such acts as Teddy Brown, the swing band Nat Gonella & His Georgians, and the comic magician Sirdani ('Don't Be Fright!'). A review in *The Era* described it as 'little more than a name for linking together a team of very fine artists, each doing their own stuff in their own jolly way'.[54] The only thing to distinguish this from straight variety was the finale, 'South American Joe', in which the whole company appeared.[55] This mixture of production numbers and sketches interspersed with variety acts was sometimes referred to as 'produced variety'.[56] As late as 1953, Florence Desmond was complaining about 'the tendency to get a collection of music-hall acts together and call it a "revue"'.[57]

Unsurprisingly, early music hall historians also tended to dislike revue, albeit for different reasons. Macqueen-Pope said they were 'sapping the strength of Variety' because 'the Individualists were joining in with the crowd – chorus girls and big ensembles were taking the place of those mighty men and women who, unaided, had been able to command the rapt attention of huge audiences.'[58] Some of these Individualists also disliked the new form, and Marie Lloyd's song 'Revue' referred to 'Maudies and Bessies' wearing 'pretty dresses' and having to 'Show a little bit of leg'. The main gripe seemed to be:

> Well you've got to do this,
> And you've got to do that,
> If you want to get on in revue.[59]

Whereas variety acts produced themselves and enjoyed a lot of control over their work, performers in a revue found themselves under the control of a director. On the other hand, there were compensations for this. As variety comedian Jack Seaton pointed out, whereas in variety 'you provided all your stuff', in a revue 'if you was in any sketch, the producer'd provide it. Sometimes they had suits made for you. Especially if there's a finale where it's all like a colour scheme finale. The suits would be made for you.'[60]

If revue eventually became subsumed into the variety tradition, cinema posed a much more serious threat. Ironically, some of the first films to be shown in Britain were shown in music halls, and topical film footage became a common feature of music hall bills in the 1890s. One of the 26 items on the 1897 Oxford Music Hall bill was R. W. Paul's 'Theatregraph' which showed 'animated pictures' of Queen Victoria's Diamond Jubilee Procession. As actual cinemas started sprouting up, they became serious competitors to variety, not least because they offered entertainment at a cheaper price.[61]

By the 1920s, variety had another competitor, and one that could provide entertainment for free in the audience's own homes – radio. The owners of the variety theatres viewed it with great suspicion, seeing it as another rival at a time when they were already experiencing a crisis. As Moss Empires' chairman Walter Payne put it:

> Offers of the BBC with its vast and growing resources may easily cause chaos in relation to what I may term [the acts'] market value. Salaries could be raised temporarily to prohibitive heights – only to be followed

by complete collapse of the permanent value and freshness of the artistes themselves.[62]

Theatre managers imposed an almost total ban on live broadcasts from 1923 to 1925, and even after that artists could be forbidden by contract to appear on the radio.[63] Disputes over variety artistes appearing on the radio were significant enough to form the plot of a feature film, *Radio Parade of 1935*, in which Will Hay appears as the Director-General of the National Broadcasting Group (NBG), a thinly disguised parody of the BBC. Banned from using variety performers in the big show they are planning, the NBG recruit acts from among their staff, although ironically, these parts are actually played by actual variety acts like Ted Ray, Ronald Frankau, Beryl Orde and Stanelli & his Hornchestra.[64]

Junior and senior

The coexistence with rival forms of entertainment and the new influences from America meant that variety was much more of a hybrid than music hall had been. Music hall is often seen as indomitably British, and variety was certainly more cosmopolitan. The difference between the two is nicely highlighted by the contrast between the two George Formbys, senior and junior. They had similar personas, taking on the role of the Lancashire underdog, and the similarity between their voices is unmistakable. One of the biggest differences was their respective musical styles.

Most of George Formby senior's songs were in the classic music hall style, and the basic joke of his act was that in spite of the fact that he was a gentle, unsophisticated Lancashire lad, he laboured under the illusion that he was good-looking, fashionable and savvy. One of his recordings, 'John Willie's Ragtime Band', sees him sending up the latest American craze by plonking it down in Lancashire. He boasts about his band playing 'on Wigan Pier' to the delight of mill girls and colliers:

> In Bury now they do it grand,
> They 'op round with black puddings in their hand,
> When they hear – John Willie's Ragtime Band.
> Baby dear, listen 'ere – *zim!*[65]

In this last line, the pure music hall musical style is infected with a hint of ragtime's rhythm and hearing Formby singing this in his slow, deliberate Lancastrian when the phrase is clearly designed for a dynamic American delivery is a good gag in itself, even on a crackly mechanical recording dating from 1914.

Formby senior was in his mid-forties when he died in February 1921, and his *Times* obituary noted that his type of music hall comedian was 'rapidly disappearing'.[66] Nonetheless, when his son, the better-remembered George Formby, started his career shortly afterwards, he initially did so by slavishly imitating his father. In 1926, Formby recorded six of his father's songs, including 'John Willie's Jazz Band', which was based on essentially the same gag as 'Ragtime Band'.[67] As he developed his own style, based more on innuendo than playing the deluded innocent abroad, he continued to poke fun at jazz convention. For example, in 'All Going Back', he gets comic mileage out of 'women...who sing upon the stage' singing about living 'in places where they've never been' like Arizona, Alabama and Texas:

> But just one thing worries me,
> When they go back to Tennessee,
> There'll be no one left in Wigan,
> But me.[68]

There is an important difference, though. Here, the entire tune is thoroughly jazz-inflected. By the time Formby junior became a star, all of his songs were driven by the rhythm, style and energy of American popular music, not least because of his choice of the ukulele, an instrument built for rhythmical flourishes. He might have made fun of jazz and swing, but his music was steeped in them. In 1939, he even recorded 'Swing It, George' parts one and two, a couple of medleys of popular American tunes like 'Tiger Rag' and 'Sweet Georgia Brown' sung relatively straight.[69]

He continued to play on his Lancashire origins in songs like 'With My Little Stick of Blackpool Rock', singing American-style music in his own native accent, but the joke had changed. The synthesis of New Orleans and Wigan was no longer funny in itself, and instead the laughs came from double entendres in the lyrics, playing on the penile possibilities of his 'little stick of Blackpool rock' which meant that 'every girl I danced with stuck to me tight'.[70] Like the ukulele-playing, swing-singing Lancashire lad George Formby, variety could take in new influences from elsewhere and yet remain unmistakably British.

4

The Golden Age of Variety, 1928–52

Variety is coming back

Press coverage of the variety bill at the London Palladium in the week commencing 3 September 1928 excitedly describes the 'overwhelming crowds' it attracted, with hundreds or even thousands milling around in Argyll Street 'struggling' to get into the theatre.[1] The show was such a big success that even in the week itself, it was seen as being of historical importance. Journalists were rightly anticipating that this was a pivotal moment in variety theatre.

It was a strong bill, with such diverse acts as comic singer Gracie Fields, comedian Billy Bennett, trapeze artist Mademoiselle Tamara, acrobats the Seven Hindustans, Alfred Jackson's English Dancing Girls, and a new Ivor Novello sketch starring Novello himself and Phyllis Monkman. However, even though as a review in *The Era* put it, it was a programme that 'that no lover of vaudeville could resist', it was not the acts themselves that gave the show its significance, or even drew the overwhelming crowds to the theatre.[2]

What made this show important was that it was a conscious attempt to bring variety back from the brink, to rescue it from the slump of the 1920s that had threatened its very existence. This is how the show was sold to the public. With a genuine flair for marketing, George Black, who had recently taken control of the theatre, had splattered London with yellow and black posters bearing the slogan 'VARIETY IS COMING BACK...', later completing the slogan by adding the phrase 'TO THE PALLADIUM'.[3] In doing so, he was picking up on an idea that was already floating around at the time: that variety was ripe for revival. A *Times* review of a show at the Coliseum in June 1926, for example, talked about people wondering whether 'variety, as distinguished from *revue*, is about to come into its own again'.[4]

Black's publicity not only brought in the crowds, it also established the idea that this was a historically significant moment for variety. *The Era* talked of 'Variety's come-back', while the *Manchester Guardian* called it a 'Music-hall rally', and *The Stage* announced that, 'The return of the Palladium to variety is certainly to be numbered among the most important events of the year.'[5] What the press coverage also makes clear is that this was seen as a popular victory. As *The Observer* put it, 'Eager crowds in Argyll Street testified each night last week to the public's joy over a music-hall that had repented of its attempts to be something else.'[6]

The threat that variety was facing at this point was very real. Not only were many of the famous music halls shutting down in the face of competition from revue and radio, but variety's most dangerous rival, cinema, was about to pose even more of a challenge. The *Manchester Guardian* pointed out that the timing of Black's variety revival was crucial: 'Apparently the "talkies", which are now, so to speak, at the door, will have something to fight when they come.'[7] Sound cinema really was at the door, as just over three weeks later, on 27 September, *The Jazz Singer* opened in London.[8]

The Palladium itself had responded to the variety slump by, as *The Observer* pointed out, attempting to be something else. Shortly before variety came back in 1928, it had staged a musical, *The Apache*, tried a hybrid of cinema and variety, and screened a controversial film called *Dawn*. All of these had enjoyed such a conspicuous lack of success that the theatre had changed hands more than once – Charles Gulliver sold it off to Walter Gibbons, who was later forced to resign.[9]

Black took over at around this time, but his background did not make him a likely candidate to stage such a conspicuous attempt to pull variety back from the brink. In fact, he had come from cinema rather than theatre. In the early years of the twentieth century, he had built up a chain of 13 cinemas in the North of England, selling them off in 1919, before building up another 11-cinema chain. In 1928, his cinemas were amalgamated into the newly formed General Theatre Corporation (GTC), and he became director of the new company.[10]

High-speed variety

In 1938, ten years after the Palladium relaunch, *The Performer* published an article about Black in which a 'well-known critic' claimed that he had 'done more to revolutionise the music-hall profession than any other living man, and can be rightly called a pillar of strength to the music-hall profession'.[11] What was it that made a former cinema proprietor take such active steps in rescuing this form of live theatre?

One crucial influence was his colleague Val Parnell, who had been brought in by Walter Gibbons as booking manager for his season of cine-variety. It was apparently Parnell who suggested the return to full-blooded variety, but Black responded enthusiastically.[12] He saw it as his role not just to rescue, but also to reinvent variety, arguing that, 'It is not enough...for the old Variety to return with its cobwebs and dust; its go-as-you-please methods and similarity of turns. A new structure is being built on the old foundations, replete with new ideas, new methods, renewed vitality and, above all, fresh powers of amusement.'[13]

Perhaps the most important innovation was to change the way variety was staged. One of the first-week reviews noted a 'cause for congratulation': 'Instead of a series of turns separated by yawning intervals, the performance was without a break, apart from the "intermission".'[14] Before Black, variety had moved at a more leisurely pace, and Max Wall recalled that in his father, Jack Lorimer's time, singers would leave the stage between numbers to change, and would be off long enough to have a drink and a chat with the stage manager, because 'speed was unheard of in comparison with contemporary times'.[15]

Increasing the speed was a crucial change. Later variety acts such as Valantyne Napier were conditioned to see stage waits as an 'unforgivable sin', but before the innovations of the Palladium relaunch, any show could have regular momentum-killing pauses, not just between the acts but also within them. Black not only made performers speed up and cut out gaps between numbers, he also eliminated stage waits between the acts. He did this by bringing in the system of alternating front cloth acts with ones that used the full stage, and others that could 'close in one', thus allowing the stage to be set for the next act while the current act was still performing.

This new approach, known as high-speed variety, was not Black's invention. It had been used in American vaudeville since the late nineteenth century, and was often referred to as 'American-style'.[16] In Britain, Walter Gibbons had tried a similar approach at the Holborn Empire some years earlier, booking more acts and forbidding them to leave the stage to change.[17] More importantly, Parnell had done much the same in response to fierce competition from Moss theatres when he was booking manager for the Birmingham Hippodrome shortly after the First World War.[18]

What Black did was to embrace such ideas as part of a more general overhaul of variety's format. He also improved the quality of sets, backdrops and drapes, put pressure on agents to nurture new talent, tried to fend off song-pluggers who bribed singers to sing the songs they were pushing regardless of quality, pressed comedians to spend money of material rather than stealing each other's gags, and generally encouraged performers to try new things instead of trotting out the same old act. His attention to detail was such that even the theatre's drinks policy was changed, with the introduction of soda fountains.[19]

Jack Seaton, who got to know Black while running errands at the Palladium as a boy in the Second World War, described his approach:

> He was like my grandfather. He used to have that kind of warmth, but a very strict man as far as the business was concerned... and everybody admired him for it. For instance, when the show was on, he used to creep into the Royal Box, and stand at the back of it to watch it. And if anything shouldn't be there, like he said to Bud Flanagan once, 'So-and-so, you shouldn't do that'. He said, 'It just crept in, guv'nor', he said, 'Well let it creep out again'. Now, Tommy [Trinder] knew when he was in, because George Black wore glasses. And when he went on first, he always used to look in that box... if it hadn't been sold to anybody, and he could see the reflection of the lights in his glasses... And he came on, he used to go, 'Watch out, the guv'nor's this afternoon'.[20]

Black's marketing slogan, 'Variety Is Coming Back', was not as hyperbolic as it sounds, because his sights were set higher than just the Palladium. A history of that theatre published in 1952 claimed that:

> [H]is aim was to revive variety throughout the country, for he realised that his one big theatre could exist only as the apex of a solid music-hall structure. He need not run the small halls, but they would have to be there to supply him with audiences and, more importantly, with artists.[21]

He certainly succeeded in making the Palladium the pinnacle of the variety profession, and Jimmy Jewel recalled that playing there 'was everyone's ambition'.[22] Having achieved great things at the Palladium, the high-speed variety policy was rolled out in all GTC theatres. From there, it continued to spread out across the national variety circuit, not least because the powerful Moss Empires chain soon came under Black's command when he became a director in 1932, and managing director in 1938.[23]

Variety's survival in the face of the crisis of the 1920s might have been partly the result of broader social and economic forces, but there is no doubt that Black's deliberate and conscious intervention had a profound effect. This becomes clear when British variety is compared with American vaudeville, where the theatres were subject to similar forces, but the intervention of an individual had the opposite effect. As in variety, vaudeville had seen individual theatre owners replaced by large chains run by entrepreneurs like B. F. Keith, Edward F. Albee and Martin Beck. In 1927, the chains converged into one enormous organization, which came into the hands of Joseph P. Kennedy, who sold his controlling shares to the Radio Corporation of America, thus forming the film company RKO. The chain's theatres were converted to cinemas and, at a stroke, vaudeville was effectively dead.[24]

Variety and its rivals

Something else which helped variety to survive the competition from revue, cinema and radio was the fact that it developed more of a symbiotic relationship with its rivals. Revues became common in variety theatres, and began to closely resemble a standard variety bill. In fact, revue was just one of a series of variants on the standard formula.

In the early 1930s, for example, the London Pavilion experimented with 'Non-Stop Variety', in which shows ran continuously from 2 p.m. until midnight. The audience paid anything from 1 shilling and 3 pence to 5 shillings to get in, and once inside, they could stay as long as they liked. The whole programme played four or five times a day, part of it being described as 'Our Cabaret', compèred by performers like Peter Godfrey and Naunton Wayne.[25]

Similarly, after the Second World War, road shows became increasingly common. *The Stage Year Book* of 1949 defined these as 'bands of vaudeville performers who travel together from town to town giving the same music hall show at each venue'.[26] As opposed to weekly-change variety, where each act had to be booked separately, road shows allowed management to book the whole bill as a total package. The difference would probably not have been particularly obvious to audiences. Both weekly-change variety and road shows offered a string of unconnected acts presented in essentially the same way.

However, for the acts themselves it would have felt very different, performing with the same acts every week, rather than saying good-bye to their fellow performers after the second house on Saturday nights. It is possible that as each act got to know the others and the dynamic of the way the bill played out, the show would get slicker and more balanced. There were also distinct financial advantages for the star act, bringing them a large share of the profits rather than a fixed fee. Vera Lynn explains how it worked: 'When I was touring I used to be responsible for my own show – you know, all the other performance ... through my agent I would engage these people and pay them their salary.' In this arrangement, the supporting acts might actually change week by week, but 'you would naturally have repeat artists that you knew were good'.[27]

Variety also found productive ways of coexisting with cinema. Just as music halls had screened early films between the acts, so cinemas began to employ variety acts to perform between the movies. The hybrid form was known as cine-variety, and it became an important enough section of the variety business to warrant its own regular column in trade paper *The Era*. The smaller cinemas would put on two acts doing about 25 minutes between them, but the big super cinemas would stage shows of up to an hour before the main feature started.[28]

The cinemas were influenced by Black's innovations at the Palladium in booking their acts. In October 1931, Arthur Jarratt of Gaumont-British Pictures Corporation spoke of needing 'silent or dumb-show acts' because acts that used patter could not be heard properly at the back of cinema auditoriums: 'We need "Rapid-fire" turns, such as those developed by George Black at the Palladium, but they must be cast in the silent technique.'[29]

A show at the Regent, Stamford Hill in January 1937 gives an idea of just how spectacular cine-variety could be. As well as the film, the capacity audience enjoyed live performances from Cooke's Pony Revue, Ju Lio San with a performing sea lion, acrobatics from the Eight Frilli Troupe, and trapeze artists the Stanley, Tony and Mae Four. The Great Andos family's act involved 'a young lady' who 'climbs from the stage to the circle on a wire, and then slides down it at alarming speed on to the stage', while Pinder's performing elephant and ponies saw the trainer 'put his head into the elephant's giant chasm of a mouth'.[30] It is hard to imagine seeing any kind of live entertainment in a modern multiplex cinema, much less something that involves a man putting his head in the mouth of a trained pachyderm.

In America, cinemas provided pretty much the only stage for vaudeville acts after RKO took over, but in Britain, cine-variety was merely an offshoot of the main variety circuit, albeit an important one. By the early years of the Second World War, it had started to disappear – in 1942, *The Performer* referred to cine-variety coming to an 'untimely end', before reporting the first West End cine-variety show since the Blitz taking place at the Regal, Marble Arch.[31] In fact, cine-variety continued to crop up here and there right into the 1950s, with Max Wall recalling a booking at the Empire cinema in Leicester Square as late as 1954.[32]

The success of cine-variety meant that some venues, such as the Empires at Woolwich and Wood Green, reverted back from cinemas to variety theatres, and in 1937, Harold Ramsey of Union Cinemas announced that he was going to experiment with a 'complete change from films to variety'.[33] Then there were the variety theatres which used films as a source of extra income. The Empress, Brixton would run as a regular variety theatre from Monday to Saturday, and rake in extra money by showing films on Sunday afternoons.[34]

Cinema also helped variety in other ways. For a start, it documented variety acts, in anything from Pathé Gazette films, in which they were simply filmed in a studio, to feature films such as the 1930s *Elstree Calling*. This was described as a 'modernised form of variety forming a "portable" bill which can, and will, be taken from town to town', and featured a series of acts like Tommy Handley, Will Fyffe, Lily Morris, Teddy Brown and the Three Eddies strung together in a loose frame. When it was shown at the Alhambra, it was supported by a live act from Barbara Austen.[35]

The bigger names in variety went further than just doing their act for the camera, supplementing their theatre careers by starring in feature films. Some, such as Max Miller, found that their style did not transfer well onto celluloid and their cinema careers were never much more than a sideline to their live performances. Others, such as Gracie Fields – in such movies as *Sally in Our Alley* (1932) and *Sing as We Go* (1934) – and George Formby – with films such as *Boots! Boots!* (1934) and *Let George Do It* (1940) – became bona fide movie stars. There were clearly advantages to the variety industry in this, because the cinematic success enjoyed by the likes of Fields and Formby made them much more of a box-office draw when they did their acts in the theatres.

Radio could give performers similar audience-pulling power. When the owners of the big variety chains were still viewing it with suspicion, Roger Eckersley of the BBC wrote to Charles Gulliver and argued that 'the fact that we can give no representation of the visual sense makes it to our minds so tremendously non-competitive that it should not be considered nearly so much a rival as, shall we say, the cinema.'[36] The non-visual aspect of radio was seen as a positive advantage to variety, because it was popularly believed that audience went to the theatres to see radio stars in the flesh. Even today, Vera Lynn argues that:

> [T]he more people heard you on the radio, the more popular you became, therefore when they saw your name up outside theatres and things, they'd say, 'Oh I'll go and see what she looks like'... You know, you're used to hearing the voice but no way of knowing what they look like.[37]

Some performers were still suspicious. Clapham & Dwyer, for example, who first broadcast in 1926, were worried that 'we had only one act at that time and we really didn't want to give it away to thousands listening in'.[38] Others realized that success on the radio could significantly boost their variety career, increasing their popularity and helping them to jump significantly further up the bill.

Vera Lynn claimed that broadcasting meant that, 'In one single month, my career had made more progress than it had in the whole previous decade', while Jimmy Jewel believed that his radio show *Up the Pole* 'had done more for us in a month than all the years of working on stage'.[39] For Arthur Askey, radio success did more than boost his variety career; it actually brought it into being. He had never played in variety before he enjoyed massive success in the radio comedy series *Band Waggon*. The reputation he built on air meant he was offered joint top of the bill engagements at the Shepherd's Bush and Hackney Empires, and these led to regular theatre appearances. Radio brought variety success to band leaders such as Henry Hall, Jack Hylton and Billy Cotton, and there were even theatre engagements for the BBC organist Reginald Foort and the disc jockey Christopher Stone.[40]

Theatre owners clearly recognized the commercial potential of radio. Popular radio programmes such as *Band Waggon* and *Garrison Theatre* were turned into stage shows at the Palladium and elsewhere. Radio also saw the advantages of variety, seeing it as 'the "bread-and-butter" of broadcasting'.[41] From the late 1920s onwards there were regular live broadcasts from theatres such as the Palladium. In March 1932, the long-running series *Music Hall* began, featuring variety acts recorded in front of a live audience, and surveys found that it attracted 60 per cent of the total audience for radio. Half of all listeners 'listened to all studio variety programmes' and 'variety or theatre relays were by far the favourite programmes'.[42]

While variety clearly reaped great benefits from radio, George Black continued to view it with suspicion and would sometimes stop the acts he engaged from broadcasting for the BBC. For example, at Christmas 1932, the GTC forbade Gracie Fields and Max Miller from appearing on a BBC programme, only relenting at the last minute. Norman Long had already publicly stated that he was going to ignore Black's instruction and had an engagement at the Palladium cancelled as a result.[43]

The interaction with rival forms meant that the stars of variety tended to have more multifaceted careers than their music hall predecessors. They were film stars, radio performers, and recording artists as well appearing on the variety stage, and the competing demands of each strand of their career could make for a punishingly hectic lifestyle. Max Miller, for example, would play two houses a night in variety, getting home about midnight, and then have to be ready to start work on a film set for nine o'clock the next morning.[44] Similarly, while Gracie Fields was filming *Queen of Hearts*, she was also playing every night at the Holborn Empire. However, her demanding schedule was also lucrative. While appearing as Lady Weir in the play *SOS* at the St James's Theatre, she was also doing her act at the Alhambra and going on to play in late night cabaret at the Café Royal, earning her £100, £200 and £300 respectively, as well as making records in the daytime.[45]

Variety comes back – again

Although Black enjoyed immediate success with his relaunch of the Palladium in 1928, the variety circuit as a whole was not revived quite so instantaneously. Other theatres continued to struggle, and at the annual meeting of the Victoria Palace in January 1930, Sir Alfred Butt made a speech in which he was extremely pessimistic about variety's future, pointing out that his theatre's profits had dropped from £21,848 to £16,260 within the space of a year.[46] Before Black took charge of Moss Empires in 1932, there were rumours that the circuit was about to switch over from variety to film.[47]

However, by 1938, *The Performer* was talking 'about the now past slump' and arguing that variety 'continues to thrive'.[48] *The Era* was even more bullish, announcing, 'This autumn will be variety's best season for four year' and warning that the demand for variety was enough to threaten 'a coming famine in first-rate variety acts... Obviously the star-material, of which there is already a very severe shortage, will not be sufficient to serve the new demands. Bookers are at their wits' ends to find enough suitable acts.'[49]

Ironically, having rescued variety from potential oblivion by reviving and reinventing the form, Black went on to move away from it, instead increasingly staging revues at the Palladium. This started when he programmed the first Crazy Month in 1931. As an experiment, he booked three comedy double acts, Nervo & Knox, Naughton & Gold and Caryll & Mundy, along with 'Monsewer' Eddie Gray, and the acts were encouraged to fool around and interrupt each other's acts. More Crazy Months were staged, and this led to the core performers being dubbed the Crazy Gang, with Flanagan & Allen replacing Caryll & Mundy. Gradually, the Crazy shows moved from being variety bills enhanced with impromptu clowning to being fully-fledged revues like *O-Kay for Sound*.

During the Second World War, Black staged a series of long-running revues at the Palladium, with shows such as *The Little Dog Laughed*, *Apple-Sauce!* and *Happy and Glorious*. Revue so dominated the Palladium's schedule at this point that when Black staged a straight variety bill in the summer of 1943, the marketing for this show echoed that of the 1928 relaunch, using the slogan 'Variety Comes Back'. Max Miller topped the bill, supported by acts such as Billy Cotton and His Band, 'aerial gymnasts' the Four Kenways, and Gaston Palmer, who was billed as an 'Anglo-French Juggling Humorist'.[50] The bill ran for 11 weeks with one or two changes in the line-up, and was seen by 320,000 people. It was successful enough for Black to launch a further 20-week season starring Miller on Boxing Day 1943.[51]

Inevitably, the war caused difficulties for variety, not least the problem of finding the people to work in the theatres, with able-bodied men and women being called up into the armed forces or munitions factories, and American and European acts being cut off by wartime transport restrictions.[52] In 1942, *The Performer* voiced serious concerns about the situation:

> Temporary deferments have done something toward relieving the position here and there, but on the whole the situation is such as to cause really grave concern to managements who are having it increasingly impressed upon them by facts that the supply of artistes, members of staffs, orchestras and technicians is becoming perilously inadequate.[53]

More seriously, some of the theatres themselves became casualties of war. The provinces lost famous variety halls such as the Argyle, Birkenhead, which went in a bombing raid on 26 September 1940, and seven major London variety theatres were destroyed by enemy action, including the Hippodromes at Balham, Ilford, Poplar and Rotherhithe, the Stratford Empire and the South London Palace.[54] Perhaps the most serious loss was the Holborn Empire, which was hit by a bomb after a second house performance of the Max Miller revue *Apple-Sauce!* in the autumn of 1940 and never reopened. This had been a key theatre, not least because as its manager Bertie Adams argued, it stood 'straight as a larch for strict "variety"' – the Miller revue being a rare exception.[55]

In spite of all this, though, variety played an important part in keeping up the nation's morale through the darkest days of the war. Vera Lynn – who came to represent British pluck in the face of the Nazi threat thanks to songs like 'We'll Meet Again' and 'The White Cliffs of Dover' – made regular wartime appearances in variety. Indeed, 'We'll Meet Again' had been an important number in her variety repertoire even before the war began. She recalls how in bombing raids, the theatre manager would come out onto the stage and offer the audience the chance to leave to go the shelters or stay and enjoy the show, which would continue in spite of the danger:

> I remember once when we had a blackout...everyone was warned, you know, because all the lights were going to go out – in the street and every-where – to have torches. And everyone turned up with torches – small ones, big ones, those that'd got seats up in the gallery came with great big lamps. And there was a microphone on the side of the stage that was run by a battery. So when everything went out, all the torches came on in the theatre you know, and I just walked over to the other microphone and picked that up and carried on with the singing ... We just sang over the sirens ... and just carried on as though nothing had happened.[56]

This extraordinary kind of solidarity helped to make the war a prosperous time for variety. Some theatres had to adjust their opening times to allow audiences to get home in the blackouts, but audiences held up, with the glamour, gags and spectacle offering a welcome form of escapism. In the year ending 31 March 1941, the GTC's profits were hit by the bombing of the Holborn Empire and the temporary closure of the London Palladium, but in the following tax year, net profits rose from £202,389 to £347,638, an increase of over 71 per cent.[57]

Just before the war ended, on 4 March 1945, George Black died following an operation, aged 54. *The Performer* commented, 'Through his passing, Variety is robbed of one who has been a very considerable factor in its progress during the last two decades'; and *The Stage* said it was 'an irreparable loss'.[58] His place at the head of GTC and Moss was taken by Val Parnell, a natural successor given the role he had played in the revival and reinvention of variety. The booking policy he would pursue at the Palladium and in his lesser theatres would bring continued prosperity to variety theatre, even if it would create divisions among its performers.

Danny Kaye at the Palladium

Initially, Parnell continued to stage big revues at the Palladium, with the odd variety season in between, topped by acts like George Formby. One such season had Laurel & Hardy topping the bill, and this was significant because they were booked through the agent Bernard Delfont.[59] They proved enough of a box-office draw to have their engagement extended from two weeks to three, which might have been one of the factors that led Delfont to become theatre proprietor himself. He took over the London Casino, which had been a venue for boxing and wrestling, and reopened it as a variety theatre. According to his nephew Michael Grade, Delfont was not trying to directly compete with the Palladium or challenge Val Parnell, but had simply seen a gap in the market: 'The Palladium was doing big revues still and Bernie took a lease on the Casino and started doing big variety bills, and doing it very successfully. And that was what prompted Val to reintroduce the variety policy at the Palladium.'[60]

Just as the Palladium had its resident dance troupe the Palladium Girls, Delfont's theatre started each half of each show with the Casino Girls.[61] Chico Marx topped the bill at the first show, which opened on 9 June 1947. Delfont marketed his shows as 'international variety', and the *Manchester Guardian* commented slightly cynically that by 'variety', Delfont meant 'turns by figures familiar on the screen'.[62] That was a reasonably fair comment, given that Delfont's bills, each of which ran for several weeks, tended to be topped by imported American stars such as Laurel & Hardy, Sophie Tucker and the Ink Spots, who were famous for either film or recording careers.

The Casino's first night audience was speckled with agents and rival theatre owners, among them Val Parnell and his wife.[63] Parnell was unhappy at this new competition and tried to persuade Delfont to give up at the Casino. Delfont refused, and Parnell launched into a savage commercial battle against him, adopting the same strategy of straight variety bills topped by mostly American stars at the Palladium. His first attempt with Mickey Rooney was not overburdened with success, but the next bill was topped by Danny Kaye, who proved to be a phenomenal draw.

Parnell and Delfont were in direct competition for the big names of American show business, and hard economics meant that the odds were in Parnell's favour. The Palladium could take a maximum of £11,000 per week at the box office, whereas the Casino could only take £8,000.[64] By the summer of 1948, Delfont realized he could not continue, because, as *The Stage* put it, 'acts of international repute are asking so much money now, and there is such keen competition to get them, that it is no longer a commercial proposition, as far as he is concerned, in booking them'.[65] On 16 October, international variety at the Casino finished for good.

Danny Kaye's success at the Palladium was a key moment in the history of British variety theatre, and it shaped what would happen from then on until the circuit collapsed a decade or so later. He was known in Britain for his films, and had never performed in variety, although he had years of experience playing several shows a day between the movies in the American equivalent of cine-variety. His first Palladium appearance on 2 February 1948 drew a capacity audience and a *Times* review said his hour-long act had them 'roaring with delight'.[66] The *Sunday Express* called him, 'The most sensationally successful single performer to appear in London in living memory', and there is plenty to suggest that this was no exaggeration.[67]

In his first six-week Palladium season he played to around 250,000 people, and by the time of his third, this had risen to 320,000 in eight weeks.[68] When he appeared in the Royal Variety Performance in November 1948, there were fewer than 3,000 tickets available, but 80,000 people applied for them[69] Kaye also toured provincial variety theatres, and in Birmingham, people queued for 26 hours in a mile-long queue to get tickets.[70]

Public reaction to him anticipated the kind of hysteria that would later be whipped up by rock stars such as Elvis or the Beatles. During one seven-week season, he received 70,000 fan letters.[71] In Manchester in 1949, a crowd of around 1,000 people turned up to see him arrive at the Midland Hotel, surging past the police with what was described as 'a high, wordless shrilling' and rocking the car he was riding in. 'It was terrifying... I thought once they were going to turn my car over', he said, but reflected on this kind of hysterical reaction, 'Better me ... than joining a Hitler Youth Group'.[72] In his first Palladium season, King George VI went to see Kaye, the first time he had attended an ordinary variety show since coming to the throne.[73]

Kaye's extraordinary success meant that not only did he come back regularly over the next few years to perform in variety, but he also established the pattern of booking big American stars to top the bill at the Palladium. He was followed by acts such as Frank Sinatra, the Andrews Sisters, Jack Benny, Ella Fitzgerald and Judy Garland. The bankability of American stars was crucial to Lew and Leslie Grade, because it allowed them to get a foothold in the Palladium. Previously, Moss Empires' booking had been dominated by Harry Foster's agency, because not only was Foster Val Parnell's golf partner, he also had a deal with the powerful American agency, William Morris. The Grades had a similar deal with GAC, an agency run by Buddy Howe which represented a lot of the big recording artists – something that William Morris lacked. According to Michael Grade, Parnell 'realised that he couldn't do without them and that was how Lew and Leslie broke the Foster–Moss Empires axis, and they really took over. They broke that cartel and became very, very close with Val, because Val couldn't do without them because he needed these attractions'.[74]

The Palladium became known 'virtually without challenge, as the leading music-hall, not only of London or the British Isles, but of the world'.[75] The policy of bringing in American acts became so well established, that it inspired a Lenny Bruce routine, 'The Palladium', which was recorded on his 1959 album *Togetherness*. In it, Bruce – a young, iconoclastic American stand-up whose scabrous work was light years away from the front-cloth comics of variety – imagines a desperate Las Vegas comedian called Frank Dell persuading his manager to book him a date at the Palladium. 'What, are you out of your nut? That's a vaudeville house!' says the manager. 'Joey Bishop played it, Alan King played it', Dell replies. Bruce has Dell perform a disastrous first show, and shows us Val Parnell coming into his dressing room to sack him.[76]

Max Miller overruns at the Royal Variety Performance

Bruce was not the only one who took a jaded view of Parnell's policy at the Palladium. The British press also criticized the idea that American acts were starting to dominate British variety.[77] Such arguments were

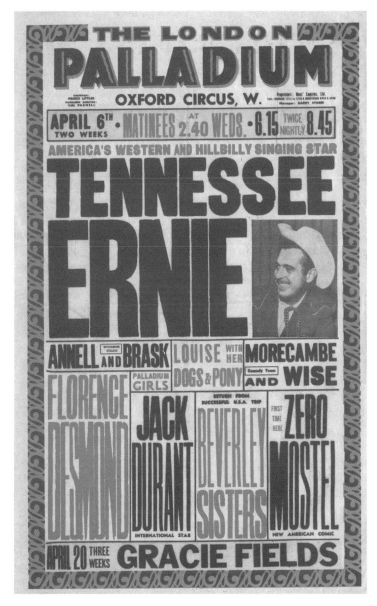

Figure 4.1 A London Palladium bill topped by American singer Tennessee Ernie Ford in April 1953. Unusually, the next bill would be topped by a British act, Gracie Fields.

far from new. Those who disparaged variety in comparison with music hall tended to paint the earlier form as pugnaciously British – 'One Englishman was worth half a dozen foreigners' as J. B. Booth put it.[78] On the other hand, as W. Macqueen-Pope argued, American slang 'was alien to Music Hall, though it might have a place in Variety'.[79] This kind of rhetoric conveniently ignored the fact that many music hall stars had come from overseas, like R. G. Knowles (Canadian), Florrie Forde, and Albert Whelan (both Australian).

In fact, Parnell's policy was nothing new, and debates about 'foreign acts' had raged in the trade press throughout the 1930s. In 1931, the agent Harry Foster defended the international market for acts, recalling George Black's argument that 'that if the Palladium were barred from having foreign artists, they could not keep the place on as a music hall for more than a few weeks'. *The Era*'s response to this was furious: 'There is not the smallest doubt that the English public is roused, as it has never been roused before, by the extent to which foreign imports, whether they be of art or the artisan, have undermined national stability.'[80]

Later in the decade, the Variety Artistes' Federation (VAF) campaigned against foreign acts. This was probably driven more by economics than xenophobia, the point being that while acts were still coming from overseas to appear in Britain, foreign markets were being closed to British acts. The VAF explained that it had 'no desire to create enmities among foreign artists' but complained about 'the closing off of Continental engagement markets in such countries as Germany, Hungary, Italy, and Russia, by the imposing of financial restrictions, etc., and the further non-engagement of British variety, circus and cabaret artists in the USA'.[81]

Ironically, what this dispute and the general antipathy towards foreign acts reveals is just how important internationalism was to variety. As Australian speciality act Valantyne Napier put it, 'A true Variety act was of its essence an international act.'[82] Dancers, jugglers, acrobats and other visual acts that didn't rely on speech could work in many different countries, and there were forms of variety theatre in Europe, Australia, New Zealand, South America, Singapore, Hong Kong, China, Japan, India and South America.[83]

The British strong woman Joan Rhodes performed in 36 different countries, including Denmark, Norway, Sweden, Finland, Portugal, Belgium, France and Italy. While performing abroad, she would go to local restaurants in order to translate the patter she used to introduce her feats of strength: 'I would get one of the waiters and get him to tell me in his language, and I would write it all down, and learn what I could.'[84]

In spite of variety's long-established internationalism, there was bitter resentment towards the American acts who were brought over to top bills at the Palladium and across the country after the war. *The Stage* saw it as a minor victory when the Palladium put on a bill in which as many as six of the ten acts were British, and later talked with barbed irony of the headliner Dickie Valentine doing well there 'despite the handicap of being British'.[85] It also offered its support to the new wave of British comedians who were coming into variety having cut their performing teeth while serving in the armed forces in the war, arguing that comics such as Reg Dixon, Peter Sellers, Johnny Lockwood, Michael Bentine, Jimmy Wheeler and Frankie Howerd 'could throw out a healthy challenge to cousins across the herring pond' and 'again justify the old-standing claim of the British music hall to be the very heart of Variety'.[86]

The acts themselves also felt some resentment towards the incoming Americans, seeing their status and even their money being reduced by these usurpers of the precious top-of-the-bill spots. When Max Bygraves appeared on a Palladium bill topped by Judy Garland, he found his salary cut from £100 to £75 so that the theatre could afford Garland's enormous fee.[87] The singer and *siffleur* (i.e. whistler) Ronnie Ronalde still resents the fact that although he could get bookings at prestigious American venues such as the Radio City Music Hall, the top British theatres were reluctant to put him on. He refused to play the Palladium because they only offered him second top to an American act. He argues that Parnell's policy devalued British acts: 'It made us look as though we were a low-class lot.'[88]

Max Miller brought the conflict right out onto the stage. A long-standing argument against foreign acts was that they were taking money out of the British economy, and as early as 1931, *The Era* had argued that, 'It is a national duty, practically an emergency regulation, to stop the export of money.'[89] Miller was one of the few British acts booked to top the bill at the London Casino, and when he appeared there in August 1948, *The Stage* reported that he got 'on good terms with the audience ... by telling them that "no dollars are going out of here tonight"'.[90]

When he appeared in his third Royal Variety Performance in 1950, he was annoyed that he had only been allotted six minutes when the American Jack Benny had been given 20. In a show in which all material is carefully selected and controlled, he threw caution to the wind, casting aside what he had done at rehearsal and instead doing a different and much longer set of routines.

As he started to overrun, he saw the stage manager Charles Henry signalling for him to come off but ignored this, saying, 'The others have had their chance. Let me have mine. The Americans do.' The argument he had with Parnell after the show has become one of variety's most enduring anecdotes. Apparently, Parnell told Miller he would never book him again, and Miller responded that he was £70,000 too late.[91] If the story is accurate, Parnell's threat was an idle one. By March 1952, Miller was back at the Palladium, opening a new variety season with a three-week engagement.[92]

Despite such disputes and resentments, the middle decades of the twentieth century saw the heyday of variety theatre. The intervention of Black and Parnell not only saw off the slump of the 1920s, but also reinvented the form itself, and it proved itself to be both hardy and adaptable, drawing on the best that foreign markets and rival forms of entertainment could offer. It survived the challenges of the war years and thrived in the immediate aftermath. As late as the early 1950s, the variety circuit was still rude with health. *The Stage Year Book 1951* reported, 'Once again it can be said that Variety has had a successful year. This is true not only in London but in the provincial theatres up and down the country.'[93] Some of the smaller theatre circuits were continuing to grow. F. J. Butterworth, who had started his circuit in 1935 by converting cinemas into variety theatres, was continuing to acquire new venues right up to 1954 when he took over the Northampton New.[94]

Ian Bevan's history of the Palladium, written in 1952, summed up variety's continuing vitality: 'One of the few things that can be counted on to annoy [Parnell] is hearing someone say "Variety is dead". After all, the surest proof to the contrary is the flourishing condition of his own company, whose music-halls entertain about 500,000 people a week.'[95]

5

Variety Falls Apart, 1953–65

Final and undisputed extinction

When the end finally came for variety theatre, it came with remark-able speed. A popular theatre tradition that had lasted for 100 years or more fell apart in little more than a decade. In late 1960, Ian Bevan – who had written so confidently about variety's 'flourishing condition' just a few years earlier – penned an article called 'What Is Light Entertainment Today?', in which he argued: 'Now that teen-agers have joined their elders in scorning variety theatres, the extinction of this form of amusement is final and undisputed.'[1]

The press reports from this period trace the calamitous decline. In the mid-1950s, *The Stage Year Book* glumly stated that, 'Variety had a difficult year. Almost every week came another announce-ment of another music hall closing or being sold...Music halls started to become a vanishing race of buildings during 1955.'[2] In 1958, the rumoured closure of a number of variety theatres led *The Stage* to propose the forming of 'the equivalent to a National Trust for Variety Halls', quoting Tommy Trinder's suggestion that patrons should be able 'to place a blue plaque on their own seats in the halls'.[3]

In 1959, John Betjeman mourned the fact that, 'Even the variety hall, which our elders recall with apologetic delight, has been shut or turned to secular purposes', leaving behind nothing but 'dust and silence'.[4] In 1961, *The Times* lamented that, 'The day of the music-hall singer, dancer, musician, story-teller, juggler and acrobat – loved and honoured with applause in the past – is now nearly over; with variety theatres closing down all over the land they are moving into the shadows of the past.'[5]

Roy Hudd, who started playing variety theatres in 1959 in the double act Hudd & Kay, looks back with rueful amusement on these times:

> [I]t was an interesting time to come into it, but it was a bloody sad time as well – because Eddie [Cunningham, aka Eddie Kay] and me still talk about it, and he says, 'We used to finish off the Saturday night, and they started pulling it down on Monday morning.' He said, 'We closed more variety theatres in England than anybody – in a year and a half!'[6]

Throughout the decade, the list of closures mounted up. In 1957, the Brixton Empress closed. In 1958 the Camberwell Palace, the Woolwich Empire and the Portsmouth Empire shut their doors for the last time. In 1959, the Chiswick Empire and the Sheffield Empire were among the casualties. 1960 saw the end of the Dundee Palace, the Chatham Empire, the Norwich Hippodrome, the Leeds Empire, the Ramsgate Palace and the prestigious Finsbury Park Empire, which had lost £13,933 in the previous two years.[7] At the end of 1950, there were 21 variety theatres in London, with a total weekly capacity of 424,745.[8] By 1960, there were just four left – the Golders Green Hippodrome, the Metropolitan, the Palladium and the Victoria Palace – and the total weekly capacity had fallen by over 80 per cent.[9]

A few theatres struggled on into the 1960s. The Glasgow Empire, so notorious among English comics, moved from traditional weekly-change variety to a resident show in 1960, and in September the following year, according to head of Moss Empires Leslie A. Macdonnell, it was losing 'between £600 and £1,000 a week'.[10] By 1963 it finally succumbed to the inevitable, staging its 'grand farewell Show of Shows' on 31 March.[11]

When John Alexander got a job as a doorman at the Metropolitan, Edgware Road – or the Met, as it was better known – in 1958, it was still running twice nightly variety, albeit closing over the summer months. Monday and Tuesday nights were busy, thanks to being papered with complimentary tickets, Wednesdays and Thursdays were quieter, Fridays were busy and Saturdays were 'often full or nearly full'.[12] By 1962, it was down to two shows a week on Thursday nights, with wrestling on Saturdays, and it was trying to rebrand itself as 'London's Irish Music Hall' in a desperate attempt to attract a niche audience. The gallery of the theatre had fallen into disuse.[13]

On 6 December 1962, the last night of the farewell variety season was witnessed by a 'pathetically small audience', who heard Randolph

Sutton, topping the bill, give a curtain speech in which he recalled his first appearance there 50 years earlier.[14] In April 1963, the Met hosted a variety show in aid of the Variety Artistes' Benevolent Fund, attracting a healthier audience which included 'a surprising number of young people', and the last-ever show was a benefit for Unity Theatre, taking place on Sunday 6 May.[15] The Met was demolished shortly afterwards, to make room for a road-widening scheme.

The relentless haemorrhaging of theatres in the 1950s was an utter catastrophe for variety. There had been crises before, but as W. J. Bishop put it in 1949, 'whilst on its last legs it has always revived with a stubbornness which is one of the characteristics of the British way of life'.[16] What was going on in that decade that caused the final extinction which it had avoided for so long?

The tax menace

There have been many theories as to what killed the variety theatres, particularly among those who performed in them. At the time they were disappearing, many believed the culprit was entertainment tax. This had long been resented by theatre managers, as it bit a considerable chunk out of their profits. In 1950, 1s1d was levied on tickets costing over 2s9d.[17] When the Wood Green Empire shut down in January 1955, *The Stage* baldly stated that, 'Excessive entertainment tax is the reason'.[18] Similarly, when the Hackney Empire closed in 1956 Prince Littler of the Stoll Corporation blamed 'the burden of entertainments tax, added to continually rising costs'.[19]

In 1954, *The Performer* called it a 'tax menace', and reported on the formation of the Theatres Entertainment Tax Committee, which was preparing a memorandum for the Chancellor on the effects of a tax worth around £2,250,000 to the government. *The Performer*'s view was that for many theatres, this sum would 'constitute the marginal 15 per cent between survival and disaster'.[20] It is easy to see why theatre managers disliked the entertainment tax, but while it could not have helped matters, blaming it for variety's demise seems like a bit of a red herring.

To start with, it was by no means a new form of taxation. It had been introduced in 1916, and variety theatres had managed to shoulder its burden for decades, even in the dark days of the 1920s. Perhaps more importantly, entertainment tax was abolished several years before the last theatres disappeared. Its abolition was announced by the Chancellor of the Exchequer in April 1957, but in October of that

year an article in *The Stage* was cynical about the effects of this: 'Tax
has been repealed, but it has meant little difference. The public don't
attend.'[21]

Television murders variety

The same article boasted a rather dramatic headline which accused
television of 'murdering variety', and this was a popular theory. Even
today, TV is the prime suspect when the death of variety is discussed. In
1958, Welsh comic Wyn Calvin called it a 'dangerous medium'.[22] In the
1980s, speciality artiste Valantyne Napier argued that, 'By the late 1950s
many theatres were closing. Most people could afford television sets and
this new novelty kept them at home for their entertainment now.'[23]

Variety was still thriving in the late 1940s, but there was a 15,000
per cent increase in TV ownership between 1947 and 1953, by which
point 2,142,452 households had television licences.[24] It was then that
the effects of a shrinking audience were serious enough to make major
theatres start to disappear from the circuit.

Ironically, when television was in its infancy, variety had offered
it a cradle, just as it had with early film. In August 1930, a bill at the
Coliseum which included Bob & Alf Pearson, Nat Mills & Bobbie,
and the performing dogs of the Gaudsmith Brothers, also featured a
demonstration of television, in which images from John Logie Baird's
studio were transmitted onto the stage.[25] Like radio, television was
quick to exploit the talents of variety performers, and variety shows
were often a feature of the early BBC broadcasts of the 1930s.

In the 1950s, when television became available to a mass audience, variety tried to use its publicity value, just as it had with radio a
few decades before. In 1952, for example, Jack Hylton put on a show
called *Televariety* at the Adelphi Theatre, in which a stage version of
the popular TV panel game *What's My Line?* was the centrepiece of
a bill featuring acts such as Frank Randle, Joan Turner and Ali Ben
Hassan's Whirlwind Moroccans.[26]

Similarly, a poster from the Wood Green Empire for the week
commencing 13 September 1954 advertises a bill presented by Carroll
Levis, 'IN PERSON WITH HIS SENSATIONAL TE*LEVIS*ION
SHOW'. The other acts on the bill are culled from his well-known
TV talent show, and to emphasize the connection with the exciting
world of television, they are announced with phrases like 'The TV
Eyeful', 'TV's Three New Star Comics' and 'TV's Wonder Boys'.
(See Illustration 5.1.)

This kind of marketing could be very successful. The Beverley Sisters got their own TV series in 1953, and Teddie Beverley believes that 'at first, television helped the theatre, because everybody rushed to theatres to see television stars…we filled every theatre we ever played to capacity no matter what the season was – because we were on television'.[27] Reports in the trade press tell a similar story:

> Benny Hill…was not an established comedian until 1954, and late in the year at that…It is interesting to note that he has gained his fame from consistently funny television appearances as compère of 'Show Case' and to prove how quickly it can change your box office importance, one need only record that in June Benny Hill played Chiswick Empire as third top of a not-too-strong bill to houses that were none too good and returned in November as the star of his own show, playing to 'house full' business all the week![28]

Nonetheless, there was still caution about the new medium. An editorial in a 1954 edition of *The Performer* argued that, 'Television may in some instances prove quite a useful publicity provider and a tonic to the box office of a show that seems to need such a tonic – but the doses must be administered with discretion so that the public's attitude is whetted and not satisfied'.[29] For Teddie Beverley, the problem was that 'some of the television stars disappointed in person…very few stars were able to come and do live theatre. So then, television started to ruin the theatre…it was the changeover then from filling theatres to gradually emptying theatres'.[30]

A particular concern was the fact that television is a visual medium. In the 1920s, BBC producers had reassured theatre owners by pointing out that as a non-visual medium, radio was less of a threat to variety than cinema was. Similar arguments cropped up in the 1950s. In *The Stage*, Ross Wade argued that:

> It's the word 'see' that kills the theatre…In the good old days of radio, folks flocked to the music halls to see what Arthur Askey, Jack Warner, the Lyons, Ted Ray, Jack Train, Eric Barker and the rest of them looked like. Today, it doesn't happen…Variety is the worst sufferer. The words 'Direct From Television' mean nothing. They're deadly, in fact.[31]

Looking back with hindsight over 50 years later, Wyn Calvin makes a similar point: 'Radio filled theatres. Television emptied them…people wanted to go and see those that they liked on radio – and that's when radio filled theatres. But then television came – and the attitude became, "Well I'm not paying to go and see them, I can see them at home for nothing".'[32]

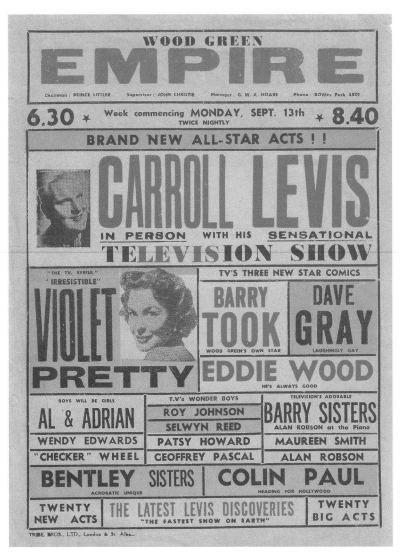

Figure 5.1 The bill for the Wood Green Empire, week commencing Monday 13 September 1954, uses television as a selling point. Ironically, the theatre would close soon afterwards to be converted into a TV studio.

Sunday Night at the London Palladium

The problem worsened with the arrival of commercial television in 1955, which had been anticipated with cautious optimism in the trade press. A report from the end of 1954 argued that:

> [I]t will not be known till later in 1955 what effect it will have on either theatre attendance or extra work for variety artists, who have contributed extremely well to the enjoyment of BBC televiewers throughout the year and although this may be thought detrimental in helping theatres to maintain audiences, in the long run it must bring more people into theatres.[33]

ITV proved very adept at adapting the variety format for television. One of the jewels of its early years was *Sunday Night at the London Palladium*, which was first broadcast on 25 September 1955. The first bill was topped by Gracie Fields, possibly the greatest star variety theatre had produced, and was introduced by one of its most successful front-cloth comics, Tommy Trinder, who had been appointed as the show's regular compère. The show had been specifically designed to give the television viewer the feel of enjoying a night out at the theatre. Initially, it began with a shot of a young woman in the stalls looking through a programme, and a sweeping shot of the auditorium which showed the audience as well as the stage. As Val Parnell put it, 'I'm offering television viewers a seat in the circle at the greatest Variety theatre in the world to watch the finest artists money can buy.'[34]

The formula proved enormously successful. In 1960, a show topped by Cliff Richard attracted 19.5 million viewers, another starring Max Bygraves brought in 21 million, and a third with Harry Secombe was watched by 22 million.[35] This kind of popularity meant that appearing on the show became an important milestone in a performer's career. Bruce Forsyth became the regular compère in September 1958, and as he has recalled, 'Almost instantaneously, I was one of the biggest names on television ... and, after six weeks, an established one.'[36]

The problem for live variety theatre was that TV shows like *Sunday Night at the London Palladium* gave audiences unrealistic expectations. When Roy Hudd started in variety in 1959, he found himself playing on bills with an odd mixture of generations. Alongside raw, young acts such as Hudd & Kay there were older, more established acts such as Max Miller, and even the remnants of the last generation of music hall singers, such as G. H. Elliott, Randolph Sutton and Hetty

King. As Hudd points out, this made for a much more ramshackle kind of bill than those seen on ITV:

> [T]elevision really was the killer – that was the one that finally put the nail in the coffin, simply because they could see and hear and everything, and you could stay at home and you could see the biggest stars in the world at home. Who've you got down at the local Empire? Me and bloody G. H. Elliott![37]

For Don Smoothey, who worked in various double acts in the latter years of variety, the discrepancy in quality was particularly stark for the lesser theatres, the number twos and threes:

> [W]hen you play your Boltons, your Barnsleys and your Keighleys and your Castlefords... your Bearwoods, and your Salfords and those places... when ITV started you started getting all these big stars on there, the local people couldn't understand why they couldn't see those people at that theatre. You see, it didn't register, they'd say, 'Why can't I see them at the theatre?'[38]

At the same time, the sheer expense of buying a television set was blamed for reducing audiences for variety theatre. The cost of a TV was comparatively much higher than it is today, and many people bought them on hire purchase. It was thought that television instalments would 'make buyers stay in and get their money's worth and cut down on paying to see live entertainment'.[39]

Television literally replaced live variety in the sense that many of the theatres that shut down were taken over by TV companies and turned into studios. The first to fall was the Shepherd's Bush Empire, whose last show closed on 26 September 1953, the BBC taking possession of it three days later.[40] Others quickly followed. Associated-Rediffusion spent £150,000 buying and converting the Walham Green Granville, which had closed on 11 December 1954, only to shut it down again two years later.[41] In the summer of 1955, the Wood Green Empire was converted into ABC's 'theatrical HQ', a camera runway being built from the back of the theatre to the stalls.[42] In early 1956, ATV took a lease on the Hackney Empire, and in 1957 Granada took over the Chelsea Palace.[43]

Bingo and office blocks

When he announced that variety's extinction was final and undisputed, Ian Bevan also described it as being 'as out of fashion as whalebone corsets'. Reviewing one of the last shows at the Met for *The Guardian* in April 1963, Norman Shrapnel wrote that variety theatre 'seems to have little in common with the London of bingo and office blocks'.[44] What both of these statements vividly suggest is that variety was failing to adapt to a changing world, and if television was one of the challenges it was failing to address, there were also other social shifts that were contributing to its demise.

The 1950s saw a general decline in all live theatre, with repertory theatres closing down just like the variety halls.[45] This was partly due to the changing face of British towns, with the demolition of traditional working-class neighbourhoods and the resulting shifts in population. The closure of the Glasgow Empire was partly blamed on the fact that its traditional audience were being moved out to the housing developments that were being built several miles out from the inner city. This meant that, 'No longer was there a demand for early performances; it was nearly midnight when you got home to the suburbs from second houses.'[46]

In spite of the problems caused by the Glasgow Empire's traditional audience being moved out of reach, *The Stage* reported that even in the early 1960s 'financially, there was hope' for the legendary theatre, but 'the directors saw in it greater value, property-wise, largely through its central position on Glasgow's fashionable Sauchiehall Street, at the pivot of Glasgow's commercial life'.[47] Moss Empires made the most of this prime city centre location when they tore the Empire down, putting up a modern building with a basement car park, ground floor shops and a four-storey office block.[48] As Don Smoothey points out, this was a common trend:

> Now I had a couple of ... acquaintances in Leeds who ... started these drug stores. And one of them came to me one day, in 1958, I was there in pantomime at the Empire, Leeds, and ... he said, 'Don', he said, 'you couldn't get us any shares, could you? Do you know how we can get hold of some shares in Moss?'... I said, 'What the hell do you want to start buying shares in theatre for?'... Of course, the reason they wanted shares is because all these Empires, your Empire, Leeds, your Empire, Sheffield, your Glasgow Empire ... were all in the centre of town with the most valuable, valuable property spots.[49]

By 1960, it was argued that Moss Empires was 'in the property business first and the entertainment business second'.[50] With audiences in decline and city centre property values increasing, variety theatres were being torn up all over the country to make way for more modern buildings. In 1961, Mollie Ellis painted a vivid picture of the situation:

> Where once stood a proud, ornate building of the worst type of Edwardian architecture, housing that warm, rowdy, slightly vulgar, and certainly very smoky atmosphere of the true music hall, there now rises a stately block of offices, bowling alley, supermarket, flats or shops, stark in their modern outlines, very much more realistically in keeping with the growing trade of the district, of course, but not half so interesting as the monstrosity of a building they replace.[51]

Where the theatres were allowed to stand, they were converted to other purposes. Wyn Calvin identifies one of the main trends: 'Theatres began to close down or go over to bingo. That was the movement – over to bingo.'[52] The lure of cash prizes made commercial bingo a popular new form of entertainment and it was viewed by most performers with a mixture of derision and dread. In 1975, Max Wall wrote 'that word "Bingo" will never do anything except cause me to shudder'.[53]

The same dreary formula

Variety theatres undoubtedly faced huge challenges in the 1950s. Urban redevelopment was stealing their audiences and making the ground they sat on too valuable to let them stay there and struggle on. At the same time, they were faced with a new rival form of entertainment much more deadly than the earlier competitors which variety had managed to coexist with so well. Television had the visual appeal of cinema but could be enjoyed for free in the comfort of the home like radio.

However, it may not have been inevitable that these difficulties should mean the end for the national network of variety theatres. Perhaps the biggest problem they faced was that there was a lack of willingness among the people who managed variety to rise to the challenge of changing times, as George Black had in the slump of the 1920s. At a time when competition from film and radio could have finished variety, Black's response had been to invest money and update the form. He had argued that, 'Variety has suffered a decline...because it has stubbornly refused to come into line with the cinema theatres...you see music-halls with dirty and uncomfortable seats, tawdry scenery and decorations. Not even cheap prices can reconcile an audience to dirt and discomfort.'[54]

In the 1950s, there was nobody like Black with the will to meet the challenge by investing money in order to innovate and raise standards, despite increasingly desperate calls for action in the trade press. In January 1955, *The Stage* reported the views of an unnamed agent who had various suggestions about how variety could be updated. He proposed increasing the number of top acts on the bill even if that meant putting up prices, and dropping the name 'music hall', as it 'conjure[d] up in the minds of the younger generation something too old to want to know'. He also argued that underinvestment was a vicious circle, making the point by invoking Black's name:

> Another fact that is killing variety, he says, is the practice of bookers saying: 'How much do they take in a poor week?' and then putting in an inferior bill costing a hundred less than the lowest figure possible for that theatre. 'This means a poor show and drives people from the theatre for a few weeks.' It was the late George Black's motto to spend more in order to lose less. That must be the variety theatre's motto in 1955, says the agent.[55]

An editorial the following year was more strident:

> Why, instead of shouting the odds about poor business and poor shows, don't they DO something positive? *Like giving us really tip-top variety bills. Like improving tatty sets and costumes, and giving sparkle to shows. Like making their public relations system friendly and really 'wooing' the public from their television sets.*[56]

On the whole, the managers of the theatre circuits failed to act to stop the rot. The trade press fingered falling artistic standards as a major reason why audiences could not be tempted back into the empires and hippodromes. Journalists complained that, 'The same dreary formula, the same old routines, are being trotted out week by week; all too rare is an artist or a bill with new, refreshing ideas.'[57] Another article made the case even more starkly:

> Audiences dwindled despite the fact that the country was enjoying a boom period, with full employment and high wages ... Cinema chains declared high profits. Why not the music halls? The blame could not, obviously, be put entirely onto television. Poor shows, tatty scenery and costumes, under-rehearsed pit orchestras, shoddy auditoriums and nudes did more than television to keep people out of smaller music halls. At a time when the variety theatres should have been putting on bigger and better entertainment, the general average went down with a bump.[58]

By the mid-1960s, when the theatres had all but disappeared, Sidney Vauncez summed the situation very simply: 'Standards fell, receipts likewise, until to all intents and purposes Variety became non-existent.'[59]

As for those falling standards, there are numerous shudderingly vivid descriptions of the depths variety had sunk to in its final days. The comedian Jimmy Wheeler wrote an article asking 'What Killed Music-Hall?', in which he described a visit to 'a decaying building alleged to be a theatre', where the box office is staffed by 'a black-dressed biddy, who has put a teapot on the seating plan', and the barmaid – who will 'get up for nobody' – serves a light ale which has 'been next to the radiator all night'. The 25 people in the audience watch a couple of dancers, a 'young novice comedian' who has 'pinched everybody's material', a juggler who drops his clubs, and at the end of the first half a 'star act you've never heard of'. The article concludes with a lovely punchline, as Wheeler describes the top of the bill: '[A]nd then a voice says "Ladies and gentlemen, will you please welcome a star of variety, TV and radio, the one and only Jimmy Wheeler". And I walk out pissed – and that's what killed music-hall.'[60]

In the 1920s, George Black had warned that audiences dislike dirt and discomfort, but by the late 1950s the theatres really were dirty and uncomfortable. At the Met, the paintwork had 'mellowed to a sort of cigar colour'.[61] Clarkson Rose wrote of theatres in which 'the gilt-and-plaster cupids and cherubs decorating the private boxes were chipped and broken' and a 'plaster figure of a goddess, as part of the proscenium decoration, which couldn't have been Venus de Milo, because not only had she no arms, but she was minus her left breast and one leg.'[62] If the tatty auditoriums let off a whiff of desperation, this could also be smelled backstage. At the Regent in Rotherham, a notice warned the acts that 'JOKES ABOUT THE SIZE OF THE AUDIENCE ARE NOT APPRECIATED AT THIS THEATRE'.[63]

The mere theatrical marketing of naked girls

Instead of investing to stop the rot, managers and agents looked for desperate short-term solutions. Nude revues became increasingly common, particularly in the lesser theatres. Roy Hudd recalls appearing in a show called *Striptease Vin Rouge* at the Aston Hippodrome: 'That was the last knockings of variety. They thought this might bring them in – couldn't get that on telly, you know.'[64]

Nudity was nothing new in variety. In 1937, an American striptease artist called Diana Raye was booked to appear in a George Black revue at the Palladium, but the furore that followed led Black to drop her from the show. Striptease was deemed to be an unwelcome American import, unacceptable to British audiences. At a meeting of the London Theatre Council, Sydney W. Carroll said he resented 'the mere theatrical marketing of naked girls' and 'vulgar and selfish exploitation of nudity on public platforms'.[65]

Some journalists defended striptease, labelling detractors like Carroll 'gymnophobes' and arguing that 'the nude in the theatre can be clean and elevating'.[66] In any case, after being dropped by the Palladium, Raye went on to appear at the Victoria Palace, where a reviewer from *The Era* described her act: 'First a full gauze curtain came down, then on the dimly lighted stage Miss Raye slowly took off her frock revealing glittering brassiere and more clothing than any chorus girl generally wears these days.'[67]

By the 1950s, revues with titles such as *Nudes of the World*, and *We've Got Nothing on Tonight* were a regular feature of the schedules at the number two and three theatres, and nude performers such as Phyllis Dixey and Chrystabel Leighton-Porter – better known as 'Jane' of the *Daily Mirror* comic strip – were famous enough to play the number ones. Barry Cryer saw Dixey when he was working at the Leeds Empire, and describes her act as 'quite decorous' and 'all rather prim'.[68] Roy Hudd is less complimentary about the Aston Hippodrome show he appeared in, calling it 'pretty seedy' and describing the women in the show as 'very nice, but they were horrible ... with no clothes on, for God's sake!'.[69]

A 1956 article sombrely declared, 'Nudes have spoiled the family trade', and it was widely believed that these shows brought in the wrong kind of audience.[70] Hudd had been going to variety theatres since the 1930s, when his grandmother used to take him to the Croydon Empire, and as he puts it: '[T]hey were really just basically waiting to see the nudes and you wouldn't exactly get a family audience in there ... that was the final nail in the coffin ... I mean I know that my Gran would never have taken me to see a nude show, you know.'[71]

This is a vital point. The respectable family audience had been the mainstay of variety throughout its existence. The impresarios who had built the big chains had advertised their theatres as places 'you can with safety take your Wives and Families',[72] and the wooing of the family audience had been an important part of the transition from music hall, with the bawdier, rowdier aspects being expunged along with the prostitutes who had plied their trade on the promenades. With traditional family audiences already dwindling in the face of falling standards, nude revues positively chased them away, replacing them with what Hudd has described as 'raincoat-on-laps businessmen'.[73]

Modern rhythm singers

The theatre chains had more success in attracting another new type of audience, defined in *The Stage Year Book* as 'youths – male and female – between 16 and 24, unmarried, living with parents, with no television instalments to pay off (a factor that kept many would-be theatregoers indoors during the year) and thanks to strong Unions, having pay packets much fatter than they would have had a few years ago'. Bringing in a teenage audience meant that the bookers had to start topping the bills with the 'modern rhythm singers' who were now dominating the pop charts.[74]

When skiffle became a national craze in the mid-1950s, variety was quick to jump on the bandwagon. Skiffle was simple, energetic music, played with passion on cheap guitars and homemade instruments like washboards and tea-chest basses. The repertoire was drawn from blues and folk, with songs like 'Rock Island Line', 'Freight Train' and 'Cumberland Gap' among the favourites. It was a profoundly democratic craze, anticipating punk's do-it-yourself ethos. The simple chord structures, accessible instruments, and crucially the emphasis on enthusiasm over technical brilliance, meant that skiffle fans could quickly form their own bands.

The first big star of skiffle was Lonnie Donegan, who had a seemingly endless string of hit singles in the 1950s and 1960s. Chart success led to frequent variety appearances, and by 1957, Donegan had reached the pinnacle of the circuit, topping the bill at the Palladium alongside the Platters. The Chas McDevitt Skiffle Group were probably the second biggest act of the new genre, and McDevitt recalls, '[W]e did this Moss Empire record breaking tour, everywhere we went we broke the records. We were on a percentage, you know, 60–40 percent, we were making a fortune.'[75] The publicity value of chart success was absolutely clear: McDevitt's group was billed in the Moss theatre programmes as 'Oriole's great recording stars'.[76]

Some promoters were utterly cynical in their exploitation of skiffle. Stanley Dale, for example, ran a 'National Skiffle Competition' in variety theatres around the country – bringing in not only the young skifflers, but also their friends and families – but the promised grand final which the groups were competing to get into was never held.[77] The bookers were as keen to cash in on the popularity of rock and roll. In November 1956, there were at least five revues with 'rock'n'roll' in the titles touring the major circuits.[78] American stars Gene Vincent and Eddie Cochran shared the top of the bill in a show which toured the Moss theatres, while other shows were topped by home-grown rockers like Cliff Richard or Marty Wilde. A review of an appearance by Wilde at the Finsbury Park Empire in 1958 acknowledged that 'teenage singing sensations have done their share in keeping alive the general public's interest in variety and they induce many young people who would not think of entering a variety theatre into taking the plunge'.[79]

Awkwardly amateur

In a sense, skiffle and rock and roll were just the latest in a long series of imported American musical styles which had featured in variety since the transition from music hall, like ragtime, jazz and swing. Yet somehow, these new styles sat less easily in the format of a variety show. Skiffle's do-it-yourself approach was slightly out of step with the polish and professionalism of the other acts, and singers who were used to performing to excitable audiences tightly packed into cellars or cafe bars sometimes found the transition to big stages and 1,500-seat auditoriums challenging.

The Chas McDevitt Skiffle Group got their first taste of variety when Joe Collins and former bandleader Bert Ambrose booked them to play the Met, Edgware Road in January 1957, and McDevitt recalls: 'We'd never been on a professional stage like that, you know, for a week, ever. And I've even got photographs of Ambrose sort of giving me mike technique and things like that...the business was OK, but it wasn't a particularly successful show.'[80] A review of the same show in *The Stage* was less than impressed by the quality of the performance:

It is surely a healthy sign that the music hall should so swiftly reflect current enthusiasm like Rock'n'Roll, Skiffle and so on...But there are risks, too, of course, and I cannot help thinking that the top of this week's bill at the Met represents one of them in a pretty obvious form. For the Chas McDevitt Skiffle Group has enthusiasm, lots of it, but little else. The presentation is awkwardly amateur in its uncertainty ... where competence might reasonably be expected, the beat of the washboard percussion is not always sure ... I am left wondering that the act should top the bill.[81]

Enthusiastic amateurism was not the only reason the show was not particularly successful. The other problem was timing, and as McDevitt recalls, the decision to book his group was 'a little bit premature' because they played the Met in January but 'the record didn't get in the hit parade until April'.[82] As established recording stars they went to enjoy great success touring the Moss theatres, but even then the basic energy of skiffle made them different from most of their fellow acts. A review of a show at the Chiswick Empire in 1958 makes this very clear:

It's teenage variety again at the Chiswick this week, which means that artistry takes a back seat as the big beat pounds its way across the footlights. But what the artists lack in the way of finesse they make up in energy. Cheerful Chas McDevitt, for instance, is bathed in perspiration at the end of his act, as are the members of his Skiffle Group, and small wonder, for theirs is an invigorating and toe-tapping session with a gaiety and swing which is not lost on the older members of the audience.[83]

Most variety acts were built on what the reviewer calls 'finesse': a performance style honed over time, polished through frequent repetition. There was precision in the way that performers interacted with the audience. Each feat which got a round of applause cued when it finished with a flourish, each carefully turned punchline which got the requisite laugh was part of a series of moments designed to elicit a response, and the entire act was made up of these.

McDevitt, on the other hand, was all about 'energy'. The value of his performance could be measured by the perspiration which he and his fellow band members were bathed in by the end of the act. Like most present day pop or rock singers, McDevitt's performance favoured energy and commitment over precision, spontaneity over the polish of repetition. The sweat-soaked energy of the performer seeks a less controlled, more frenzied audience response than traditional variety, and it was this recalibration of the relationship between performer and audience that made it so difficult for more traditional variety acts to share a bill with them.

Nonetheless, skiffle bands tried to adapt what they did for the variety stage, and tangible sign of this was the costumes they adopted. As McDevitt explains:

> We played jazz clubs and things like that before we went on tour just dressed as we were, you know, as musicians. As the rock groups do now, really, they go onstage with what they wear. When we hit the theatres ... we sort of spruced up a little bit, and gradually were sort of more accepted by the showbiz regime, you know. [84]

Sprucing themselves up meant wearing a kind of band uniform, initially consisting of matching shirts, jean-type trousers and basketball boots. A firm called Jaytex supplied two sets of shirts as part of a sponsorship deal. One set was red and one yellow. When the band wore the yellow shirts, McDevitt wore a red one – and vice versa – to mark him out as the leader. Later, they adopted matching sweaters decorated with a giant letter M. Lonnie Donegan was even more successful in becoming accepted by the showbiz regime, embedding himself very nicely into the world of variety. Some of his singles were recorded live in the theatres, like 'Gamblin'' Man'/'Putting on the Style' taken from the London Palladium show in 1957.[85] One of the last records Max Miller ever made was a single featuring duets with Donegan, the two generations of performer singing and joking together in front of a live audience. In one of the songs, Miller gets a big laugh for one of his gags, then crows triumphantly:

> Nah, look at that, look at that! A round of applause! That'll be the best joke of the evening![86]

By 1960, Donegan had broadened his appeal, putting gags into his act to appeal to older patrons, and expanding his repertoire beyond skiffle, notably with novelty songs such as 'My Old Man's a Dustman'. Even so, putting skiffle into variety theatres was never an entirely comfortable fit, and Donegan's adaptation into a more middle-of-the-road showman was viewed with suspicion by some in the skiffle community. Asked whether the other skifflers thought Donegan had sold out, Chas McDevitt replies, 'Yes. And the purists, as there are in all lines of music, were not interested in that.'[87]

Over-amplified groups of teenage idols

Rock and roll was even harder to fit into a night of variety, and it was positively loathed by some critics. Writing in *The Stage* in 1959, Reg

Barlow contemptuously described the typical rock band as 'an over-amplified group of teenage idols whose only call at the barber's in months is for a change of oil and grease'.[88] Like skiffle, it successfully drew in a young audience, but their expectations and the wild energy of the performance did not always fit the other acts in the supporting bill. A scathing review of Cliff Richard at the Chiswick Empire in 1958 gives some idea of the problem:

> Then there is young Cliff Richard, another artist in the long line of those who find it necessary, in order to express themselves, to jerk a leg or wave an arm as they string together a succession of extraordinary words and phrases, often repetitive, each jerk or wave producing more or less non-stop screams from youthful fans who hang on to his every word and gesture.[89]

The youthful fans with their non-stop screams could completely unbalance the normal reactions of a variety audience. Roy Hudd appeared on a bill topped by Richard at the Met, the show being made up of an odd mixture of comics, dancers and speciality acts like the tap-dancing roller skater 'Checker' Wheel. He recalls that Richard 'pulled in all the kids', but, 'They didn't know what the fuck it was all about.' Hudd and Kay's act was well received – 'We got away with it because we were as young as Cliff' – but others were not: 'They didn't give them a rough time. They were just bored because they were waiting for Cliff, you know.'[90]

Des O'Connor found himself particularly in demand for shows topped by rock and roll stars, and has written about a far more chaotic Cliff Richard show at the Chiswick Empire. One of the Friday night performances was disrupted by two local teenage gangs, who pelted the supporting acts with 'an avalanche of foodstuffs', and the show was abandoned on the advice of the police.[91]

As the Cliff Richard review suggests, rock and roll embodied a certain kind of frenzy, in both stage and auditorium, which would never sit easily alongside more sedate acts like magicians, comics or tap-dancing roller skaters. This is still the case in the twenty-first century, as present-day comedian Arthur Smith acknowledges: 'Stand-ups now think...if there's a band on, it's a fucking nightmare, you don't wanna be on with a sodding band. You know, they're loud and you can't compete, they're a different thing.'[92]

Like the nude revues, bills topped by skiffle singers and rock and rollers – with young, excitable audiences liable to descend into frenzied screaming or hurl objects onto the stage – must have helped to scare away what was left of variety's traditional family audience. On the other hand, the new younger audience could not last. The skiffle craze died out comparatively quickly, and rock shows soon moved on to other venues, where the bands could be enjoyed without having to sit through a bill of supporting acts with such a different kind of appeal. This was what Ian Bevan meant when he wrote about teenagers 'scorning' variety theatres as their elders had previously done.

Another problem with booking pop singers to top the bill was that it upset the traditional hierarchy built into the structure of a variety show. Types of act that had traditionally occupied the star spot now found themselves usurped. For example, an article in *The Stage* complained that, 'The comedian is, or should be, the most important person in light entertainment', but his or her place was being taken by 'the current rock'n'roll hero or recording artist on the bill'.[93] Naturally enough, this led to tensions between the acts. Barry Cryer, who worked backstage at the Leeds Empire in the late 1950s, witnessed the kind of situation that occurred:

> A very young Petula Clark ... had a hit record. And Jimmy James ... bridling because she was top of the bill and he wasn't, got his music down very quickly. And she was standing on the side of the stage watching this old comic and his colleagues, and he'd had a quick word with the MD, the Musical Director, and the band. No music for it obviously, he hadn't got the music, but they sang an atrocious version, with the band busking, of her hit. And she's standing there transfixed and horrified and apparently she said, 'Mr James?' 'Yes, dear'. 'That's my record, I'm doing it in my act, tonight.' 'I'm terribly sorry love, we've been doing this for years, we finish the act with it.' It was really cruel, he had her going for about half an hour before he owned up.[94]

The same kind of friction was generated by American stars who were imported to top variety bills. If this caused the kind of resentment that led Max Miller to rebelliously overrun at the Royal Variety Performance, it had even more corrosive effects as the policy moved beyond the London Palladium and spread through the circuit. The problem was, as Ronnie Ronalde put it, 'the vast sums paid to the so-called American stars caused the theatres to cut down on the rest of the artistes and charge higher seat prices which in turn frightened the family audiences away'.[95] This was known as the 'one top' system, and it was bitterly criticized in the press because 'the patron of a better class music hall has to pay more than he would at a cinema to see one good turn and a lot of acts of mediocre quality'.[96]

None of them seemed to care

If nudes and pop singers proved to be short-term solutions to shrinking audiences, there was little will among the agents and booking managers of variety to take the kind of steps that George Black had taken in the 1920s, or to make the kind of improvements that the trade press was crying out for. Naturally, the lack of real investment in variety's future rankled with the acts whose livelihoods depended on the theatres. Don Smoothey recalls that when Dickie Valentine's road show was going around the variety theatres, his manager Tommy Layton 'was sending back to the Grades weekly, on an average between 1,300 and 1,500 quid for their share. But it wasn't being ploughed back. So that's another side of what closed the theatres.'[97] Similarly, Jimmy Jewel wrote: 'Those who pioneered commercial TV had huge vested interests in Moss Empires, yet none of them seemed to care about the theatres one way or another.'[98] Jewel's point is crucial, because the fact is that the early days of ITV were dominated by the theatre managers and agents who had been running variety, including Prince Littler, Jack Hylton, Bernard Delfont, Lew Grade, Hugh Beaumont and Henry Sherek.[99]

There was some effort to stop the rot. Notably, when Leslie Macdonnell became managing director of Moss Empires in 1958, he experimented with a policy of running spectacular, Palladium-style shows in some of his provincial theatres, bringing in big names such as Harry Secombe, Ruby Murray, Tommy Cooper and Benny Hill to top the bills. These would run once nightly for a period of three or four weeks before changing over.[100]

There was also an attempt to reinvent the theatres themselves, reintroducing food and drink into the auditorium for the first time since the heyday of the Victorian music hall. The London Hippodrome closed in 1957, and was opened the following year as a theatre restaurant called The Talk of the Town, which seated about 800 people, who paid an admission price of 42s6d for an evening which included a meal, a show and dancing.[101] A few theatres followed this example. The Palace Theatre in Hull, for example, was reinvented as the Hull Continental Palace. The fixed seating was replaced by tables and chairs, there was drinking and dancing, and the evening ended with 'Old-Tyme Music Hall', with audiences joining in with chorus songs.[102]

However, while The Talk of the Town ran successfully for a couple of decades, finally closing down in 1982, the trend for theatre restaurants failed to revive the variety circuit. Bruce Forsyth has claimed that Robert Nesbitt, who pioneered The Talk of the Town, had made plans for similar conversions with at least ten more Moss theatres, but had failed to get the necessary backing. Forsyth concluded that 'people on the management side of show business, although very happy to take money out, are not always so happy to risk putting money in'.[103]

What is perhaps most significant about the lack of meaningful action from variety management is that Val Parnell was still in charge of Moss Empires through much of the 1950s, but he did as little to help as anyone else. Parnell had been George Black's right-hand man in the 1920s and 1930s, and had thought up many of the innovations which Black had used to revive variety's fortunes in that earlier crisis. By the 1950s, he was an older man and his interests lay elsewhere. While continuing to work for Moss Empires, he became one of the pioneers of commercial television, sitting on ATV's board of directors. Indeed, *Sunday Night at the London Palladium* was very much his show.

You'll never lose money with Miller

Perhaps the agents and managers were right to disinvest in variety. It may be that it was inevitable that it would be crushed by the march of modernity. However, there is evidence to suggest that at the very point when some theatres were being converted into TV studios, others were still doing good business. Summing up the state of the circuit in 1954 in *The Stage Year Book*, Andrew Gray wrote: 'Prosperity for the number-one music halls; adversity for the smaller music halls – that sums up the business year in the variety profession during 1954', adding that, 'The larger theatres did record business'.[104]

A good example of the prosperity that some theatres enjoyed even in these turbulent years was a show at the Globe, Stockton in 1954, with big names like comedian Ken Platt (catchphrase: 'I won't take me coat off – I'm not stopping'), singer Lita Roza (who sang 'How Much Is that Doggie in the Window?'), and Harry Secombe (then famous from *The Goon Show*) topping the bill. Even with a maximum ticket price of 4s6d, the show broke the theatre's records, bringing in nearly £4,000 over the course of the week.[105]

In 1955, it was reported that 'the Moss circuit has kept its theatres well filled with American recording artists and top-line, talent-packed variety bills'.[106] At this point, some of the super cinemas were still putting on as many as five variety acts along with the films, and in January, the Leigh Hippodrome announced that it was giving up film and reverting to variety.[107]

With some theatres thriving and others going under, continued survival seemed to rely on the quality of the shows. In such a time of divided fortunes, the big names of variety started to emphasize their market value. In spite of cultivating a reputation for meanness, Max Miller also used to boast that managements would never lose money if they booked him. The agent Billy Marsh recalled that after performing to a week of small audiences at New Cross Empire, Miller rang his agent, Julius Darewski, to arrange to have his salary cut so that the venue would not lose money and he could maintain his boast.[108]

Even the smaller theatres – which could not afford the big names – could still pull audiences in if the shows were good enough. Jack Seaton, who started working as a comedian in number two and three theatres like the Woolwich Empire, Collins' Music Hall and the Granville, Walham Green recalled:

> If you got them off on the right foot from the beginning, or if there was a good bill, which there was sometimes, in even these theatres, you set them alight. Then the word'd go round the town and by the time you got to the Saturday, you'd probably finish up with a practically full house on a Saturday.[109]

A solid music hall structure

In the 1920s when George Black revived the Palladium, he had built up the GTC and Moss chains because he recognized that his theatre could exist 'only as the apex of a solid music-hall structure'.[110] The terminal crisis of the 1950s revealed that variety was less a solid structure, more a delicate, complex web, made up of hundreds or even thousands of interdependent threads – the performers, the agents who booked them, the companies who ran the theatres, the trade press, the Variety Artistes' Federation (VAF), the professional clubs such as the Water Rats, the theatrical landladies, and so on.

As audiences dwindled, the web started to pull itself apart. When the theatres closed, the number of acts touring from town to town was reduced. With fewer performers to accommodate, theatrical digs started to disappear. In the 1940s, the list of approved digs published by the Actors' Church Union had run to 30 pages, but by 1962 it was down to eight.[111] The trade press also disappeared with the theatres. The only publication exclusively dedicated to variety was *The Performer*, the official organ of the VAF, which had been published since 1906. On 26 September 1957, the cover was headed with the phrase 'OUR FINAL ISSUE', and the editorial read:

> It is with profound regret that we have to announce that with this issue 'The Performer' ceases publication ... with the disintegration of the music hall business, through the development of Television and the consequent changes in booking and other practices, support from those whom the paper set out to serve and has served so declined it has been impossible to continue publication.[112]

A situation of prosperity for the big theatres and adversity for the smaller ones meant that the traditional hierarchy of the halls, with acts progressing from the number twos and threes to the number one theatres – and perhaps, eventually, the Palladium – could not last. The training ground, where young performers could hone their acts in relative anonymity, was disappearing.

It could be that the rot set in with the post-war policy of bringing in American film stars and recording artists to top bills at the Palladium. This may have pulled in record audiences in the short term, but it undermined Black's idea of that theatre being the apex of a solid music hall structure, and meant that the management of Moss Empires no longer had the same need to protect variety's survival across the country.

As Valantyne Napier pointed out, variety artistes were much better paid than legit actors, and the cost of putting a bill together was based on filling large theatres twice nightly, six nights a week. In changing times, with the massive challenge faced by the new competitor, television – which could provide the finest quality bills for free in the comfort of the living room – it is hard to say whether variety could have possibly sustained an audience big enough to sustain a national network of halls. Certainly, Michael Grade bluntly argues that, 'The theatres were unsustainable'.[113]

However, given that most of the key figures running variety had thrown in their lot with commercial television, there was simply not the will to take significant action to keep the theatres open. Instead, they were allowed to decay and falling artistic standards meant there was no hope of winning back the respectable family audience which had always been at the heart of variety's identity. Grade recalls an anecdote which sums the situation up well: 'Val Parnell's great line when variety was in decline, he was interviewed and somebody said, "What are you going to do about the decline in the variety theatres at Moss Empires?" And he said, "Well, we're gonna close Liverpool Empire, and if that works we'll close them all".'[114]

Part Two

Performance Dynamics

6

Personality

The first requisite

What was it that drew the crowds to such large theatres up and down the country for twelve shows a week throughout the middle decades of the twentieth century?

Perhaps the simplest way of explaining the appeal of variety is to say that its purpose was the honest, unashamed pursuit of delight. The Futurist F. T. Marinetti put it well when he wrote: 'The Variety Theatre is absolutely practical, because it proposes to distract and amuse the public with comic effects, erotic stimulation, or imaginative astonishment.'[1]

Delighting the audience was variety's most essential intention, and as Marinetti suggested, this was absolutely practical because the intention was to please the people so they would come back week after week. Success in performance was openly judged in terms of profitability. In 1952, Ian Bevan wrote:

> Profit and loss may not be the best yardstick to apply to all forms of creative work, but it is possibly the best to use in judging music-hall, which is, by definition, a 'popular entertainment'. What better criterion of popularity can there be than whether or not people are willing to pay for it?[2]

Performers were equally open about the fact that they were motivated by money. It was certainly an important factor at the beginning of the Beverley Sisters' career, as Teddie Beverley recalls:

> [O]ur mother did not want us to go into the theatre. But...when the first cheque arrived...15 guineas, we put it on the kitchen floor and danced round it, you know. Because naturally we needed the money, I mean

everybody...was very poor in those days...and it meant everything. It wasn't a question of 'Shall we go into show business?' It was, 'Let's go and pick up this cheque'. [3]

Money was also an important motivation in helping the performers to get through a working week in variety. Peter Prentice remembers:

> It's very bad to be paid before you work. It takes all the heart out of you, somehow. Sometimes they'd come round and pay out and you think, 'Oh'. It's not like waiting [until] after the second show on Saturday night [for them to] come round with the money. And of course you were always paid in cash in those days.[4]

The intense practicality of variety performance meant that it tended to shun theory. From the late nineteenth century onwards, the legitimate theatre saw wave after wave of innovation, as actors, directors and playwrights explored the possibilities of their medium, pushing at the boundaries and publishing the results of their creative experiments. As a result, the legitimate stage built up an intellectual superstructure, surrounding itself with a huge range of theories on acting, directing, design and the nature of theatre itself. Nothing like this happened in variety. There were no Stanislavskis, Craigs, Meyerholds, Artauds, Brechts or Grotowskis among its performers. Quite the opposite, in fact. Brian O'Gorman, the son of Joe from the comedy double act Dave & Joe O'Gorman, wrote, 'The performers...were, in general, not anxious to intellectualise their work...The intellectual sphere has been, notoriously, poison'.[5]

This lack of theory makes analysing the appeal of variety difficult. Roy Hudd's autobiography offers a good place to start, because it describes what made variety worth paying for from a customer's point of view. As a child, he was taken on 'almost weekly' trips to the Croydon Empire by his grandmother, who could scarcely afford the cost of these treats, but reasoned that 'two hours with pretty, handsome, graceful, smiling people doing amazing things, singing songs she liked and, very best of all, making her laugh, was well worth missing a meal for'.[6] Unpicking this description reveals a lot about variety performance. It was participatory and the audience were expected to actively respond to it ('very best of all, making her laugh'). It involved feats of skill and novelty, to astonish the audience ('doing amazing things'). Crucially, it was performed by 'pretty, handsome, graceful, smiling people'.

In 1953, variety critic Reginald Barlow wrote that, 'Personality is still the first requisite when it comes to pleasing an audience.'[7] Reviews of variety theatre are liberally strewn with references to the 'personality' which the best acts were said to possess. For example, a review of bandleader Harry Roy at the Leicester Opera House in 1936 said 'he has a pleasing personality', and after an appearance at the Holborn Empire in March 1937, Max Miller was said to be 'a man of personality'.[8] In an interview in *The Observer* in July 1933, Gracie Fields – who was herself said to have a 'far-reaching and transcendent personality'[9] – argued that 'personality is probably the thing that our whole music-hall business rests on'.[10] The problem is that while the word 'personality' was often bandied about, the lack of introspection among variety people meant that it was rarely discussed or explained. One way of trying to understand the term is to examine those performers who were said to possess it.

Harry Roy

Harry Roy led a big band that topped variety bills for over two decades. As well as conducting the band, he was a vocalist on some of the numbers, and played more than one instrument. Between the songs, he would talk to the audience, and was known as 'an accomplished comedian'.[11] The laughs he got came not just from what he said but how he said it. He starts his act at the Holborn Empire on 24 October 1938 by saying, 'Good evening!' in an excitable falsetto, and exhales in a tiny ghost of a laugh. The audience laugh at the contrast between the sophisticated figure of the bandleader – hair stylishly slicked back, evening suit immaculate – and the silliness with which he greets them (see Illustration 6.1). He then flips back to a delivery that matches his clothes – friendly but formal – and makes reference to a recent tour of South America:

> Good evening everybody, thank you very much for your very nice reception, very sweet of you, and we're all happy to be home again – especially in London, because London reminds us of South America. The sun is always shining. *HEE-HEH-HEH-HUH-huh-huh-huh-huh!* [laughter][12]

The basic gag is simple. Clearly the sun is not 'always shining' in London, especially not in late October, but it is the delivery – the sudden flip from urbanity to a crazy, high-pitched laugh – that wins the laugh. This is typical of how Roy worked, and a review from 1937 gives a good description of the essence of his personality:

> And when the curtain disclosed Harry Roy, with beautifully-cut evening 'tails' and captivating air of having been born half an hour or a hundred years ago – I'm not quite sure which – and Protean ability to turn from matinee idol into golliwog and back again in a second, enthusiasm was clamorous.[13]

The flip from 'matinee idol into golliwog' – from sophistication to childlike silliness – was not reserved for the between-song patter,

Figure 6.1 A signed photograph of Harry Roy, the bandleader with a personality that turned from 'matinee idol into golliwog'.

but also crept into the numbers themselves. He sings the first line of 'Highland Swing', then goes into a repeated scat phrase:

Oh-li-hi-hi
Oh-li-hi-hi
Oh-lah-de-lah
Oh-lah-de-lah

With more repetitions, he starts to get hoarser and more manic, eventually tailing off in a kind of insane yodel:

Oh-lah-de-lah
Oh-lah-de-lah!
OH-LAH-DE-LAH! [laughter]
Aye-ee-aye-ee-aye-

Then he adopts the fanciful falsetto voice of a posh, drunken uncle and says:

Hell-o, how are you? [laughter][14]

This is personality because the laughter springs not from material but from performance, not from the song but from the singer.

Gracie Fields

Gracie Fields was the biggest name in variety, enjoying success not just in the theatres but also on radio, in films and as a recording artist to become a truly international star. Like Harry Roy, she played on different levels, getting laughs in the middle of a song by suddenly flipping into parody, switching from sentiment to burlesque in a single line. Her opening number at the Holborn Empire in October 1933 is 'There's a Cabin in the Pines', and for the first few lines she plays the song's syrupy nostalgia straight:

There's a cabin in the pines,
Hidden in the wild wood,
Wrapped in honeysuckle vine.
Where the mellow moon is always shining

Then she suddenly flips over into the grotesque, deliberately making her voice crack into a yodelling whine, sending up the sentimentality in which she had previously been wallowing:

Sh*i*-ining *o*-on my c*a*-abin in the p*i*-ines. [laughter][15]

She would pull a similar trick in her patter, for example suddenly adopting an affectedly posh stage voice – far from her usual Lancashire accent – then flipping over into stage Cockney:

> Ladies and gentlemen, aye do want to thenk yew so veddy veddy mach. [laughter] Neau, really, I do wish to thenk yew so *aw*-fully, a-heh! [laughter] No really, *honest to gawd*, I mean – [laughter][16]

Playing on different levels suited Gracie Fields's personality, because her whole identity was based on contrasts. She was at once humble and glamorous, ordinary and extraordinary, a big star who managed to give the impression that she was absolutely on the same level as her audience. She grew up above a chip shop in Rochdale and started her stage career in cheap revues directed by her first husband, Archie Pitt, which toured the number twos and threes. Her working-class background was well known to her audience, her entry in Moss Empires publicist Lawson Trout's card index noting that in her 'early days' she had 'revealed her gifts as a singer' by 'entertaining the other girls' when she 'went to work as a winder in a cotton mill'.[17] In her Holborn Empire performance, she directly plays on her humble background when she asks the audience to sing along with her most famous number, 'Sally':

> Now before we go any further I think you know this chorus as well as me, and I *don't think* it'd be a *bad idea* if we all *sang it together*, do you? [laughter] I'll sing it with you and when it comes to a fresh line I'll – I'll shout the words over, see? Those that don't wanna sing can go out and the others can stop and sing. [laughter] Now – come on now, let's – let's forget we're in the 'olborn Empire, let's imagine we're in our front room and we're having a bit of a do. [laughter] Had a nice tea, some boiled ham and lettuce and a tin of salmon, we're all right now. [laughter][18]

Some of the laughs come purely from her delivery. In the first line, her voice becomes jokily bad tempered, with an over-deliberate emphasis every few syllables creating a silly rhythm which turns a simple request into a joke. The next laugh comes when she adopts the kind a voice a shy child might use in a school assembly, as she tells those that don't want to sing that they can go out. As with Harry Roy, the laughter comes not from what is said but from how it is said.

The next two laughs strike at the heart of what made Gracie Fields so popular. By asking the audience to imagine that they are not in some big, grand theatre, but in a vividly evoked working-class front room enjoying an informal sing-song, she explodes the distance between the star and her audience, making the intimacy between them as close as possible by pointing out – even in the spirit of fun – their shared roots.

Max Miller

Although he lacked her success in radio, records and film, Max Miller was probably as big a star as Gracie Fields in the variety theatres themselves. Long-term fan Roy Hudd describes who Miller was while he was onstage:

> He was a rogue, he was a sexy rogue, you know. And funnily enough, I always thought that if I could have been anybody in real life, even when I first sort of saw him in variety, I'd like to have been like him, you know. A bloke who could pull all the birds in the world, you know, but could still get up in the pub with the lads and make them laugh and tell them a story and a joke ... he would be the one who'd chat the barmaid up and he'd win.[19]

Hudd recalls Miller's opening line when he appeared on the same bill as him at the Finsbury Park Empire in the late 1950s: 'Max Miller walked on, "I went to the chemist's yesterday", a big laugh. 'Cos he'd only go to the chemist for one thing, Max – not a toothbrush!' The audience picked up on what Miller was implying – that he had gone to the chemist to buy condoms – because they knew his reputation as the sexy rogue.

Miller played directly on his reputation for bawdiness. At an appearance at the Holborn Empire in 1938, he is quite brazen about it:

> I don't care what I say, do I? [laughter] I don't, I don't care, honest I don't! You want to hear me on Sunday on Luxembourg, I'm *filthy!* [laughter] I don't care, I don't! [laughter continues][20]

As the routine continues, it becomes harder to tell just why the audience are laughing:

> I look better since I came back off my cruise, don't I? No, I *do* look, I was poorly, wasn't I poorly? [laughter] No, I was – I was, I was dyin'! [laughter] Before I went away. I look nice now, don't I, duck, don' I? [laughter]

As with Roy and Fields, it is the delivery as much as anything else that wins the laughs. As he tells them about how poorly he was, he becomes gossipy and camp. Then be becomes gleefully boastful about how 'nice' he looks, becoming ever more intimate by flirting playfully with a particular woman in the audience.

Once again, the comedy is entirely based on the identity of the performer. As a review in *The Stage* put it in 1958: 'Max Miller's comedy is timeless because it exists in the man himself rather than in anything he says. He has but to raise those cheeky, challenging eyes in delighted incredulity and the audience is laughing.'[21] As this suggests, part of the appeal was rooted in Miller's physical presence. In 1947, A. Crooks Ripley wrote that Miller had 'physical charm equivalent to that of an attractive woman, or, in vulgar terms, sex-appeal', mentioning 'the scrumptious expression Max wears in particularly big moments, pinching his teeth with his cheeks as if he were sucking a pungent acid-drop, the yolks of the eyes looking towards the heavens through his panama'.[22]

If the way Miller looked was important, the way he dressed was crucial. Onstage, he wore a succession of gaudy suits, generously cut multicoloured monstrosities with billowing plus-four trousers, in loud checks or enormous floral prints. On his head he wore a white panama, on his feet shiny co-respondent shoes, and in his hand he sometimes carried a cane. In a time when male fashions were far dowdier and more restrictive than today, dressing like that was extraordinarily exotic, something that could not be seen outside of the world of the variety stage. The outrageousness of the clothes provided a context for the outrageousness of the innuendo in his gags. A reviewer in *The Times* declared that, 'Mr Miller is a sartorial outrage, and a man must have a way with him before he could bring himself to don such deplorable garments. Mr Miller has that way.'[23]

At the Holborn Empire, Miller uses the costume to establish an immediate connection with the audience. It is the first thing he mentions when he comes onto the stage, alternately asking another lady in the audience to share his own delight in his appearance, and chiding the rest of the audience for laughing at him:

> I wear some nice clothes, don' I lady, some nice clothes, don' I? No, listen, no, shaddap! [laughter] Weeeell, shaddap! [laughter] I do wear some nice clothes, don' I, lady? Real taffeta, I wear, weeell! [laughter] Nooo, shaddap! [laughter] Weelll! [laughter][24]

Your own personality

Clearly, what 'personality' suggests is that the identity of the performer is at the very centre of the performance. It was certainly more important than material, as an article from *The Stage* in 1952

clearly acknowledged: 'The art, of course, lies not so much in learning a comic song or any other routine, but in improving the presentation of the offering and infusing personal charm into it.'[25] That same
year, Max Miller advised young performers: '[W]ork out your own
individual style. Then do all you can to develop yourself. Trust in
your own personality, select and arrange your own material.'[26] What
this is implies is that material did not need to be original. Rather
than being created by the performer, it could be merely selected
and arranged. The real act of creation was to create the onstage
self – to work out an individual style, to develop the self, to trust the
personality.

This advice certainly reflected Miller's work. What made him so
appealing was the person he was while he was onstage: the Lothario
and the gossip, the intimate show-off in the peacock suit. However,
personality also implies more than that. Max Miller is not the creation of a playwright's imagination. He is not a character in a play, a
role that can be played by many different actors. Laurence Olivier,
who played the grizzled old comic Archie Rice in John Osborne's
The Entertainer, clearly explained the difference between acting and
variety performance:

> Surely you must know that all actors are saying, 'Look at me! Look at me!'
> And this is fundamental, but more so for the Variety Artiste, because,
> while the straight actor is playing a part, creating a character and hoping
> to lose himself in it, the entertainer is projecting his own personality. He
> offers himself for approval.[27]

This is the true implication of 'personality'. The term implies that the
role played onstage is a projection of the performer's actual self. Max
Miller appears onstage as 'the man himself'. This idea was commonly
expressed in variety. Appearing for troops in the Second World War,
George Formby is welcomed onto the stage:

> He's been out and found his ukulele for you, so now you're going to see
> George as he really is – George with his banjulele![28]

The implication is very clear: the person the audience is seeing in
stage is the genuine article, an authentic portrayal of Formby's personality. The way the audience react suggests that that is exactly how
they see things: they are seeing the real George, and they are communicating with him directly. As well as greeting him with torrent of
cheers, applause and whistling, individuals shout out to him, trying
to engage him in direct conversation. Between the first two numbers

this gets slightly out of hand, and Formby sounds almost rattled as he calms them down:

> Now wait a minute, lads – I can't tell yer if yer talking back to me, can I?[29]

Many acts saw their onstage personalities as projections of self. Joan Rhodes put it simply: 'I was just myself, you know. If something came into my head I would say it. And I used to get big laughs sometimes.'[30] Asked whether she was aware of playing an exaggerated version of herself onstage, Vera Lynn replies: 'Well no, not really, you're not aware of playing anything except being on the stage and doing what you do, and that is sing... you don't have to sort of put on an act as it were.'[31]

To be authentic, the act had to build the onstage personality from the offstage self, and avoid superimposing anything artificial. After seeing Bruce Forsyth struggling at the Empress, Brixton, Bernard Delfont advised him to adopt a 'pseudo-American accent'. Forsyth rightly rejected the advice: '[I]n the end I thought, "This just *isn't* me. I have a high voice – so what? – *that's me!*" One of the hardest things in our business is to go on stage and be yourself – not how you or others think you should be, but how you are.'[32] It could be disastrous to impose inauthentic characteristics, as it was for Barry Cryer when he started out as a comic in variety:

> I thought I was Terry-Thomas. I can't believe it looking back, but I wore a dressing gown and sat in an armchair and had a cigarette holder. I'm not making this up. And an old comic said, 'Oh, you must be a London act'. I always remember that, me from Leeds, you know – with a Leeds accent. Oh, it was just dreadful.[33]

Teddy Brown's special rebate

The emphasis on the self meant that the way a performer looked became a vital part of the act. Whereas actors can disguise themselves, using costume, wigs and make-up to distinguish the character they are playing from their offstage selves, variety artistes played on their own inherent physical properties. Their hair, their face, and their body were part of the texture of the act, part of their appeal. Comedians would often play on the quirks of their own appearance. The impish, pocket-sized comic Arthur Askey, for example, joked about his height. Turning to his taller partner Richard Murdoch, he asked, 'Am I standing in a hole, or are you on horseback?' [laughter].[34] Similarly, Tommy Trinder told gags about his distinctive, jutting chin: 'A woman kept looking at me side-faced, have you ever seen me side-faced, look. She said, "Excuse me, didn't I back you at Newmarket?"' [laughter].[35]

The physical identity of the act was important enough to put effort into maintaining it, so that the appearance that had become familiar to the audience would not change. Roy Hudd has a distinctive gap between his front teeth, and he argues that:

> If you do change, people get upset. I always remember years ago when I was doing a lot of variety... my dentist said, 'I'm going to close that gap up.' I said, 'Don't do that for Christ's sake... People will say, 'What's up with him? What's he had done? Oo look, he's had his choppers done!'[36]

The strongwoman Joan Rhodes recalled, 'I did my best to be glamorous' because she recognized that 'glamour was necessary.' Performing two shows a night was enough to avoid the need for training to maintain her strength, but she would walk five miles a day to keep her slim figure.[37]

The xylophonist Teddy Brown had the opposite problem, because he was as famous for his fatness as for his musicianship. His own bill matter – 'The "Great" Xylophonist' – punningly played on his enormousness, and jokes about his size were common, like the spoof advert in a theatre programme which reads: 'Are you going tenting? Teddy Brown's shirt to let'.[38] In June 1927, Brown was arrested and temporarily imprisoned for non-payment of income tax. The background to the case was convoluted, but significantly Robin Humphreys, the manager of the Café Anglais who intervened on Brown's behalf, argued that his huge size ought to have been taken into consideration by the Inland Revenue:

> I think there is a number of reasons why Mr Brown should have special rebate. Owing to his immense size – he weighs 25 stones – his suits cost three times as much as those of an ordinary man. Then he has to consume big meals. To him a two-pound steak is only a d'oeuvre.[39]

Humphreys was clearly implying that Teddy Brown's fatness was such an important part of his act that the money spent on buying the food to maintain such an unhealthy and abnormal girth and the outsize clothes to fit it should quality as legitimate business expenses. At the same time, of course, he was also helping to maintain Brown's image as a famous fatty with the comment about the steak being a mere starter to a man with such an extraordinary figure.

The Beverley Sisters in the absolute raw

The Beverley Sisters had, as one reviewer put it, 'the not inconsiderable advantage of possessing three delightful personalities'.[40] On the face of it, these delightful personalities might seem rather exaggerated and artificial, and Teddie Beverley freely acknowledges that they had a 'very strong image'.[41] It was a visually arresting act, not just because the sisters were pretty and 'beautifully dressed',[42] but also because of its striking symmetry. Their costumes were identical, and the older sister, Joy, always stood between the identical twins, Babs and Teddie, who mirrored each other. They came across as glamorous girls next door, modest and bashful, like children performing for their parents at a party. A 1963 review of a show at the Palace, Manchester praised their 'delightful shows of nervousness' and noted that 'they are made up like girls who are as hard as nails, yet they hit an oddly diffident note in their patter'.[43]

The twist was that their songs sometimes contained a milder version of the kind of innuendo that Max Miller traded in, and they were even criticized in the *News of the World* for their suggestive material.[44] They responded by writing themselves a song called 'We Have to Be So Careful':

> We've been told we look ethereal,
> And so in our material,
> We have to be so careful what we sing.
> We're allowed to have our festive times,
> But mustn't have suggestive rhymes.[45]

Later, they include an example of such a suggestive rhyme, in a line about a bank manager who liked 'to make advances, but they're not the kind we need'. The comedy partly works because of the contrast between the slightly racy gag and the innocent image, as Teddie Beverley acknowledges: '[W]e looked like three innocent little angels, and we were in fact three little angels, and then we'd come out with something naughty, but it amused us.'[46]

However, she strongly denies that there was anything affected about this, arguing:

> It's not an act really, it was *us*, you see. It wasn't assumed. It was us. It was us in the absolute raw ... It doesn't succeed with the public over time if you put on an act. The public, on the whole, can see through that after time. And it's only if you are *the* real person ...[47]

She explains that the distinctive aspects of their onstage personalities were entirely 'natural': 'We were horrendously shy and that came across and although it was painful for us, it sort of helps your image a little bit, you know? It's rather endearing to be shy. You don't wanna be too brash.'[48] Similarly, the striking visual symmetry reflected their offstage lives:

> It all came very, very naturally, and our mother, as children, dressed us alike because she could just afford one yard of material from the shop and she'd make three dresses out of it...So if, you know, the twins had a brown checked dress, Joy had a brown checked dress – and the other way, you see.[49]

Off the stage I am nothing

On the other hand, others suggest that the stage persona of the variety artiste was a long way from the performer's offstage self. In a seminal article on the identity of the popular entertainer published in the 1970s, Clive Barker argued that the stage persona is 'a fabrication...played as consciously as the actor assumes his role'.[50] Some performers support this idea. As well as arguing 'I was just myself', Joan Rhodes also wrote: 'On stage I became a different person, very glamorous and strong.'[51] Similarly, Barry Cryer says, 'You become a creation of your own. Something else...People are always, in a sense, playing a character. A larger-than-life projection of themselves.'[52] Florence Desmond, who was probably the most famous impressionist in variety theatre, once wrote: 'Do I like to meet the person I am impersonating? No, I find this confusing, I like to give impressions of the stars as they are known to the public. Very few stars behave in private life as they do in their professional appearances.'[53] Max Miller is a good example of this, and the contrast between his loud, brash stage persona, and the quiet, soberly dressed private man has often been noted. Miller himself is supposed to have said, 'Off the stage I am nothing and only when I'm working in front of an audience can I come to life and become an interesting person.'[54] An obituary in *The Stage* made a similar point: '[O]ff-stage except perhaps when joining in the fun of a party with friends and drinks, he was a quiet, still man.'[55]

It might seem impossible to reconcile these two positions. Either variety performers were simply 'being themselves' onstage, or they were playing a character. In fact, there is an element of truth in both. They might have been drawing on their own personalities to create a stage identity, but the traits they showed to audiences must have been selected and exaggerated. Undoubtedly, they adapted themselves to the demands of the stage, not least because as Max Miller suggested, acts would usually merely select and arrange their material rather than actually creating it.

Vera Lynn was often praised for her 'sincerity', but in her autobiography she points out how misleading this word is: 'On the whole – and it was certainly true in 1941 – a popular singer uses other people's words, and she hasn't necessarily been through the experiences she's describing... So she has to use her imagination, which is not a matter of sincerity so much as conviction.'[56]

Another adaptation was that variety performers would put money and effort into making sure the clothes they wore onstage were as immaculate as possible. Even when they wore nothing more exotic than a smart suit onstage, this would have been treated as a formal stage costume. Front cloth comic Jack Seaton recalled, '[W]hen we put on our stage suit, we never sat down... As soon as you came offstage, you took it off, and put a dressing gown on.'[57] Similarly, Peter Prentice says, 'Never sit down in your costume – because it creases. My father would be very furious if you got creases in your trousers. Because satin creases across where you sit down, so you don't sit down.'[58] In a world in which booking managers might refuse to engage an act for wearing dirty shoes, it was important to maintain a clear division between offstage clothes and onstage costume.

For Max Miller, the costume was an important part of what divided the 'quiet, still' offstage man from the 'interesting person' he became onstage. The costume took him out of the ordinary world, because the vast majority of men dressed far less garishly than he did onstage. Wearing those clothes seems to have helped him to transform into the sexy rogue he played onstage. There is a story about an early engagement at the Palladium in which George Black insisted he wore an ordinary lounge suit. He went down badly, and only started getting the usual laughs again when his agent, Julius Darewski, made him wear his usual outlandish costume.[59] He would wear the trademark clothes whenever he performed, even on the radio, as Barry Cryer recalls:

> I did Midday Music Hall with Max Miller at the Playhouse, Northumberland Avenue... They showed me to a dressing room, and I thought, 'Dressing room? For radio?' And I'm sharing with the great man. And he put on his full stage costume... The hat and the plus fours and everything, he said, 'Can't work in ordinary clothes, son'.[60]

The clothes Miller wore onstage might seem like an entirely artificial element, a clear symptom of the fact that the person he played
onstage was a purely fictional character. However, even a costume as
colourful and stylized as this had its origins in Miller's offstage life.
As a child, he had a reputation as a dandy, wearing paper collars and
spats in spite of the scruffiness of the rest of his clothes.[61]

On the stage, you're alive

Variety performers might have played themselves, but there seems to
have been a definite transformation into the strong, glamorous, interesting version of themselves that they became on the stage. For Peter
Prentice, personality simply meant 'smiling' and making as much
effort as possible:

> You're doing these things, it's no good doing it with a glum face and not
> taking any notice of the audience, they've got to enjoy what you are appar-
> ently enjoying. And never, ever went on intending not to perform at your
> very best. My dad used to say, 'You never know who's in front'.[62]

Going onstage meant becoming energized and adopting a heightened state of being. A biography of Danny Kaye written in 1959
describes the stark contrast between Kaye's onstage and backstage
selves: 'The man on the stage is high pressured, completely zany,
hyper-tense, driven by nervousness. The man in the dressing room
is relaxed as a rag doll.'[63] Illness or injury could be put to one side
while the performer was onstage. Don Smoothey was once hit on
the head by the heavy bottom of the front cloth just before his act:
'I went on and I did me spot, and came off and had delayed con-
cussion. I had no recollection of doing the act – but I had done, you
know.'[64]

The heightened state of being became particularly visible as the performer crossed the borderline between dressing room and stage, and
it was vital that this transformation was immediate. Don Smoothey is
incredulous when today's entertainers talk about needing 15 minutes
to establish themselves: 'I say, "What are you talking about?" Miss
Williams used to say to us, "You establish yourself as you walk on
my stage".'[65] According to Jack Seaton, '[Y]ou learned that art by just
walking on. It's not anything people can teach you ... you have to learn
it by sheer experience.'[66]

At the end of the act, as the performer came back across the
boundary from stage to dressing room, and became their everyday

self again. Morris Aza, who was Gracie Fields's nephew by marriage and saw her perform many times, remembers: 'She came off the stage in the dressing room and she wasn't the person that'd just been out there. She just went right down and she was just ordinary – just an auntie, as far as I was concerned.'[67] An interviewer encountering Fields in the dressing room between two houses at the Palladium in July 1933 noticed another difference between her onstage and off-stage selves:

> Miss Fields has a dresser in the room and a secretary. To the speech of all three of them clings a soft Lancashire burr. Which is curious. For on the stage (unless she is doing specifically Lancashire dialect songs) Miss Fields herself has a clear precision of articulation that all the gods and all the politicians might envy.[68]

Fields herself was aware of the distance between her stage persona and her private self. In her autobiography, she recalled her friend, the artist John Flanagan, telling her, 'On the stage, you're alive, you're bubbling, everyone wants to feel the way you're obviously feeling', whereas offstage 'your eyes always look miserable, half dead'.[69] She was worried that her audience, who only knew the person she became onstage, would be disappointed if they actually met her:

> They knew me – but *how* did they know me – as someone who could make them laugh, make them sing, cheer them up, perhaps help them a bit here and there. They didn't know me as the tired, inadequate woman I felt, and if they ever found out, I was sure they'd feel I'd let them down.[70]

Always be funny in public

Gracie Fields was not the only performer who thought like this. The personality seen onstage might have been different from the private person, but there was no clear distinction between the two in the audience's eyes. This meant that the act often spilled offstage into everyday life. Sometimes, performers were expected to hobnob with the public as part of their contract, and George Black would get star comedians to greet the audience coming into the Palladium.[71] John Alexander, who worked front of house at the Metropolitan, Edgware Road at the end of its life, recalled how Max Miller would do this voluntarily while appearing there:

> He seldom used the stage door, preferring to arrive by taxi at the front, often in the company of a statuesque blonde who once or twice made an

appearance in his act. He would walk in, larger than life, greet everyone in sight and with a 'Hello Boys' for the staff.[72]

Many performers felt they had to become their stage selves not only in and around the theatre but whenever they were in public. Vera Lynn has written that it was 'part of the job' for women in the profession to look glamorous 'whether you were on the stage or not'.[73] Tommy Handley's scriptwriter and biographer Ted Kavanagh believed that the famous variety and radio comedian had to 'always be funny in public', adding, 'It was expected of him – he must not disappoint anyone ... He could only relax in the privacy of his home.'[74] Eric Morecambe's children have explained what a burden this could be, his daughter Gail talking of, 'Not being able to go on the beach with dad, not being able to just walk into a café, because people felt they knew him', and his son Gary saying that, 'He never wanted to let anyone down, so he'd be Eric Morecambe for them all the time.'[75] Even in retirement, Don Smoothey talks about slipping into anecdotes while drinking with his neighbours, leading one of them to comment, 'The curtain's gone up'.[76]

Gracie Fields offers a particularly striking example of the way a variety act could spill out into everyday life. She may have been well aware of being very different onstage and off, but there is no doubt that the stage personality she adopted was based on authentic parts of herself. She certainly had the common touch, and would have been no stranger to the working-class teatime of boiled ham, lettuce and tinned salmon which she conjured up so vividly on the stage of the Holborn Empire. Morris Aza tells a story which shows not only that she tended to shun much of the luxury associated with stardom, but also how easily she could slip into performance mode, even in everyday situations:

> She loved going on buses. She loved upstairs on buses. Wherever she was going, 'No, I don't want taxis.' 'We'll send you a car Miss Fields.' 'No, no, I don't want a car.' She never did, she either walked or she went on a bus or something like that. And I was with her on the top of a bus once going along ... Oxford Street, I think it was. And we were sitting at the back, she liked that back seat upstairs in the bus. And she's looking out, looking at people, and watching them, and shops and everything. Then she suddenly – she starts singing 'Sally' – at the top of her voice. And I went cold, I thought, 'What is she doing?' And of course everybody in the bus all stood up and turned round, said, 'Oh look, there's Gracie!' And she sang this song for them. Then got up and got off the bus. You know, 'Hooray!'[77]

Selling himself

Given that variety was such an openly commercial form of theatre, with performers motivated by the cash payment after the second house of Saturday night and success measured by the yardstick of profit and loss, creating a stage personality effectively meant turning the self into a saleable commodity. Some performers certainly talked in these terms. Harry Secombe, for example, described the Met, Edgware Road as 'a very good "shop window" theatre ... because it was easily accessible for all the London agents and bookers'.[78] Similarly, an official ENSA report on Tommy Trinder praised his 'artistry' in 'selling himself' to the troops he had been entertaining in Italy.[79]

Like any product, personality had to be properly marketed. Writing about variety's American cousin, vaudeville, Trav S. D. argues that, 'Just as Coca-Cola, Burma Shave, and Nabisco were learning how to sear impressions of their products into the consumer's mind, vaude-villians began to apply the principles to their own market. The smart acts branded not only their act, but themselves.'[80] Ken Dodd described the tickling stick he carries onstage in terms of product branding: 'It's like the golliwog on the jar of marmalade – it's the little symbol that stands for the whole.'[81]

Bill matter was important not just for the theatres who wanted to bring in the audiences, but also for the individual acts who wanted to build a personal following for themselves. In a sense, it was their own personal advertising slogan. The value of bill matter was brought home to front cloth comic Wyn Calvin when he was forced to change his: 'I was at one point billed as "The Clown Prince of Wales". And then in 1959, Charles was declared Prince of Wales. And I had a note from the Press Office at Buckingham Palace, saying it would be wise if I no longer used that.' A change in bill matter was significant enough for a Sunday newspaper to run a competition among its readers to find him a new billing: '[T]he one that the editor liked was "The Daffy Taffy". I didn't like it ... I preferred "The Welsh Prince of Laughter". And that's what it's been ever since.'[82]

There were also other ways to build a personal following, and like all forms of advertising, this meant spending money. Glamorous strong-woman Joan Rhodes recalled, 'I used to get a lot of fan mail – and they all wanted photographs. And of course I was paying for the photographs.'[83] Ronnie Ronalde produced a newsletter for fans called *Voice of Variety* twice a year, with print runs of up to 55,000.[84] Eddie Gray produced a delightfully eccentric form of self-promotion, in the form of a tiny blue booklet which he could give out to fans as a kind of calling

Figure 6.2 This little booklet was 'Monsewer' Eddie Gray's calling card. Inside, the pages are all blank.

card. On the front is a cartoon of the moustachioed comic juggler, and the title: 'What I know about Women!!! By "Monsewer" EDDIE GRAY'. Inside, the pages are completely blank (see Illustration 6.2).[85]

The master of self-publicity was Tommy Trinder. During the Second World War, he paid the Borough Bill Posting Company £265 a week for hand-painted hoardings to be displayed at 26 sites across London, bearing a cartoon of his face and the slogan 'If it's laughter you're after – TRINDER'S the name!' On one of them, opposite Aldgate tube station, he had the slogan translated into Hebrew.[86]

Whereas some acts used marketing techniques to sell their personality, other used the personality as a form of marketing for other products, turning themselves into living advertisements. Morris Aza's surname stems from the early twentieth century, when his father Bert Aza was part of a music-and-dance act. He gave up his original family name – Selinger – as part of a commercial transaction that provided the act with free costumes:

> Because they had no money for clothes, they went to a firm and said if they called themselves the name of their cloth, would they give them a length of their cloth for nothing, and they said, 'Well ... what we could give you is a new cloth that we're just getting out, and it's called the Aza cloth, A-Z-A'. They said, 'Oh that's fine, that's lovely'. So they called themselves the Three Aza Boys.[87]

Catchphrases

Tommy Trinder's stunt with the advertising hoardings suited his style, because the appeal of his act was built on a shared enjoy-ment of his outrageous self-promotion. Appearing at the Embassy Theatre, Peterborough in November 1940, he starts off by telling the audience:

> Good evening now ladies and gentlemen, the name is Trinder, T-R-I-N-D-E-R, pronounced Chumley, and I'm going to sing to yer, ha ha, you lucky people!

'You lucky people' is Trinder's catchphrase, and it is so well known to this audience that they actually say it along with him, then break into laughter at their own silliness. Trinder continues to drop his own name throughout the act that follows, for example telling a man in the audience:

> Don't look at the programme sir, the name's Trinder. [laughter]

And commenting:

> Gentleman doesn't believe I'm Tommy Trinder, if I'm not Tommy Trinder I'm having a hell of a time with his wife! [laughter][88]

When the ENSA report described him as 'selling himself', it was not referring to the way he marketed the act offstage but the way he engaged with the audience while onstage. This was something that all variety acts had to learn to do, and an important part of it was making themselves as familiar as possible with the audience. The catchphrase was ideal for this purpose, because it works precisely through its familiarity. Catchphrases only became established through repetition, and the fact that the audience recognized them was a tangible sign of their familiarity with the act, helping to close the gap between stage and auditorium.

This made using a catchphrase a great way of starting the act. The Western Brothers were a pair of monocle-wearing musical comics who sang witty songs in an upper-class drawl that suggested mock-bored contempt for the rest of the world. Their onstage personalities were crystallized in an admirably succinct two-word catchphrase: 'Hello, cads'. A radio broadcast begins with George tinkling away on the piano and Kenneth intoning this catchphrase, which is enough in itself to get a round of applause.[89]

Establishing catchphrases which would successfully latch onto the audience's imagination was not easy, and they were often discovered by accident. Sandy Powell got his catchphrase – 'Can you hear me, mother?' – when he dropped his script during a live radio broadcast, frequently repeating the line as he struggled to retrieve it. The following Monday, the manager of the Coventry Hippodrome persuaded him to use the line to open his act that night, and when he did, it got 'loud and prolonged applause'. He would use the catchphrase as his opening line for the rest of his career.[90]

Some acts had other devices to create a feeling of familiarity in the audience, like Ken Dodd's tickling stick or Gracie Fields's whistle. Sometimes a particular piece of material would become strongly associated with the act, a trademark routine that they would always be expected to perform. For Gracie Fields, it was the song 'Sally', which was written by Will E. Haines, Harry Leon and Leo Towers for her debut film, *Sally in Our Alley* in 1931. By the time of her Holborn Empire performance in October 1933, the song is so well established that she reacts to the audience's shouted requests for it with joking annoyance:

'Sally', 'Sally', every time 'Sally', I'll be singin' 'Sally' when I'm nine hundred and ninety-nine! [laughter][91]

Small men and bullies

If familiarity was one way in which variety artistes connected with
their audience, another was status. In 1898, Max Beerbohm wrote an
article in which he argued that music hall comedians 'make themselves as unsightly as they can', because 'The mass of people, when it
seeks pleasure, does not want to be elevated: it wants to laugh at something beneath its own level.'[92] Similarly, when Wyn Calvin started in
variety, he found his Welsh accent 'useful for comedy, because it was
unusual. And because it was easy to feel superior to, which is what an
audience wants to feel about a comic…the fact that an audience can
also feel superior means that they will like him or her.'[93]

Others argue that far from allowing the audience to feel superior,
variety performers dominated their audiences. According to Roy
Hudd, 'They're leaders…And they are people who observe things in
a different way to you. You've noticed these things as well, but they
point out the ludicrousness of it all…I don't know any performers
really who try to be less than their audience.'[94]

It might seem impossible to reconcile these two positions, but in
fact both approaches were used, with some acts lowering their status
and others raising it, as Ivor Brown pointed out in an article for *The
Observer* in 1943:

> The music-hall has often relied on the small, shrinking man whose
> attack on the audience was superficially a form of retreat…he drew our
> hearts over the footlights in terrible concern for his starved affairs and
> windowed raggedness. The other type triumphs by exactly the opposite
> method…He bestrides the orchestra-pit and batters us into submission
> with his cudgelling of quips. Max Miller may appear to be standing there
> upon the stage, but his personality, ogling and leering in its zest for life,
> is lording it over the auditorium. Impenitently aggressive, he reaches out
> to annex his fascinated public. Here is the bully-boy – and audiences love
> to be bullied.[95]

The different status levels of different stage personalities did not
only define their relationship with the audience, but also with each
other when they shared the stage. The classic variety double act was
based on the contrasting status of the two performers. Don Smoothey –
who worked as the funny man in both Lowe & Ladd and Smoothey &
Layton – defines the double act as: 'The little silly character against
the rather pompous'.[96] Arthur Askey had a much more colourful
definition, which he once shared with Roy Hudd: '[H]e was doing a
season in Blackpool and they had a double act on the bill and I was
quite interested in double acts having been one myself, and I said,

"What are they like, Arthur?" He said, "Oh, you know, the usual", he said, "The toff and the cunt" '.[97]

Both of these definitions imply the same thing. The straight man played higher status. He was 'rather pompous', a 'toff' – the one who was in charge, middle class rather than working class, sophisticated and debonair. The funny man was quite the opposite – a 'silly little character', a 'cunt' – the down-to-earth working-class underling, more goofy than glamorous. The laughter echoed from the clash of one against the other, as the funny man constantly undermined the status of the straight man. This was the basis of a long line of variety double acts – greater and lesser – including Flanagan & Allen, Dave & Joe O'Gorman, Jewel & Warriss, Morecambe & Wise, and Mike & Bernie Winters.

There were double acts which didn't play on status battles, particularly female ones like Elsie & Doris Waters and Ethel Revnell & Gracie West.[98] However, even in acts which followed the classic pattern, status was far from simple. The low-status funny man was, on the face of it, somebody the audience should have felt superior to. He could be physically smaller than the straight man or distinctly less attractive, as in the contrast between Mike Winters' slickness and Bernie's big buck teeth. In spite of this, the funny man enjoyed a much closer rapport with the audience, audibly gaining their approval in the form of laughter. The joy of the classic double act is seeing idiocy triumphing over soberness, chaos over order, the higher brought down by the lower. In this sense, the funny man is the more important member of the act and usually the bigger star.

Warmth

Successful variety performers were often said to have 'warmth', and this word crops up nearly as often as 'personality'. Don Smoothey recalls being spotted by Gordon Marsh while appearing at the Clapham Grand in 1946: 'It wasn't so much what I did, it was *me* that he liked... What he said was he loved my warmth. Those were his very words.'[99] Jack Seaton argued that Max Miller and Tommy Trinder became stars because 'they had the warmth', and Ted Ray believed that warmth was the 'greatest quality' shared by Robb Wilton, Bud Flanagan and Will Hay.[100] On the other hand, the agent Joe Collins argued that Peter Sellers enjoyed less success than Harry Secombe in variety because 'when facing a live audience with his act "Speaking for the Stars" Sellers lacked personal warmth and communication'.[101]

'Warmth' seems to have pretty much the same meaning as when it is used in everyday relationships. It implies likeability and an ability to make the audience feel affection. The trick was, as Peter Prentice puts it, 'getting them to like you'.[102] What was achieved was a very personal relationship between performer and audience – an imagined friendship in which the audience felt they knew the performer personally. In 1950, Max Bygraves described the audience as 'people to whom, after all, you are appealing as friends'.[103] This was in an interview in *The Stage*, entitled 'The importance of being yourself', and the title is revealing, because the affection the audience felt was not for a fictional character but for a projection of the performer's self. The fact that there was no clear division between the stage persona and the private self meant that the affection which the public expressed could have a very personal impact on the performer.

Gracie Fields wrote that, 'The fan mail and those audiences were like something warm and good – it was like being loved.'[104] The affection she inspired in audiences was extraordinary, as Morris Aza – who watched her perform quite often from the side of the stage – recalls:

> I could see the audience as well...I can remember it, you know, it was just so gripping. You'd see people in there, mesmerised, you know, you think, 'What's the matter with them? Are they cut-outs? They don't move! Nothing happens! They're just, you know, stuck, still, solid.' And that's what one came to realise about her...she literally mesmerises audiences.[105]

Having such an effect may have given her a feeling of 'being loved', but even such enthusiasm could have a jarring emotional impact, as she explained in her autobiography:

> In my own small way I've learned that once you let such tremendous receptions move you to tears, you're done. There comes a point when you just have to weld your heart and mind and feelings into a sort of shock-absorber so that, as wave after wave of emotion rolls towards you, you have the strength to take it, to smile, to control your voice, and to speak. Afterwards, and especially if you're alone, you feel wrung out, shaken, and often frightened. You have an impossible need to run back to all those wonderful people and start trying to explain: 'Look, I'm just an ordinary person, there's nothing about me that deserves all this, please understand.'[106]

However, it was even harder to take when the public mood turned against her. During the Second World War, sections of the British press waged a concerted campaign against her. This started very early on, in spite of her tireless efforts in entertaining the troops even at the very beginning of the war – while she was supposed to be convalescing from a hysterectomy following a diagnosis of cervical cancer. At this point, Fields's partner was the Italian-American film director Monty Banks, whose citizenship meant he was in danger of being interned as an enemy alien. To avoid this, the couple moved to America, which was seen in some quarters as a sign of treachery. The *Daily Mirror* sprung to her defence, saying:

> In one way and another there seems to have been quite a lot of mud-slinging by certain people, who from patriotic or other motives difficult to define, seem intent on besmirching a name that a few months ago inspired the greatest admiration in the bulk of the population of this country ... One would imagine that with the British Commonwealth of Nations fighting for its very life against two powerful enemies, some people's time and vocals cords could be devoted to something that really matters.[107]

Such a stink had been kicked up that a few weeks later, Fields's departure was discussed in the House of Commons, where J. J. Davidson asked why she had been allowed to take £8,000 out of the country, and Captain Crookshank, Financial Secretary to the Treasury, replied that she had sought special permission and explained that she had taken items of jewellery out of the country before the ban on this was imposed on 1 July.[108] H. B. Morgan, the MP for Rochdale, was quoted by *The Stage* as saying, 'I think it very unfortunate she should be pilloried when some rich and noble people have had the same facilities.'[109] Later, in 1943, she was criticized for cutting short a tour for the Eight Army in order to honour a contract for an appearance on American radio. The furore was serious enough for Winston Churchill to come to her defence, saying, 'It is unfair that Miss Fields should be singled out for an attack in a newspaper published for the troops.'[110]

The onslaught she suffered in the war left her with a damaged reputation even after peace was restored, and this meant the stakes were very high when she made her first major post-war appearance in a London variety theatre in October 1948. She admitted to Val Parnell that she was scared that her popularity had been harmed.[111] Morris Aza remembers that his father Bert Aza, who was her manager, 'was absolutely terrified – he was shaking like a piece of jelly, I imagine. He was ill for about a fortnight afterwards. 'Cos he thought they were going to absolutely murder her, you know.'[112]

Her opening number – an English adaptation of 'La Vie En Rose', entitled 'Take Me to Your Arms Again' – subtly addressed the situation she was in, implicitly asking the audience to forgive her for any perceived misdemeanours and give her the same kind of affection they had before the war. It was a triumphant return and the reviews suggest that it was seen as having some kind of special significance. *The Times* reported: 'Miss Gracie Fields is back at the Palladium. There is as much satisfaction in writing that sentence as there would be in announcing... the reliable return of summer.'[113] For variety trade paper *The Performer*, it was a patriotic victory in the face the Parnell's policy of importing American stars to top the bill at his flagship theatre:

> The enthusiastic roar that greeted Gracie Fields on her return to London Variety after an absence of nearly ten years was proof positive that such welcomes are not necessarily the prerogative of American headliners. And it must be said that Miss Fields lived up to the warmth of the reception and at peak form showed that she remains, as always, the best native-born female entertainer.[114]

What all of this reveals is just how significant the blurring of onstage and offstage identities could be. Fields inspired affection because of the warmth she exuded while performing onstage, but the conduct of her private, offstage life in the war had the potential to destroy her relationship with her audience. More than this, the restoration of her place in the public's affection demonstrated by her success at the Palladium went beyond a connection between performer and audience in the theatre itself and was seen as some kind of symbol of national pride.

The Most Beautiful Man in the World

If the warmth between performer and audience was a kind of pseudo friendship, occasionally it became less platonic. Even a male reviewer such as A. Crooks Ripley acknowledged Max Miller's 'sex-appeal', and there were certainly acts which played on their own sexuality by presenting a flirtatious personality to the audience. The American singer Evelyn Dall appeared regularly in British variety theatres in the 1930s and early 1940s, both as a solo act and as a vocalist with Ambrose's band. Footage from 1937 shows her performing a typically libidinous number called 'I Don't Wanna Get Hot' in a spangly sleeveless frock.

With heavily painted lips and immaculately moulded, supernaturally glossy hair, in some ways she is sending up the blonde bombshell type. She does some goofy jazz dancing between the verses, makes exaggerated gestures and pulls cartoonish faces, grinning broadly and widening her large eyes as she moves her pupils right over from one corner of them to the other. However, in spite of any parodic elements, there is no doubting her intention to exude serious, straightforward sex appeal. In the song's lyric, she may protest that she does not want to get hot – in other words aroused – but this is only because she wants to 'start slow' and wait until she can 'give it all I've got'. Ostensibly, she is singing about getting excited by the music, but her gestures make the lightly hidden meaning perfectly plain. 'I can work myself into a lather', she sings, wriggling her hips and running her hands up and down over her thighs.[115]

Male performers could also play on their own attractiveness. The magician Channing Pollock, for example, was billed as 'The Most Beautiful Man in the World'.[116] However, the most overt appeal to sexuality came from the nude acts which were particularly popular in the final years of variety. Here physical appeal is not just part of the act's charm, but its sole purpose. The market value lies not so much in the personality as the body that houses it, and the extent the performer is willing to bare it for audience's titillation. Nude acts clearly exploited female sexuality, not least because the performers were often obscure and interchangeable. Some did break through to become famous, important acts, but often the more successful nudes included other elements in their act.

The most famous was Phyllis Dixey, who presented whole revues which included music and dancing as well as nude tableaux. Descriptions of her own nude performances tend to emphasize their innocence. A *Times* review from 1945, for example, describes her treating the audience 'with the prim archness of a school-marm of fiction at the end of term'.[117] Similarly, Beryl Reid recalled appearing with her in variety: 'She had such dignity and looked as if butter wouldn't melt in her mouth.'[118] What is interesting about these descriptions is that they emphasize aspects of personality – primness, dignity, butter-wouldn't-melt innocence – rather than physical attributes. It seems that Dixey was able to project these aspects of her personality while displaying her nakedness, and it may have been this personal quality which allowed her to become more than just another anonymous nude performer.

The sexual appeal of variety acts might seem stylized, symbolic or even mocking, but it could also be surprisingly straightforward and literal. The singer and siffleur Ronnie Ronalde was a well-dressed, darkly handsome figure, and a review of his act at the Chiswick Empire in March 1957 said he had a 'mixture of mischief and charm which is the sure way to a woman's heart'.[119] Just how easily he found his way to some women's hearts is revealed by an incident which he recalled in an interview:

> This woman came at the side of me. Very nicely dressed, quite exclusive ... She said, 'I saw you last night at the London Coliseum, in a concert.' I said, 'Did you?' She said, 'Yeah, you're very good.' 'Thank you', I said. She said, 'Would you like to come round the corner? And find out how good you are in bed?'[120]

I'm shaking like a leaf, honestly

The idea of personality is nothing if not ambiguous. The variety artiste appears as him- or herself, but it is a projection of self, and as such is larger than life. Elements of grotesquery, exaggeration, and eccentricity ran through many acts, from Max Miller's peacock suit to Teddy Brown's monstrous girth to Evelyn Dall's sex kitten flirtation. However, there were also performers who achieved great success by appearing to close the gap between onstage and offstage selves, presenting a more honest and authentic personality to the audience.

In the 1930s, after adopting a series of outlandish costumes and identities – using stage names such as 'Nedlo, the Gypsy Violinist' or 'Hugh Neek' – Ted Ray had an idea which he later described as 'new, disturbing and exciting ... so vivid that I felt almost a physical shock'. His idea was to go onstage simply as himself, a very ordinary person:

> Why keep yourself aloof from the audience? Why not be *one* of them? Forget all about comic make-up, the white bowler hat, those fantastic, ridiculous 'props'. Why, there's no need even to bother about a dinner jacket. Just be human. Stroll onto that stage in an ordinary suit, just as if you'd walked in from the street.[121]

This was a radical innovation at the time, but recordings of Ray suggest that he only got so far in his attempts to be ordinary, human, and '*one* of them'. Compared with today's stand-up comedians, his delivery sounds distinctly stylized, far slicker and neater than the conversational style that currently predominates. His accent betrays little of his Wigan upbringing, and there is a distinctly American rhythm and phrasing in lines like:

> My wife's mother arrived and took off her gas mask and nobody noticed it, ho-ho boy, was she burned up? [laughter][122]

Nonetheless, his new approach was distinctive enough to make him one of the most successful front cloth comics of his generation.

Frankie Howerd took a similar approach when he started in variety after the Second World War, wearing 'an ordinary, far from immaculate, brown lounge suit' onstage, in order 'to give the impression that I wasn't one of the cast, but had just wandered in from the street'.[123] Unlike Ray, he attempted to make his delivery as casual as his costume. Turning a potential weakness into a strength, he incorporated his natural stammer into the act: 'My nervous, stammering, jabbering delivery was a bit different...People in real life don't talk precisely as though from scripts, and neither did I attempt to on stage. My act sounded almost like a stream of consciousness, which is why I often didn't finish sentences.'[124] A routine from *Variety Bandbox* in the late 1940s gives a good idea of his delivery: '

> Now, er- ladies and gentle-*men*. [laughter] Hearken. Now, hearken. This is a – no, hear*ken*. [laughter] Now, *harr-kenn*. [laughter] Hear-ever-so-ken. [laughter]'[125]

For a style based on conversational messiness, this shows remarkable comic economy, getting a laugh for each of the opening four lines. Far from sounding like the way 'people in real life' talk, it is a kind of brilliantly distinctive poetry, full of catchphrases ('ladies and gentle-*men*'), oddly placed emphasis ('hear*ken*'), and verbal oddities ('Hear-ever-so-ken'). Nonetheless – as with Ray – his apparent authenticity was bold and innovative, and quickly took him to the top of the bill.

Danny Kaye enjoyed his meteoric success by taking an approach which was both bolder and more subtle. The apparent authenticity of his personality came not just from costume or delivery, but from a disarming kind of honesty. After some big American acts had flopped at the London Palladium, Kaye opened there on 2 February 1948 to face an audience described as 'taut as a violin string':

> He was obviously nervous as he walked on: a good-looking, slightly stringy young man, with unruly marmalade hair and carelessly wandering hands.

He gave a high-pitched giggle, and said, 'I'm shaking like a leaf, honestly.' Then he smiled. The effect was miraculous. People began to clap and cheer, and the gallery girls called their welcome. Everyone seemed to realise in a rush that they were not going to witness another flop, and they relaxed in sheer relief.[126]

Kaye's frankness was surprising, even daring. He was openly acknowledging his predicament – the weight of expectation placed on him – and letting his guard down utterly. By showing his vulnerability, he allowed the audience to sympathize with him, closing the gap between them. They rewarded him handsomely for it. *The Performer* said that he 'caused enthusiasm that had not been equalled here since new-style Variety entered its portals way back in 1928'.[127]

One of Kaye's most famous techniques was to break away from the rehearsed routines and sit 'on the edge of the stage, feet dangling into the orchestra pit, smoking a cigarette, and chatting – chatting about things that came into his mind, sometimes humorous, sometimes observations and sometimes even philosophy'.[128] In these moments, he seemed to be taking a break from the act, shattering any barriers that may have remained between him and his audience by cadging a cigarette from somebody in the front row.[129]

However authentic this may have seemed, there was undoubtedly an element of artifice. The bit where he sat on the edge of the stage was a regular part of the act, something he repeated twice nightly. What he said as he sat there and chatted might have varied from show to show, but the idea of breaking through the formal boundary between stage and auditorium was a routine, as premeditated as his scat singing or his crazy facial expressions.

Even the famous 'shaking like a leaf' line might not have been as honest as it seemed. Kaye said he was 'sick with nervousness' before he went on, and it has been claimed that he had 'stage-fright paralysis' and had to be physically pushed onto the stage by either Charles Henry or Val Parnell.[130] However, Kaye had prepared meticulously for his Palladium debut, and it is not impossible that he thought up the line in advance, as a deliberate strategy to dispel the tension of expectation. Having done so, any account he gave of that moment would have to stress its authenticity by claiming genuine stage fright.

Ultimately, it does not matter whether the line was spontaneous or premeditated, honest or calculated. The point is that it established an instant rapport, and allowed Kaye to be, as one review of that first show put it, 'on intimate terms with his audience all the time'.[131] Like the tools other variety acts used – the catchphrases, the manipulation of status, the warmth, the sexuality – Kaye's apparent naturalness was a means for connecting with the audience. This was the ultimate purpose of developing the personality, because the audience played a central and active role in the dynamics of variety performance.

7

Participation

Getting over

An advert in a 1937 issue of *The Era* shows a drawing of a not particularly funny-looking comedian. Lacking the individuality of a Max Miller or a Robb Wilton, he is very much the smart young man – casual jacket, shirt and tie, slicked-back, centre-parted hair, handsome but nondescript face, friendly smile. His head and shoulders are drawn almost in profile, his hand practically caressing the gleaming black microphone he is supposed to be speaking into. Its circular design might look old-fashioned today, but in the 1930s when variety theatres were being fitted with such equipment, it was cutting-edge technology. The caption under the drawing reads:

> HIS JOKES WERE APPRECIATED
> ... probably not because he was a superlatively good comedian, but because he realised that he just had to 'get over'. He knew that the Standard Reproducing System would assist without the slightest distortion of his voice, and as a consequence every joke was appreciated and his audience showed its pleasure. Why not follow the example given by the Leading Stars of Variety, and always insist upon:-
> STANDARD SOUND REPRODUCING EQUIPMENT.[1]

Not everyone saw microphones as such a big step forward. They were widely derided when they were introduced, and the criticism continued throughout the variety era. In 1938, Maurice Willson Disher complained that when singers used a microphone, 'Mechanised music, in effect, tops the bill'.[2] W. Macqueen-Pope claimed that, 'The

126

microphone murders individuality. Everything is far too much of a muchness. The machine is paramount.'[3] As late as 1952, the variety column in *The Stage* was asking: 'Does the microphone spoil the music hall?'[4]

The argument was not just that amplification replaced the warmth of individuality with the coldness of a machine, but also that it was a substitute for talent. The microphone was sometimes referred to as a 'crooner's crutch', implying that it could prop up a singer with inadequate musical ability.[5] Neville Cardus looked back with misty eyes to the 'old-time comedians' of the pre-microphone music hall, arguing that what made them superior was that they 'had to hold the attention of vast audiences by means of individual talent and presence, and by their own unmicrophoned voices'.[6]

Even though he wanted to bury microphones rather than praise them, Cardus was essentially making the same argument as the advert in *The Era*. The assumption – almost touching in its naivety – was that the highly skilled and complex business of projecting a personality to create a rapport with an audience could be bypassed by the simple expedient of talking into a mike. This either seriously underestimates the talent of the likes of Gracie Fields, Max Miller and Danny Kaye, or seriously overestimates the power of the technology. (See Illustration 7.1.) Clearly a microphone cannot make a comedian funnier or a singer more tuneful, but what it does do is amplify the voice and send it out into the auditorium. Even though their arguments were essentially ridiculous, both adverts and critics of the microphone realized the importance of 'getting over' – of somehow projecting the self out over the footlights to the hundreds of people sitting out there in raked tiers of seating in the darkened auditorium.

On a simple physical level, microphones must have helped the performers to ensure that they could be heard even in the remotest back rows of the gallery. Ronnie Tate recalled what it was like to work without amplification: 'You had to learn to throw it out so that everybody could hear, but you had to shout your guts out to do it. We used to come off wringing wet, after shouting for twenty minutes.'[7] Houdini gave a slightly different account, which suggests that there was more artistry to it than simply shouting and sweating: 'I never spoke to the first row. I would walk down to the footlights, actually put one foot over the electric globes as if I were going to spring among the people, and then hurl my voice, saying, "Ladies and Gentlemen".'[8]

Figure 7.1 A Gracie Fields songbook given away free with *Woman's World* magazine in October 1933.

When microphones were introduced, performers had to adapt their technique, allowing for a different kind of connection with the audience, and a different kind of effort. Vera Lynn remembers:

> [W]hen I was younger, I had a very strong voice. And it was too loud for the microphones – because you'd blast everybody out, you see. So you had to learn to sing quieter, 'croon' as they used to call it in those days, and I had the keys dropped a little bit lower so I didn't have to use so much force on my voice. So I could sing in a quieter, more intimate way ... I didn't have to use so much *force* to get to the balcony.[9]

However, even in the age of amplification, performers still had to work to project themselves, as Danny Kaye described:

> Maybe I'm all wrong ... but it seems to me that a voice has a trajectory just like a bullet. It travels in a sort of curve – up, over, and down – so you aim for the place you want it to land. You don't just talk to the first few rows. You talk over them, to the rest of the house, and the front rows hear your voice as it goes past.[10]

Sometimes Kaye would go further, sending not just his voice but his entire body out into the audience. Footage of the Royal Variety Performance in 1948 shows him stepping out over the footlights, the audience laughing nervously as he walks across the desks and pianos of the orchestra pit towards them.[11] Tommy Trinder would pull a similar stunt in Palladium revues, walking out onto a run which had been erected across the pit to make the journey easier.[12] The Beverley Sisters would also step off the stage into the auditorium, as Teddie Beverley recalls: '[S]ometimes we'd move right down into the audience and sing it right there, in the aisle – so that people could see your throat, you know, your Adam's apple – and feel you with them. We used to walk right down and be with them.'[13]

Direct contact

The legitimate theatre of the variety era had a very different approach to the audience. The concept of an imaginary fourth wall separating actors from audience had been proposed by Denis Diderot as early as the mid-eighteenth century, and was now a central plank of Stanislavski's approach to acting. In *An Actor Prepares*, his narrator character, Kostya, is greatly disturbed during rehearsals when the curtain is opened revealing the auditorium: 'But opening that fourth wall with its big black proscenium arch made you feel that you must constantly adjust yourself. You think of the people looking at you; you seek to be heard by them and not those who are in the room with you.'[14] While the curtain is closed, Kostya imagines he is in a drawing room, but he has to face the truth that he is actually on a stage once it is opened.

The fourth wall separates not just actors and audience, but the fictional world of the play from the real world of the auditorium. It helps the actors to blot out all awareness of the audience, imagining themselves to be in whatever setting the play takes place in, and addressing only the other actors who are 'in the room' with them. Having said this, not everyone in the legitimate theatre approved of this way of treating an audience. Artaud, for example, derided the 'psychological theatre' that transformed the audience into 'Peeping Toms', suggesting that this was why 'the masses' preferred to go to variety theatre and circus instead.[15]

He was absolutely right to assume that the concept of a fourth wall was completely alien to variety. There might have been a thin, fictional setting in comedy sketches – Harry Tate on a day trip in his car, or Old Mother Riley awaiting the return of her daughter Kitty – but generally speaking there was no attempt to evoke a fictional world, and the stage did not pretend to be anything other than a stage. Variety was precisely about thinking of 'the people looking at you' and seeking to be heard by them. As Vera Lynn put it, 'The variety stage involved direct contact with the audience, then and there. Everything had to be right, you couldn't stop and start again, and reaction was immediate.'[16]

Direct contact was made easier by the shape of the theatres and the way their auditoriums were structured. As Ernie Wise put it, 'They were designed for relationships between artists and audience, and you can actually feel that contact.'[17] Bruce Forsyth realized the importance of boxes, arguing that 'they give artistes the feeling of being more intimately engaged with the audience – even when they're empty. When you have stalls with a blank wall either side of you, it's never the same.'[18] For Wyn Calvin, it was the curved shapes that gave the theatres their special character:

> The old Victorian and Edwardian theatre designers could draw a curve – and the curve of the circles, the curve around the boxes, the curves in the proscenium arches. A curve is an embrace. An embrace is intimacy – which is what theatre's all about. Modern architects in the modern halls draw straight lines, and straight lines are clinical and cold.[19]

Such views are strikingly similar to those of present-day theatre designer Iain Mackintosh, who argues that 'the chief purpose of theatre architecture is to provide a channel for energy' which 'flows chiefly from performer to audience' but also allows the performer to receive 'in return a charge from the audience'.[20] To achieve this, he recommends 'a gallery or number of galleries which wrap around the space, so as to enfold the performing area in a welcoming embrace'.[21] Like Forsyth, he dislikes vast expanses of cold, blank wall, and instead suggests 'papering the wall with people'.[22]

The curved, tiered auditoriums of the variety theatres not only made for a warm, intimate connection between performer and audience, they also divided the patrons up into different sections, each with its own distinct character. Frankie Howerd wrote about having to learn 'to perform to three layers of people at once: stalls, circle and gallery. I had to please them all.' He got his sister Betty to watch the show from all parts of the auditorium to make sure he was projecting his 'voice and facial expressions – especially those made by my eyes'.[23]

Making eye contact with every section of the audience was an important skill, which became habitual for many performers. Even filmed in a studio, without a live audience, Billy Bennett shows how he would have shared his gaze around all parts of the theatre while barking out his surreal comic poems. In the 1937 film *Calling All Stars*, he wears a vest and an army cap to recite 'Christmas Day in the Cookhouse', breaking out of the thin narrative to use a kind of direct address that he has entirely refused to adapt for the medium of cinema. Instead of locking eyes with the camera, he addresses an imaginary live audience, his thick, black moustache and heavy eyebrows knitting into a stern frown, as he looks out to the left, to the right and occasionally upwards.[24]

Double acts had to create collusion in two directions, each performer dividing attention between partner and audience. Freddie Davies has talked about the 'great affinity' between Eric Morecambe and Ernie Wise, arguing that, 'The best double acts always have eye contact with one another.'[25] Footage of a young Morecambe & Wise filmed performing on a stage set to a live audience shows how skilfully they could split their focus. Dressed in matching checked suits, bow ties and bowler hats, they stand very close and look into each other's eyes as Ernie tells Eric:

Listen – *you* – would make a marvellous bullfighter.

On the word 'you', both turn their heads out to the audience, then
back to each other, and Eric turns back to the audience as Ernie
finishes the sentence. Eric's face registers subtle but open-mouthed
confusion, and he gets a laugh by raising his eyebrows, turning back
to Ernie, pointing at himself and quietly asking, 'Me?'. 'Yeah, you're
a natural', says Ernie. As the dialogue continues, they continue to
move their heads this way and that, so that for most of the time one is
looking at the other, while the other looks out at the audience:

> *Ernie*:   Listen, I'm gonna make you the greatest bullfighter in the world.
> *Eric*:   You're only saying that.
> *Ernie*:   No I'm not.
> *Eric*:   Well somebody just did! [laughter][26]

On the punchline, they twist around away from each other, looking
behind them as if to see who might have said it. This kind of detailed
conversational choreography shows not just how carefully double acts
had to share their focus, but also how the very business of shifting
focus could form the basis of a gag.

Direct address was a central part of variety's appeal, the strong
bond between performer and audience an inherent part of its pleasure. John Betjeman described the rapport 'between the artist and
the audience' as 'an intimacy and understanding which we remember
all our lives'.[27] Studs Terkel recalled the feeling he got from seeing
shows in variety's American cousin, vaudeville: 'There was nothing separating that performer on stage from me. He was to me. He
was singing to me, he was making cracks to me, he was jumping and
tap-dancing to me, at that moment. And so it was highly personal.'[28]

Good-natured members of the lower middle class

Given this highly personal rapport, it is worth thinking about the
specific nature of the audience which the performers addressed so
directly. What kind of people came to see variety, and what kind of
habits and customs did they have when they came together to form an
audience?

In 1939 St John Ervine, a journalist for *The Observer*, wrote a vivid
description of the patrons of an unnamed London variety theatre. He
homed in on individual patrons, with vivid descriptions that give off a
distinct whiff of snobbery. For example, there is the 'oleaginous man
with leering eyes, podgy hands, and dirty nails' whose girlfriend is
'all skin and bone and lipstick'. Other women sitting near him are

criticized for being 'addicted to the foul feminine habit of wearing long, bloody talons'.

If this suggests a rather disreputable audience, for the most part they come across as a much more respectable bunch: 'The audience was mainly composed of unexacting, good-natured members of the lower middle class: small shop keepers with their wives, clerks with their girls...a collection of decent, commonplace and unpretentious people: a good average British crowd.'[29]

This was precisely the kind of crowd that managers such as Stoll and Moss had sought to attract when their chains began to dominate around the beginning of the twentieth century. The aim had been to tame the wilder music hall audiences, and curb the excesses of rowdiness. Patrons found that they could be thrown out of the theatre for hissing the acts or even told off for laughing too loudly.[30] However, there were also subtler ways of encouraging more orderly audience behaviour.

One of the effects of the twice nightly system was to discourage the habit of what J. B. Booth called 'looking in', which involved people going to the music hall 'not so much in search of a seat, in which to sit out the performance, as to meet a few friends, watch a particular turn or two, chat, hear the news of the town, and wander about in perfect freedom'.[31] A music hall was almost as much a social space as a performance venue, and many accounts note that whole sections of the audience would wander around at the back and simply ignore what was going on onstage. George Bernard Shaw was astonished by 'the indifference of the audience to the performance',[32] Arnold Bennett described the 'Fearful noise from the bar behind',[33] and Thomas Anstey Guthrie wrote that the conversation in the upper parts of the Alhambra 'renders it impossible to hear distinctly anything that is said or sung'.[34]

The habit of looking in was encouraged by the sheer length and number of acts on a music hall bill, which meant that it was perfectly normal to turn up after the show had started and leave before the end. Patrons would often turn up just to watch a particular act and go home after it had finished, and some music hall programmes printed the time each turn would appear onstage next to their name to make this easier to do.

The twice nightly system strongly discouraged this kind of behaviour, because with shorter, tighter shows, the incentive was to come along, sit down in neatly tiered seating, and watch the whole show. However, there was still an echo of the older habit in the way variety audiences would continue to shuffle in through the first couple of acts and leave to catch the bus home while the last act was still onstage.

Scared of playing the halls

Variety audiences may have been more focused and attentive than their predecessors in music hall, but they still had habits and customs which could intimidate the acts. Arthur Askey cut his performing teeth in the friendlier territory of concert party and became famous on the hit radio comedy series *Band Waggon*, but he avoided playing variety theatres for years. 'I had always been scared of playing the Halls', he wrote, 'for I never felt I was "broad" enough. I was still essentially concert party in my approach and I had seen some popular radio artistes who had "died" on the Halls.'[35] What was he so scared of?

It might have been the fact that variety audiences could get very rowdy at times. As Wyn Calvin puts it, 'heckling could have been part of any performance'.[36] While Calvin says he 'enjoyed' heckling and would 'almost encourage it', a heckle was a challenge which had to be dealt with. The performer's duty was to retaliate with something which would get a bigger laugh than the heckle, and, crucially, not show any sign of being thrown by it. A bitter or defensive response could undermine the act's authority and put a chill on the rapport that had been built up.

Ted Ray recalled someone shouting, 'When are you going to say something funny?' at him. He was 'quite at a loss for a moment' then came back with, 'When you get a little more intelligence to understand it!'. This was not good enough to neutralize the threat and Ray felt that 'the interruption had upset the audience. I had lost them and from being a very pleasant performance it became a fight, a real tussle to get laughs.'[37]

Trouble often came from the gallery – also known as 'the gods' – which was the highest tier of seating, where the people who had paid least for their tickets sat furthest from the stage. According to the agent Joe Collins, these were the 'most important' people to please because, 'They sat on hard benches three tiers up – above the stalls, the dress circle and the upper circle – and if they couldn't hear what was happening on stage or didn't like the show they let the performers know about it by stamping their feet and disruptive catcalling.'[38]

Heckles and catcalls were by no means the worst thing that could happen to an act. In Sunderland, Frankie Howerd had a shipyard rivet thrown at him, and Harry Secombe had an air pistol fired at him from the gallery of the Clapham Grand.[39] Roy Hudd recalls playing at the Chatham Empire with his double act, Hudd & Kay:

> Eddie and I are doing the act, and we die on our arse, you know, it was so bad they threw coins at us. And Eddie, my pal, picked up all these coins and the audience went dead quiet. Picked them all up and counted them. And said, 'Great. Another one and ninepence and we've got our fare home'. Wallop, loads more came down![40]

At the Wood Green Empire, someone threw a slightly less hair-raising missile at Bruce Forsyth – a packet of fish and chips. He dealt with it by eating a couple of chips and commenting, 'Too much vinegar and not enough salt'. By showing no fear in the face of this rather bizarre act of hostility and instead playfully improvising with the situation, he reasserted his authority and the audience 'rose wonderfully well'.[41]

In most theatres it was rare for the audiences to throw things at the acts, but in some cases it was a regular occurrence. More than one performer has recalled how the Grand Theatre in Byker, Newcastle upon Tyne, had wire netting over the orchestra pit to protect the musicians from the objects being hurled at the stage by rumbustious patrons.[42]

The most notorious theatre of all was the Glasgow Empire. Far from being a rough dive, it was a number one, part of the prestigious Moss Empires chain. Nonetheless, it had a fearsome reputation, being widely known as 'The Graveyard for English Comics', with the second house Friday night being the most terrifying of all. The plot of the 1940 film *Hoots Mon* entirely hinges on an English comic – Max Miller, pretty much playing himself – overcoming an impossibly hostile audience at a theatre which is the Glasgow Empire in all but name. Don Smoothey recalls Empire audiences shouting things such as, 'Get back across the border! Will ye no' piss off?'. On one occasion, while appearing there with Lonnie Donegan, the audience became so unruly that Smoothey broke out of the sketch he was performing and berated them:

> I came right out of character. And I went to the microphone, and I told the audience. I said, 'We've just returned from Malaya'...I said, 'The best audience we had were the Cameron Highlanders...We had to go in and out in daylight because it was too dangerous to go in dark...They were the finest audience, what a lovely bunch', and I said, 'It's those boys should be sitting out in those comfortable seats, and you buggers should be out in Malaya.' That's what I told the audience. 'WAAAAAYYY!' They went bloody berserk, you know. [43]

Performers enjoyed swapping such stories and a rich body of folk-lore grew up around the Glasgow Empire. Mike & Bernie Winters' act started with Mike playing a clarinet solo, which normally got a round of applause, before Bernie made his entrance by sticking his head through the curtains, getting a laugh. In Glasgow, the clarinet was received in silence and Bernie's entrance was met with someone shouting, 'Christ – there's two of 'em!'.[44] Norman Wisdom had a par-ticularly revealing anecdote about the time he did the whole of his act without talking, so that the Glasgow audience would not realize he was English.[45]

The point is that the Glasgow Empire's hatred of English com-ics was based on national rivalry – a kind of tribal hostility. In 1957, *The Stage* observed that, 'There is a definite "iron curtain" in show-business at the Scotland–England border ... Comedians from England don't think they're too welcome in Scotland. Scottish comedians find a long traditional theory that their fun won't appeal to Manchester or London.'[46] Don Smoothey recalls that the Glasgow Empire was particularly unruly after England had beaten Scotland at football.[47] Being Welsh, Wyn Calvin managed to sidestep the iron curtain: 'I have always enjoyed playing Glasgow – but I made sure they didn't think I was English.'[48]

The riotousness of the Glasgow Empire was a symptom of a wider challenge. In a time when local accents were stronger and more dis-tinct, before television had started to erode regional differences in the way English is spoken, comedians could hit trouble when they played theatres a long way from home. Roy Hudd found the best audi-ences for his double act were 'down south – because we spoke with the Cockney accents'. On the other hand, when he played the Newcastle Empire:

> I went on there and died on my arse, you know ... I couldn't understand it, I came off and I said to the stage manager, 'I was bloody awful ... I can't understand it', I said, 'I've done all this material before everywhere, all over the place, and it's sort of gone all right.'

The stage manager explained the problem to him – the Geordie audi-ence simply could not understand a lot of what he was saying because of his accent: '[H]e took me down to the theatre the next day and he ironed out all the Cockney bits for me and everything. And I got away with it.'[49]

Variety rowdiness was different from the kind of rowdiness seen in the earlier music hall audiences. Instead of people standing at the back ignoring the acts and talking among themselves, in variety they were more likely to heckle or jeer. The noise they made was less about apathy and more about positive antipathy. At places like the Glasgow Empire this might have come from national rivalry, but generally it was a judgement on the actual ability of the act. Performers got heckled or shouted at if they failed to entertain the audience, or were seen to be lacking in the talent department.

The Clapham silence

While heckling, jeering and throwing things could happen, on the whole variety audiences tended to be quieter and better behaved than the more lurid stories might suggest. Tellingly, the Moss Empires contract stated that, 'The Artiste shall not be required to perform if by the unruly behaviour of the audience his performance would be rendered inaudible but unless such unruly behaviour is due to word or action on the part of the Artiste no deduction from the Artiste's salary shall be made.'[50] It is unlikely that Moss would offer performers the chance to retreat in the face of hostility if the management were not reasonably confident that audiences would usually behave themselves.

Heckling was not a particularly common hazard. Don Smoothey argues that 'once you start working the Mosses and the Stolls...it wasn't much at all' and that it only happened further down the hierarchy of theatres 'when you worked the twos and the threes'.[51] Jack Seaton agrees: 'Well I must admit, seldom did I get heckling. Mostly, the audiences didn't react to what you were doing. And you can imagine six minutes of silence. Feels like six hours.'[52]

Silence was possibly the most powerful weapon in the audience's armoury, and it was far more common than catcalls. Certain venues became notorious for their stony-faced lack of response, like the Clapham Grand where acts faced the infamous 'Clapham Silence'.[53] Even the famously rowdy Glasgow Empire could be more terrifying for its silence than its barracking. In one legendary anecdote, Des O'Connor was so intimidated that he pretended to faint onstage so he did not have to go through the rest of his act.

The audience were in a particularly foul mood. Mackenzie Reid & Dorothy – a husband-and-wife act with a big local following – were supposed to be on the bill, but could not appear as planned because one of them had been killed in a car accident. The surviving member of the act, Dorothy, decided to honour the booking by appearing with her nephew, but on the Thursday night she was overcome with grief and had to cut the act short. There was an awkward pause in the show, and by the time O'Connor reached the stage, the atmosphere had turned ugly:

> There was no welcoming applause. The audience looked at me as though I was some kind of intruder at a funeral. I knew this was no time for telling jokes, but I wasn't experienced enough to know what else to try ... Nobody laughed. At first there was just murmuring. Then the murmuring stopped and the silence started. Real silence. The kind you can actually hear ... I was scared, confused and very, very embarrassed. All I wanted to do was run away.[54]

Such was the power of this 'real silence' that O'Connor found he would rather go to the extreme if slightly ridiculous length of faking a faint rather than putting up with it any more. This is highly revealing. Whereas Stanislavski seemed to distrust the audience's reactions and recommended an imaginary fourth wall to block them out, variety artistes thrived on them. Silence was an awful void that had to be filled. Ken Joy argues that 'going off to the sound of your own footsteps is the worst thing that could ever happen to you. That is the worst thing. You know, your tongue starts to dry up, your mouth goes behind your lips, oh it's a terrible feeling when you die.'[55]

Filling the silence was a challenge, because audience conventions were different from how they are today. It is now perfectly normal for popular entertainers to be welcomed onto the stage with a round of applause. In variety, this was by no means guaranteed, and the lesser-known acts further down the bill would often walk onto silence. If things went badly, the audience might not even applaud when they walked off at the end of the act. Only once an act was well known would their entrance onto the stage be rewarded with applause. Harry Secombe, for example, only started to get applause on entering the stage once he had become famous thanks to radio appearances on programmes such as *The Goon Show*.[56]

For less famous acts every audience reaction – even the applause at the end – had to be earned. Don Smoothey takes a dim view of shows such as *Britain's Got Talent*, because of the way that the acts are washed onto the stage on a tidal wave of whistling, yelling and ear-splitting applause: 'I used to flog myself to 12, 15 minutes to get a bleeding round of applause! And they haven't done anything yet!'[57] What he resents in that they simply have not earned that kind of reaction.

Audience as judge

Every variety act was driven by the desire to create an audible reaction in the audience. As Roy Hudd puts it, 'Everything was done towards that end – getting a good finish, you know, getting applause when you went off.'[58] A *Times* review of the Palladium relaunch in 1928 pointed out that in variety 'the performers have to stand or fall on their individual ability to please', and the implications of this are clear.[59] The audience could decide whether an act had succeeded or failed, with their pleasure – in the form of laughter or applause – or displeasure – in the form of heckling or silence – as a tangible sign of one or the other.

This meant that they played a very active role, and a powerful one at that. In Wyn Calvin's words, 'Every performance is a trial, with the audience as judge'.[60] Individual patrons could make their views known by shouting abuse or even throwing fish and chips onto the stage, but for the most part the role of judge was democratic and collective. The audience acted together to reward an act with applause or damn it with silence.

However, there was a special exception to this rule, in which the role of judge was delegated to one tiny section of the audience in the Royal Variety Performance, which was one of the most nerve-racking shows variety artistes experienced. In an age in which the Royal Family enjoyed far greater respect than today, it was a huge honour to be asked to perform for them, a kind of pinnacle in a variety career.

The audience at these events were infamous for being cold and difficult to please, but more than that for the way they would be swayed by the responses from the royal box. There is a hint of this in a review of the very first Royal Variety Performance in 1912: 'The King and Queen showed an extraordinary number of signs of pleasure and satisfaction, and the enormous audience more than confirmed the Royal appreciation.'[61] The suggestion is that audience were led by the royal couple's reactions, merely confirming them rather than making their own minds up. This is certainly the way it worked in future years, as a number of performers have confirmed. Frankie Howerd wrote of having to fight 'snob sections of the audience whose eyes were riveted on the Royal Box ... and who laughed only when the Royals did'.[62] Similarly, Harry Secombe recalled, 'Every old pro I spoke to said the same thing: "The audience always look up to the Royal Box to see if They are laughing, and if so, they'll laugh too. If They're not, they won't." '[63]

Daisy mucks it up

Seen from one angle the audience sat in judgement, but seen from another they were collaborators, helping to shape the way the act played out. In 1913, Marinetti wrote, 'The Variety Theatre is alone in seeking the audience's collaboration. It doesn't remain static like a stupid voyeur, but joins noisily in the action, in the singing, accompanying the orchestra, communicating with the actors in surprising actions and bizarre dialogues.'[64] This is echoed by performers such as Roy Hudd, who says that the audience are 'the drivers' who 'push you each way where you're going',[65] and Teddie Beverley who argues:

> It's a question of being *with* an audience. You don't sing *to* them or *at* them – you sing sort of with them. And you get on their wavelength, what *they* like. And yet all the while you're doing really what you like. But you're very much rationed by what they like.[66]

For speciality act Valantyne Napier, the only way of 'acquiring the polish of a real performer' was 'constant work in front of an audience. No amount of practice in a rehearsal room can give that sense of timing and stage presence.'[67] Similarly, Max Bygraves argued that, 'The only way to learn is from those people out there in the dark. They guide you.'[68]

The process of learning from the audience's reactions could be surprisingly systematic. George Formby's wife Beryl timed the reactions to his jokes with a stopwatch and wrote down the timings in a notebook. This would be used to select and rework material for future performances.[69] Ken Dodd drew on his experience as a travelling salesman to keep detailed records of every show, noting the size and character of the audience, and including an entry for each joke he told, with notes about how it might be improved.[70]

Because the variety stage was simply a stage and did not represent a fictional world as the legitimate stage sought to do, it made for a style of performance which was firmly rooted in the here and now. The fact that the show was happening in this theatre in this house in this evening was ever present. The particular circumstances of the show – the audience, the orchestra, the theatre itself – could be openly acknowledged and worked into the act. This led Ken Dodd to distinguish between 'Was comedy', in which 'you are trying to paint a picture in people's minds' and 'Is comedy', which plays on 'a situation taking place now'.[71]

'Is comedy' allowed performers to play on their own mistakes and turn them into jokes. Elsie & Doris Waters usually appeared in the guise of the heart-of-gold Cockneys Gert & Daisy, telling gags dressed up as everyday conversation. In one performance, Daisy gets the beginning of a punchline wrong, and as it is based on speed and rhythm, it gets no more than a mere ghost of a laugh. Drawing attention to this, she admits:

Mucked that one up! [laughter]

It is a huge laugh, and Gert laughs along with the audience. As the laughter dies down, Daisy says:

I was gonna say that's clever, but I won't now. [laughter].[72]

Again, Gert joins in with the audience's laughter. There seems to be a kind of conspiratorial pleasure in this moment of truth, as though the reaction to the mistake – the spontaneous lines and the performer's own laughter – allows Doris to peep out from behind her character Daisy and Elsie peep out from behind Gert.

Other mistakes feel less authentic. A 1939 recording of Billy Russell's act sees him acting out a conversation with his wife in bed. As he does both his wife's voice and his own, he suddenly realizes he has shown her as lying on the wrong side of the bed and comically corrects himself:

No, she sleeps this side. She says – [laughter][73]

This mistake seems to have been faked for comic purposes. Unlike Gert & Daisy, Russell does not seem to break out of the frame of the act. The tone of his delivery does not really change, and his comment does not particularly break the rhythm of the routine. It may be that this joke-mistake started life as a genuine error, and Russell decided to keep it in the act because it got a good reaction.

Certainly, there were acts which faked mistakes at every performance having found that they went down well. Max Bygraves appeared at the Palladium when Judy Garland was topping the bill, and he recalled how she once tripped over the microphone cable as she left the stage at the end of her act. Coming back on for the encore, she showed her contempt for the shoes that had tripped her up by taking them off and throwing them into the wings: 'The audience liked that, they went wild, she used that trick at every performance from then on; it was a good piece of stagecraft'.[74]

The master of this kind of thing was Danny Kaye, who was widely praised for his spontaneity and improvisation. A review of his Palladium debut in *The Performer* said he 'was obviously planning his routine just one jump ahead', citing the moment when he decided 'to call for a glass of water and proceed to drink it before proceeding with his show' as an example of this.[75] An early biography recalled how in a later Palladium appearance, he turned to his pianist, Sammy Prager, and speaking 'as casually as if we were in his living room' said, 'Sammy, we didn't have our tea this afternoon...Gee, I'd like some tea'. Shortly afterwards, the tea lady walked onto the stage carrying a silver tea tray. According to Prager: 'The audience were panicked! And they were delighted. It was obviously spontaneous, and it took Danny several seconds before he caught on. He stopped and savoured his refreshments while I tenderly played "Tea for Two".'[76]

Even at the time, there were some critics who gently questioned exactly how spontaneous Kaye's act was. A profile in *The Observer* used the telling phrase 'apparently spontaneous' and argued, 'It is wrong to suppose that the Kaye act is not planned at all, though he believes preconceived notions would be fatal to it. The framework is solid enough, but to this he adds arabesques of fantasy as the ideas come to him.'[77]

Sammy Prager recalled that the spontaneous bit with the tea tray 'was so in keeping with British psychology and wit, that we decided to keep it in the show. Of course, each time Danny went through it the pantomime was a little different but the basic idea was a great hit, the result of a completely unplanned situation.'[78] There may have been room for improvisation, but Kaye was still doing essentially the same act when he appeared at the Palladium as late as 1955.[79]

The key point is not just that Kaye improvised spontaneous moments or that he subsequently faked this spontaneity, but that he used the audience's reactions as a guide to which improvisations were worth faking in future performances. Once again, the performer was learning from the audience and using them as collaborators.

Energy

Perhaps the least obvious but most important function of audience response was to fuel the performance. As well as offering an immediate indication of success or failure and helping to shape the way the act played out, it was part of an exchange of energy between performer and audience. Songs, stunts and gags flowed out from the stage, and laughter and applause flowed back from the audience in response. The noted performance theorist Philip Auslander is cynical about this idea, describing 'the "energy" that supposedly exists between performers and spectators in a live event, and the "community" that live performance is often said to create' as 'clichés and mystifications'.[80]

Far from cliché or mystification, the idea of an exchange of energy is rooted in hard, physical fact. Performing a variety act required the expenditure of physical energy, whether this came in the form of muscles straining to achieve a difficult balance, the lungs and larynx belting out the notes of a sentimental song, or even the small amount of effort required to deliver the punchline of a joke and raise the eyebrow knowingly. Similarly, the members of an audience used physical energy to clap their hands together in applause or laugh out loud. This is more than metaphor, it is simple fact.

The connection between the two kinds of physical energy – that expended by the act, and that expended by the audience – is slightly more metaphorical, but still essentially simple and straightforward. The performance onstage generated pleasure in the audience, which was expressed as laughter and applause. In a theatre where judgement was so important and applause had to be earned, we can be fairly sure that the physical energy expended by the audience was stimulated by the efforts of the act.

Meanwhile, the energy the audience put into their laughter and applause stimulated confidence in the performers, which helped them to keep expending energy in their performance. Again, we can be fairly sure of this, given the accounts performers have given of how they relied on audience reaction. Vera Lynn explains it very clearly: 'If I could see that they were enjoying it and pleased, you know, with a little smile maybe on their face, then it ... relaxes you and [you] think, "Oh well, they are enjoying it". But if ... you don't get any reaction, it's very difficult.'[81] Harry Secombe described how he was helped to recover from being badly received in Bolton by a more generous audience at the Oldham Empire: 'From the moment I went on, the audience was ready to laugh and my confidence grew with every second.'[82] Similarly, Danny Kaye asked, 'How can a comedian write away from the people? I ... need the contact of the large crowds of people to stir me to do my best. I need the response of an audience, for they give me as much as I try to give them.'[83] On the other hand, a silent audience – one which is not expending energy on laughter or applause – had a terrible reaction on the acts, giving them nothing to fuel their performance.

Variety performers had to not just gain a response, but to build the energy, so that the audience were livelier at the end than they were at the beginning. This was not just a tangible sign of audience approval, it also helped to set things up for the next act. A front cloth comic performing second on the bill was, in Calvin's words, 'warming them up for acts that were to follow. A second spot comic would've been one who had an ability to create an atmosphere – turn seven hundred, eight hundred people into one thing called an audience.'[84] Meanwhile, an act that failed to build the energy of the audience's responses would make things significantly harder for the following one, as Peter Prentice recalls: 'It's easy to follow a good act, but to follow a poor act, it's ever such hard work to lift the audience.'[85]

In place of a conventional theatrical narrative which shapes and drives a play, variety was given shape and purpose by the audience's response – the energy which built up not just in each individual act, but throughout the entire show. At the beginning, the audience's responses would be cool, not least because some of them would still be filing in, but they would get warmer and louder as the evening progressed, with the top of the bill offering a natural climax. This pattern was mirrored across the length of a week's engagement, with the auditorium getting fuller and livelier from first house Monday through to second house Saturday. As Jack Seaton pointed out, this made for a rather disconcerting rhythm of work:

> Saturday night. Bingo! You were away like a dream, you know. The place'd be packed and everybody's waiting, it's their big night out of the week. Now you've had that on a Saturday, you go the next town on a Monday, dead as a dodo, and you walk out, the first house, it's about a third full – and they don't want to know you.[86]

Working the audience

The active role that audiences played meant that learning how to manipulate their responses was vital. Variety artistes drew on a whole range of skills when it came to working an audience, including some very formal elements. Performers energetically pursued applause, and once it was won, there were ritualized conventions for acknowledging it.

'Taking a call' was how they described the process of how they took applause at the end of the act. In her glossary of variety jargon,

Valantyne Napier is rather dogmatic about the correct way to do this: 'Amateurs say "taking a bow". Pros did not bow. They stood with arms outstretched to receive the applause, looked up to the gallery, then circle and to the stalls, acknowledged the Musical Director and pit orchestra, particularly the drummer, and then exited to the wings.'[87] In fact, many performers would receive applause with a bow, often a rather shallow one, arms kept neatly by the sides, head bowed, upper torso bent very slightly forward. They would bow like this to the various sections of the audience, taking in the centre and both sides.

At the end of the act, the tabs would swish down from the sides and part again to allow the act to bow (or use Napier's stretch-arms gesture), the process being repeated if the applause lasted long enough. Eventually, the tabs would stay closed, and the performer would come through for a final call.[88] There is an excellent example of this in the film *Variety Jubilee*, which shows famous adagio act, the Ganjou Brothers & Juanita taking their call. Juanita skips daintily through the curtains to stage left, giving the merest wisp of a curtsy before looking back and raising her arm to welcome the three brothers back onto the stage. They come through the curtain, the first of them taking her hand, and they all give a simultaneous shallow bow. As they exit, one brother stays behind, and brings Juanita back one last time, allowing her to give a full curtsy, then a shallow bow to right and left.[89] It is an extremely elegant sequence, with the kind of precision that made their act exceptional. Taking a call in the proper manner was more than just a convention; it was also governed by regulation. The standard Moss contract rather officiously stipulated that, 'Artistes shall respond to encores or not as the Management shall reasonably direct'. This was probably to stop acts from milking the applause and thus throwing the strict time schedule of the show off course. Certainly, acts had to learn to how to adjust their material to account for laughter and applause so as to stop their tightly timed act from overrunning. Jack Seaton recalled that he would have to 'cut a couple of gags out' towards the end of the week to compensate for the longer laughs he got from the audience. He also describes how theatres would help acts keep track of the time using coloured footlights:

> Most of the variety theatres in those days, they had footlights. And invariably in the footlights, was two lights, a red and a green one. As long as the green one was on, you was OK. Well, when it changed to red, you had a minute. But you see, most of us, you had an inbuilt clock.[90]

Would you care to try?

Some performers asked the audience to participate in the act, either en masse or as individual volunteers, and managing this process was another important skill that had to be mastered. As in the music halls, variety theatres were often filled with the sound of the whole audience singing along with a popular song. Vera Lynn points out that most of her repertoire was eminently singalongable because 'they were easy songs to learn. The tunes were easy, and the lyrics were basic, and so…people used to pick up the tunes quite easily.' Furthermore, her songs were structured so as to cue the audience to participate:

> [Y]ou'd sing a verse and a chorus, and maybe you might do a second verse and a chorus, and then you repeat the chorus and you just gesture to the audience – invite them to sing along with you. 'Cos they'd already heard the chorus the first time around, then by the time they got to the second chorus, the second time round, they were a little bit familiar with it.[91]

Audiences were not always straightforwardly cooperative when asked to join in. Around the time of the Second World War, Joe Loss's band were recorded at the Edinburgh Empire, and their act included a section of community singing, with the audience joining in a series of well-known numbers: 'Ain't She Sweet', 'Beer Barrel Polka', 'In the Quartermaster's Stores' and 'The Music Goes Round and Round'. Loss sets this up by drawing attention to the fact that the audience is peppered with people in uniform, and asking them to 'imagine that you're attending one of the camp concerts'. Then he gets them to prepare to sing:

> So tonight I just want you to let yourselves go, just clear your throat first.

He leads the way, giving a couple of coughs to demonstrate what he wants them to do, and this unleashes a boisterous torrent of exaggerated coughing from around the auditorium, and a general hubbub of muttering and laughing. There is a tangible feeling of mischief in this response. As the noise dies down, Loss starts to continue with what he was saying, but he is interrupted by another comical cougher. He sounds slightly rattled as he responds to this:

> Ha ha. Your throat's pretty good there, you should leave that.[92]

Loss is a big-name act – one the audience is unlikely to want to challenge too much – and his words are enough to quell their insubordination. Seconds later they join in good-heartedly with the songs, but this tiny incident shows that variety audiences were not always easy to tame.

This meant that acts which brought individual volunteers up onto the stage to join in the act had to take particular care. A volunteer brought an element of potential chaos into the act, not least because it would be impossible to predict exactly how someone would behave once they were standing under the gaze of a large audience. The strict time limits which an act had to stick to meant that the process of picking somebody out, physically getting them up onto the stage, and getting them off again afterwards would have to be swiftly and neatly managed.

The 1943 film *The Dummy Talks* shows exactly how an act called the Skating Avalons did this. A farcical murder mystery set in a variety theatre, the film includes a number of scenes of genuine acts filmed in what looks like a genuine theatre complete with large live audience. As such, it offers a good approximation of how the act would have been performed in an actual live show.

After some impressive stunts in which a male roller skater spins a female roller skater around at dizzying speeds, the man leaves the stage and the woman is joined by two more female skaters on either side of her. She brightly asks:

Is there any member in the audience who would care to, er, come up and take a little ride with us this evening? May we have a gentleman, please?

As she says this, she is already scanning the audience for volunteers, and finishes her question by holding her arms out in invitation. The other two women move outwards, each actively searching their half of the auditorium. The one on the left points to a man close to the front and asks:

How about you, sir? Would you care to try?

When he fails to respond, the one on the right points out somebody standing to the side and says:

How about you, sir? Would you care to try?

The skater in the centre reinforces the question, asking:

Yes, how about you, sir? Will you come up?

The audience sense his assent, and applaud him. He makes his way to the stage, getting up onto it via some small steps by the side of the proscenium. The whole process has taken less than 25 seconds.

What happens next is a gag that has clearly been set up for the film rather than a normal part of the stage act. Their volunteer is the bumbling detective character played by Claude Hulbert, and when he is spun around by one of the skaters, the comedy is crudely heightened by speeding the film up. Having said this, some of the business does genuinely seem to be part of the act.

As Hulbert arrives onto the stage, the three women hold out their arms to greet him, leading him over to centre stage. One of them takes his hands, so that he thinks she will be the one who will spin him around, but then the male skater taps him on the shoulders and he realizes that it is this man rather than one of the three lissom ladies who is going to spin him around. The gag shows just how skilfully the whole situation has been manipulated. They have deliberately chosen a male volunteer ('May we have a gentleman, please?') and led him to believe he will be spun by a woman. The male skater taps Hulbert on his downstage shoulder, so that when he turns around his face will be turned out towards the auditorium to allow the audience to enjoy his look of surprise. This is effectively the punchline to the gag, and the laughter comes from the visible realization that he has been duped.[93]

The kind of technique used by the Skating Avalons is surprisingly similar to the conventions that govern audience participation today. Even in the rough and tumble of a modern comedy club, individual punters are often addressed with a rather formal 'sir' or 'madam', and the normal pattern is for the audience to applaud as a volunteer takes to the stage. This is vital, because it helps to confirm the choice of volunteer, putting pressure on him or her actually go ahead – in the film, the applause starts before Hulbert has visibly accepted the invitation. Even more importantly, the applause covers the time it takes to actually get onto the stage, thus avoiding the unforgivable sin of a stage wait. The audience also applaud Hulbert as he leaves the stage having completed the stunt, thus rewarding him for his bravery and again, covering the time it takes to get off the stage.

A slightly safer bet was to use audience volunteers who were not actually members of the audience. Ken Joy, who appeared in his parents' 'comedy-knockabout-musical' act as a child, was actually used as a plant. They would play a range of unusual instruments – bagpipes, a sousaphone, 'comedy violin'– and at a certain point they would ask if anyone in the audience would like to come and have a go at playing one of them. Joy recalls:

> I'd be at the back, what we used to call a plant, this little lad of 3 or 4 years old, and I'd shout, 'Hello, I'll do it, mister!' And they'd get me up there and of course I'd play 'Home Sweet Home' or something like that, and of course it brought the house down in those days – to see a little lad playing this great big bloody sousaphone.

He says that, 'A lot of the old acts used to do that', and particularly mentions double acts where the funny man would be placed in the gods or in one of the boxes, and would deliver his lines from there. The point of this was that, 'It breaks down the barrier. If you work to somebody in the audience, then the audience becomes involved and become part and parcel of the act.'[94] This worked even if the individual patron joining in was a plant, although they would often come clean at the end of the act, with the plant taking the call alongside his or her fellow performers.

Boom-boom

Taking applause, managing participation and using plants were all part of the craft of working an audience. These were the tangible aspects of it, and they were often governed by customs and conventions which formed a kind of grammar of audience interaction. The real poetry lay in the less tangible ways in which the performers related to the people sitting watching them. One of these was the ability to read and interpret the reactions from the auditorium, and to judge from the particular quality of laughter and applause what the character of that particular audience was like. A 1938 article in *The Times* argued that 'perfect timing is essential, and a shrewd estimate of "the house" is part and parcel of every act'.[95] For Vera Lynn, estimating the house meant getting the lighting right:

> I liked to be part of the audience. I used to make sure that the limes weren't too strong so I could see at least one or two rows of people that I could perform to ... so I could see their faces and how they were reacting to what I was doing.[96]

Even when this was not possible, there were other ways of gauging the audience, as Peter Prentice points out: 'Well you can't really see them. The front row you might see a few ... We used to just work to the lights.

But you can tell whether it's a good house or not…from the sounds and in those days from the amount of cigarette smoke.'[97]

Reading the audience helped the acts to time their delivery correctly. 'Timing' is a word which is often invoked but rarely precisely defined, although Ted Ray passed on a pleasingly straightforward definition to Roy Hudd: 'Well, what timing means is you don't talk when they're laughing – you wait till they've stopped laughing, and then you talk. That's all there is to know about timing.'[98] Talking over a laugh – or 'treading on a laugh' to use the performers' jargon – risked foreshortening the audience's hard-won response.

Important as this was, there were also subtler aspects to reading an audience. Danny Kaye claimed that:

> I can tell within seconds after I step out on the stage what that particular audience is like and what it expects of me…I don't know why or how I know this, but I do. Maybe it's a sixth sense or, more likely, the result of many years of experience.[99]

What he suggests here is that this 'sixth sense' allowed him get a sense of what the audience wanted him to do, and thus what to include in the act. Teddie Beverley implies much the same thing in describing how the Beverley Sisters worked: 'You gauge the audience. You gauge whether songs should be faster, slower, whether it should have two choruses or three, whether it'll sustain another chorus.'[100] It was only by reading an audience that performers could enlist the audience as collaborators in this way, using their responses to shape the act.

The art of working an audience meant not just knowing how to interpret and acknowledge responses, but also how to solicit them. In Harry Secombe's novel *Twice Brightly*, an older performer, Jimmy Long, tells the inexperienced Larry Gower, 'An audience is like a child, it has to be told clearly and distinctly how to behave. If they are supposed to laugh at a certain point, tell them so beforehand. They might not laugh, of course, but at least give them the opportunity.'[101]

There were various ways of cuing a response, an obvious example being the convention of finishing a front cloth comedy act with a song. As Wyn Calvin points out, this was 'useful' because, 'It's a natural communicative climax'.[102] As well as giving the act a sense of completion, the end of the song would normally cue a round of applause which the act could exit to. Similarly, singers would plan their sequence of songs to create a sense of climax at the end of the act and cue the appropriate response, as Vera Lynn explains: '[Y]ou'd always make sure that you finished on your strongest song, so you could finish on a high...that was important. It helps to tell the audience that, "Oh well, this is the last song...we must give her an extra hard clap".'[103]

Music could also cue applause in other ways. Valantyne Napier noted that, 'For speciality acts the orchestra was most important. "Up and down for tricks" would be written on their band parts and the Musical Director could bring the applause for the difficult tricks performed on the stage by the way he conducted in the pit.'[104] Drums were particularly useful for cuing applause. As a 1938 *Times* article put it, 'a roll of the drums at the critical moment is as necessary as the stage itself'.[105]

Sometimes, this was about building the excitement for a great feat. The strongwoman Joan Rhodes would have a drum roll when she tore telephone directories in half: 'To accent it...when I was tearing the book there was a drum going BRRRRRRR and I would sort of go with it'.[106] On other occasions, the drum could act as a cue for a laugh. Harry Secombe recalled seeing Norman Vaughan giving detailed instructions to the drummer in rehearsal, for example telling him: 'Give me a "boom-boom" at the end of the lion-tamer gag.'[107] Drummers would not necessarily need to be told what to do, because the conventions were well established, and as Roy Hudd points out, 'in the days of variety, every drummer knew what following the act meant. You didn't have to give them band parts.'[108]

Particular performers might have particular tricks for manipulating a response in the audience. Max Bygraves recalled how Billy Bennett 'stood stock still with his feet at twenty-to-eight, until he came to his punch-line, and, to telegraph to his audience that the funny bit was coming up, he'd wiggle his moustache once then throw one hand up in the air.'[109] The singer and *siffleur* Ronnie Ronalde set up the whole of the beginning of his act so as to manipulate the audience into applauding his entrance even before he was famous enough to have earned such a response:

> When I really got starting to go well as a single act, I remember I made...a letter R on a piece of cardboard and sewed a piece of cloth to it, white cloth, and that white R, I put on my red jacket, which was a blazer type of jacket...another thing is that on the back of the stage, I had a single leg behind me with an R, which I also had made, with all glitter on. So all the tabs would open, and pick up that R with the glitter. And then I'd whistle a few notes offstage, and...I'd walk on to applause. I mean, you know, I wasn't a star, but...they would think, 'There must be *somebody* good coming on'.[110]

Don't laugh in the wrong places

Some of the best acts went beyond simply cuing laughter and applause. Tommy Trinder, for example, would draw attention to the way the audience were reacting, getting laughs by playfully critiquing their responses. At the beginning of the 1950 Royal Variety Performance, he was sent on to warm up the notoriously chilly audience, which he did by pulling out some press cuttings and announcing, 'I'm going to read your notices from last year... If I'd had such lousy write-ups I'd never show my face inside a theatre again.'[111] Appearing at the Embassy Theatre, Peterborough in November 1940, he gives a running commentary on the audience's responses throughout the act. After a small laugh, he says:

> Ha haaargh, don't bother with the small jokes. [laughter]

When one patrons gives a particularly raucous laugh, he says:

> Uh, please – [laughter] If it hurts, loosen something. [laughter]

One gag gets a slightly uncertain laugh, which leads him to tell them off:

> Don't laugh in the wrong places please, it makes the jokes sound dirty. [laughter][112]

Clearly he is joking here, but it is a revealing joke because innuendo was a mainstay of variety comedy, and acts could actually get into trouble for using jokes with hidden sexual meanings. The Moss Empires contract specifically stated that:

> Any Artiste giving expression to any vulgarity or words having a double meaning or using any objectionable gesture when on the stage shall be liable to instant dismissal and if dismissed shall forfeit the salary for the current week. Any question under this Clause to be decided by the Management whose decision shall be final and binding on the Artiste.

Given the number of comedians who laced their acts with innuendo, this was normally a bit of an empty threat, but Don Smoothey remembers the management of the Coventry Hippodrome telling him and his comedy partner to take a joke out of the act because – just like in Trinder's impromptu quip – 'anything that gets a sustained laugh like that did' must have had a hidden dirty meaning which he could not work out.[113]

Innuendo was a delicious comic technique not just because of the naughtiness of hinting at forbidden subject matter, but also because it bound audience and performer together in a conspiracy against the kind of restriction stipulated in the Moss contract. Trinder's great comic rival Max Miller was the supreme master of the double entendre, and he would tease the audience about their role in his conspiracy by playing with their reactions. (See Illustration 7.2.) For example, during a performance at the Finsbury Park Empire in September 1942, he says:

> My first number, my first, have you got 'Rhapsody in Blue?' No? No. No? I'll tell yer – I'll do 'Josephine'. [laughter] What's wrong with that, go on, make something of that, go on, make – [laughter] Nice lot of people, eh, Finsbury Park! [laughter] But there's one thing I like about you people, you're so quick, you're quick. You get all the gags right away. You're like a flash of lightning. [laughter][114]

The basic gag – playing on the sexual possibilities of the phrase 'do Josephine' – gets a good, strong laugh, which Miller exploits to the full. First he gets a couple of laughs for blaming the audience for any hidden meaning, as if he were entirely innocent of what he might have implied. Then he gets another laugh by taking the opposite tack and praising the audience for their ability to keep up with his double entendres.

Part of the power of this was that Miller was showing the audience just how good he was at reading their reactions, almost as if he could get inside their heads. Indeed, at an appearance at the Met, Edgware Road in November 1957 he explicitly tells them:

> I know exactly, I know exactly what you're saying to yourselves. You're wrong. [some laughter] I know what you're saying. [laughter builds] Oh you, you wicked lot. [laughter] You're the kind of people who get me a bad name. [laughter][115]

Settle down, that's all

Tommy Trinder adopted some of the same techniques, and even used the line 'make something out of it' after a dirty gag.[116] However, he also had gags which played on knowing what the audience were thinking which did not involve sexual innuendo. The Peterborough show took place during the Second World War, when petrol was rationed and very few were allowed to use private cars. Not long after starting his act, he tells the audience:

> I was coming here in my car –

Figure 7.2 A 1942 programme for the Empress, Brixton flags up an appearance by Max Miller the following week.

Without missing a beat, he flips into character, voicing what he imagines the audience are staying to themselves:

Huh-huh, he's got a car!

Immediately, he flips back into his own voice and asks them:

Do you wan' any petrol? [laughter][117]

It is an extraordinarily compact gag. The three sentences follow each other so fast that it is effectively a single line, in the space of which he comments on wartime restrictions, lords it over them because he has a car and they don't, and jokingly makes them a spiv-like offer of petrol. By doing so, he not only shows the audience that he understands the way they think, but also defines his relationship with them. He is the garrulous, hectoring show-off, who is perfectly happy for them to know that he is in control of them.

Danny Kaye was possibly even more adept at playing with an audience's responses, building whole routines out of them. One of his signature bits was his own version of Cab Calloway's 'Minnie the Moocher', which involved making much play of the call-and-response sections. Footage of the 1948 Royal Variety Performance shows him setting it up by saying:

I'd like you to unleash your golden throats and let the sounds of your voice drift into the still of the night. Are you ready?

After some physical comedy with the band, who are behind him on the stage, he sings the first verse before launching into the first call-and-response line:

Hi-de-hi-de-he-do-hoo-

Only a pathetic few people respond, making the faintest ghost of an echo of what Kaye has sung. He takes a fraction of a second to register their failure, and as the band dies away, he looks up at them, the disappointment on his face like that of a teacher let down by a pupil. Then he gets a prolonged but slightly uncertain laugh as he walks away from them in disgust, convincingly feigning barely concealed anger by walking upstage in a circle, kicking the stage hard as if to let it out, once, twice, three times, each kick reigniting the audience's laughter. He ends up back behind the microphone, his hands in the pockets of his stylishly baggy trousers, his right leg forward and jerking as if with annoyance. He looks up at them, and then drops his head as if he cannot bear to talk to them yet, getting another laugh. 'I'll be all right in a minute', he reassures them, still sounding upset. This gets the biggest laugh yet.[118]

It is a beautiful bit of business, filling 30 seconds of stage time and getting six good laughs. The joke is that he is treating the audience as if they are there for his amusement, rather than the other way round. Instead of allowing them to judge him, he is pretending to judge them. His mock anger and disappointment are far more effective than the genuine annoyance in Joe Loss's voice as he dealt with a rogue cougher.

As the routine continues, Kaye deals with the audience's responses ever more playfully. He pleads with them, gets tearful, and makes them practise singing 'ahh' together. When they finally hit the call-and-response sections, he shows off his vocal flexibility with increasingly silly scat singing, using falsetto, yodelling and silly-sounding nonsense:

> Reep, ba-gi, ba-gi-bom-zay.

The audience copy him faithfully, their pleasure audible in the laughter that breaks out from their own singing. All of this is accompanied by some precise, almost balletic hand gestures, as he rhythmically bends and straightens his fingers, swiping his palm sideways, pointing both index fingers downwards, or flapping like a bird. It is as if he is actually physically moulding the audience to make them sing correctly. Then he does a particularly long, complicated bit of scat – getting a laugh – and points at them and says, with a note of challenge in his voice:

> Go ahead. [loud laughter][119]

The game he plays involves teasingly showing his mastery over the audience, getting them to do whatever he pleases, then pulling the rug out from under them by deliberately catching them out. Later in the act, he points out his wife in the audience and announces:

> I'd like you all to meet her now, Mrs Danny Kaye.

The applause is long and loud, and he lets it continue for a while, before undercutting the showbiz sentimentality by saying:

> That's all, that's all, settle down, that's all. [prolonged laughter]

It is as if their applause – the applause he effectively asked them for – is too generous, so he jealously has to cut it short.[120]

Performers such as Max Miller, Tommy Trinder and Danny Kaye showed just how much more there was to 'getting over' than the simple mechanical process of talking into a microphone. They made their relationship with their audiences a central feature of their act, manipulating the patrons with imagination and perception, and shifting the balance of power so it was the acts who sat in judgement over the people out there, rather than the other way around. This kind of thing demanded an exceptional level of skill, but it was a far less visible and conspicuous kind of skill than that seen in certain other kinds of variety act.

8

Skill

Elements of astonishment

The Japanese juggler, Gintaro, has a huge tower of bricks on an elaborate table in front of him. It is taller than he is, made up of 22 bricks in all, and on top of it there is a glass of water. He concentrates hard as he slowly works his right hand underneath the bottom brick. Then, as he actually picks up the entire tower, it tilts disastrously, and he runs across the stage with it until he has found the balance point. The audience applaud the feat, and he runs backwards to centre stage with neat, controlled little steps, holding the tower up proudly atop his right hand, his left arm held out in a flourish. Finally, he throws the bricks up into the air, and as they cascade down he catches the glass of water, pouring its contents into a bucket offered by an assistant to indicate that he has not spilt a drop.[1]

June – the female half of the act Sereno & June – climbs to the top of a giant stepladder which must be at least 10 feet tall, and leaps into the arms of her male partner, balancing there upside down. Their arms disengage, forming a pure head-to-head balance. Keeping her in this precarious position, Sereno climbs right up the stepladder and down the other side. Then he walks over to the side of the proscenium, and June bends so that her feet are touching it. By carefully stepping backwards and leaning forwards, Sereno allows June to walk right down the proscenium – totally horizontally – until they are both face down on the stage.[2]

The three Chinese men in white tuxedos and two Chinese women in kimonos who make up the Five Lai Founs are spread across the stage, each holding two long poles with spinning plates on top. One of the women hands one of her poles to one of the men, who now has to keep two plates spinning in one hand, as well as the one he still has in his other hand. Keeping the plate in her left hand spinning, the woman bends backwards, her torso flexing right over until her right hand reaches the stage. Then she picks her feet up to go into an extraordinary balance, her body folded so far backwards that her legs are draped over her right shoulder, her feet level with her face, which looks straight forward at the audience, smiling serenely. It is such an unnatural position that it is hard to comprehend, and all the while, her plate keeps spinning.[3]

Valantyne Napier has had her hands firmly tied behind her back. Dislocating her wrists, shoulders and collar bones, she twists her arms around, taking them back over her head, and then freeing herself.[4] The Danny Lipton Trio are doing some very fast, sharply coordinated tap-dancing. Then the music drops away, the two women move to one side, and Lipton does some solo steps. Incredibly, he takes the pace up even faster, his legs becoming a blur, wildly criss-crossing each other. At one point, he crooks his right leg back and keeps furiously tap-dancing with his left foot only in a kind of extraordinary hopping action, at a pace many people would struggle to match using both feet.[5]

Such examples start to give an idea of the range of spectacular skills which could be seen in variety, which were as varied as they were breathtaking. One of the things that had drawn Roy Hudd's grand-mother to variety was the sight of 'people doing amazing things', and this was also something that appealed to Marinetti: 'The authors, actors, and technicians of the Variety Theatre have only one reason for existing and triumphing: incessantly to invent new elements of astonishment. Hence ... an excited competition of brains and muscles to conquer the various records of agility, speed, force, complication, and elegance.'[6]

Musical virtuosity, dance, acrobatics, escapology, contortionism, tight-rope walking, trapeze, paper tearing, hypnotism, ventriloquism, sleight of hand, and feats of memory were just some of the skills that were displayed for the delight of audiences. There were also the dem-onstrations of sporting talent, with exhibitions of table tennis, bad-minton or snooker.[7] Then there were the non-human skills offered by groups of performing animals, like Vogelbein's Bears, which rode bicycles, or Duncan's Collies, which played a football match onstage.[8]

The efforts taken to acquire these skills must have been extraor-dinary, particularly because as *The Times* pointed out in 1961: 'Most occupations have schools, colleges, universities or places where apprentices are taught – even the actor has his Academy of Dramatic Art; but the music-hall artist has none of these aids.'[9] The nearest to a formal training in variety were the small dance schools which many performers were sent to as children. This seems to have been a very common experience even in impoverished working-class families, where dance lessons might lead to professional work on the stage which would make an important contribution to the family coffers. To give just one example, Betty Clarkson was sent to dance lessons when she was just four and a half, before she had even started school. When she reached the age of 15, she joined the Danny Lipton Trio, earning £2. 10s. a week, of which she was able to send 10s.home to her parents.[10]

Clive Barker has explained how, before the foundation of acting schools such as RADA, actors would have trained in a 'proto-academy' made up of 'the large number of theatrical families who handed on the secrets of their craft from generation to generation, and jealously guarded them'.[11] This is how many variety performers who grew up in theatrical families would have learned their skills. Lupino Lane, for example, a child of two long-established theatrical families (the Lupinos and the Lanes), wrote that 'each member of my family, male or female, has been put through a course and trained from early childhood by the elders of the family'. This 'course' would have trained them in a wide variety of skills including ballet, tap, acrobatics, juggling, singing, elocution and 'The art of miming or expressing emotions, in "dumb show" '.[12]

Similarly, Peter Prentice's father taught him rope tricks and unicycling so that he could join their family act El Granadas & Peter. The problem was that this kind of training was limited by the pool of knowledge that existed within the family: 'It actually made it very difficult in some ways because, say I'd wanted to play the clarinet – how could I do that travelling week by week by week? No one to give you a lesson ... So it had to be within the scope of the family's experience'.[13]

However, the secrets of variety performance were far from jealously guarded. Those who did not have the kind of family tuition that Lane and Prentice enjoyed tended to pick things up in a more casual kind of training, with acts learning skills from each other. Roy Hudd recalls:

> That did happen quite a lot in variety ... you'd go down to the theatre in the morning, see if there's any letters for you ... all the performers used to. That's when you used to meet and have a cup of coffee and that. But people

would say, 'I'll show you how to do a back flip, you know, if you want to know.' 'I'll show you a couple of time steps.' So people used to learn a bit of tap, bit of acrobatics...Mr Pastry [aka Richard Hearne] taught me to fall off a chair backwards, which was very useful ... people would always want to pass the knowledge on.[14]

Jimmy Jewel benefited from a combination of this kind of informal tuition and family training. His father took cheap touring revues around the number three theatres, and he would hire performers specifically so that they could teach his son particular skills. Thus the young Jimmy learned tap-dancing from assistant stage manager Henry Vale, tumbling from a circus act called the Stebbing Brothers, and saxophone from a performer called Billy Childs.[15]

May all your children be acrobats!

For speciality acts, learning the skills was only part of the battle. Displaying extraordinary feats in 12 shows a week for years on end would take its toll on the body. In 1958, still in his early fifties, Freddie Dehl retired his adagio act, the Dehl Trio, because, as his son Chris put it, 'at the age of 51 his body was telling him that his days as a professional acrobat were coming to an end'.[16]

Then there was the sheer risk involved. Marinetti raved about the 'school of heroism' in variety that 'creates on stage the strong, sane atmosphere of danger'.[17] This was undoubtedly part of the appeal of many acts, and an article in *The Strand Magazine* talked about 'the *soupçon* of danger which attaches to these feats (which, as a matter of fact, is much slighter than is commonly supposed) [that] may, in a measure, account for their never-failing popularity'. [18]

However, some acts were every bit as dangerous as commonly supposed. In 1931, an audience at the Birmingham Empire got 'an unexpected thrill' – as the *Manchester Guardian* put it – during the Four Latvians' act, in which a man on a motorcycle balanced a woman on a trapeze as he looped the loop. In this particular show, when they reached the top of the loop, the woman lost her balance and fell, causing the man to fall under the bike. She escaped with bruising, but he sustained head injuries, and the act had to be replaced in the next house.[19]

Skiffle star Chas McDevitt, who toured the theatres in the last days of variety, remembers working with an aerial act called the Skylons:

[O]ne of them had broken every bone in his body, you know, at one stage, literally every bone. And whilst we were in Edinburgh, he fell off the high thing and was carried off. And I used to think, 'Well, they've been doing this for years, they're knocking themselves out ... they're getting paid a pittance, and they're not causing much of a reaction with the audience, you know. How can they continue?[20]

This highlights an interesting contradiction: the acts which showed the most extraordinary skills, worked the hardest, and took the most physical risks also tended to be the ones that were furthest down the pecking order of variety. Peter Prentice happily admits that El Granadas & Peter 'were always amongst the wines and spirits', meaning that their billing was printed so small that it hardly stood out from the bar prices: 'We were always very small-billed. It always used to annoy me ... Actually, speciality acts in booking terms were quite expensive – but we never got the glory that the comics and the singers got.'[21]

There was a traditional curse among performers, 'May all your children be acrobats!' referring to the fact that they would, as Brian O'Gorman explained, 'go on last, work hard and never earn any money'.[22] Similarly, there is an apocryphal story told about comics as diverse as Billy Bennett, Robb Wilton and Max Miller. The comic is watching an acrobat or a contortionist from the wings, and jokes that this highly skilled performer is only doing an act like that because he is 'too lazy to learn a comic song'.[23]

Obviously, the joke plays on the idea that it would be far less effort to be a comic singer, but in fact, both singers and comedians had considerable and hard-won skills of their own. The difference is that their skills would be essentially invisible. The artistry with which they projected their personality and interacted with an audience was such that it came across as being natural and spontaneous, disguising the experience and effort that lay behind it. As O'Gorman has argued, 'The skill involved in "doing your act" was truly that art which conceals art.'[24]

The question is, why was it that comics and singers, whose skills were often intangible, could top the bill, when dancers and speciality acts whose skills were remarkable, spectacular and visible for all to see were often relegated to thankless opening and closing slots, playing to people shuffling in at the beginning of the show or shuffling out at the end? Teddie Beverley offers a way into answering the question. When asked whether the connection between performer and audience is the key to variety performance, she answers, 'Well it should be, it should be. Apart from the speciality acts – and they're just visual. And everybody fidgets around in those times, waiting for the star they've come to see usually.'[25]

The suggestion is that acts which had a warm, powerful bond with the audience were very different from speciality acts, which had visual appeal but lacked rapport. Skill in itself, then, was not enough to allow a speciality act to climb higher up the bill.

Mathematical precision

In most theatres, the dance act which started both halves of the show would be a duo or a trio, but in the biggest London venues such as the Palladium or Bernard Delfont's Casino, there would usually be a resident troupe of dancers, like the Sherman Fisher Girls or the Tiller Girls. To get a job in such a troupe meant a rather contradictory position: the lowliest position on the bill in some of the most important theatres in the country.

Troupes such as the Tiller Girls featured many more dancers than the average dance act, the number of girls sometimes being trumpeted in publicity which proudly announced the presence of, for example, '16 Palladium Girls'. The implication seemed to be that the more girls there were, the more spectacular the act. Walter Benjamin, who saw the Tiller Girls when they appeared in spectacular revues in Germany, acidly sent this logic up, commenting that 'soon there will be more Girls than spectators'.[26]

Whereas the small dance acts tended to feature solos, showing off particularly flashy tap steps, the big troupes were all about uniformity and coordination, kicklines being particularly popular. Footage of the Tiller Girls onstage in 1953 shows a line of girls so long that they fill the proscenium even standing shoulder to shoulder. They dance the cancan, waving their voluminous frilly skirts and kicking their legs high and straight, always staying in perfect unison with each other. This unnaturally precise coordination is only broken by the occasional moment when two of the girls turn cartwheels across the stage.[27]

Coordination was a deceptively popular feature of variety, appearing in most types of act. There was visual coordination, with the performers that made up an act often dressing identically. There was aural coordination, with close harmony singing, words being spoken simultaneously, or the fast-paced, intercut cross-talk patter of comedy double acts such as Flanagan & Allen. Then there was coordination of movement, which was not restricted to dancers and acrobats. In one of Danny Kaye's visual gags, he turns to face the band ranked onstage behind him, as if to conduct them. With his back to the audience, he leans to one side and then the other, the band leaning with him to perfectly mirror his movements. This nicely coordinated bit of business gets sustained laughter.[28]

It is one of the fundamental facts of popular entertainment that seeing – or hearing – more than one person doing the same thing at the same time is inherently pleasing. Voices singing in harmony sound enjoyable, and 16 pairs of legs kicking in unison look exciting. Beyond the simple pleasure of symmetry, coordination is a display of skill, and the amount of effort that has gone into achieving it is shown in the level of precision achieved. The applause which greeted coordination was partly a reward for work put in.

Nowhere is this more obvious than with the Tiller Girls. Siegfried Kracauer, who like Benjamin had seen the Tiller Girls in Germany, wrote:

> When they formed a line that moved up and down, they radiantly represented the superiority of the conveyor belt; when they step-danced at a rapid pace, it sounded like 'business, business'; when they tossed their legs into the air with mathematical precision, they joyfully approved the progress of rationalization; and when they continually repeated the same motions, without breaking their line, one imagined an uninterrupted chain of automobiles streaming from the factories of the world.[29]

Kracauer might have been attempting a Marxist metaphor, but he was actually close to the literal truth. John Tiller had started out as an industrialist, working in the Manchester cotton industry, before founding the troupe in the 1880s. He set up a factory-like training system which continued throughout the variety era. The girls would work for hours on end in front of a long mirror, with kicks and 'ceaseless counting', until 'their legs, arms, heads and bodies move as one'.[30] Total uniformity was the aim, not just in movement, but also in the way the girls looked. Tiller Girls had to be of a particular physical type: 'height around 5 feet 4 inches, bust 34 inches, waist 24 inches, hips 35 inches'.[31]

On the whole, variety was about individualism, and as Reginald Barlow put it, personality was the 'first requisite' for pleasing an audience – but The Tiller Girls seem to blow a hole in this idea. The idea was to erase the personality, with training devised by a businessman which turned out identical dancers like products off a production line. To quote Kay Lambert, a 1940s Tiller Girl: 'Being Tillerised means smoothing out the individualists ... In an ordinary chorus line, although she is doing the same step, every girl has her own particular style. Usually she is hoping to be noticed and picked out for a solo part.'[32]

Well coordinated with the lyrics

On the other hand, coordination was not always about erasing individualism. Like the Tiller Girls, the Beverley Sisters based much of their act on careful coordination, and not just in their vocal harmonies. *The Stage* noted their 'three delightful personalities' and their 'extremely pleasant voices', but argued that 'it is the co-ordination of their performance that unfailingly pleases. Every gesture is aimed at gaining a certain effect, every movement is balanced within the trio, nothing is left to chance'.[33] (See Illustration 8.1.)

A performance of 'I'm Late' on *The Beverley Sisters Show* gives a good idea of their stage choreography. Standing in a line, very close to each other, the oldest and tallest sister Joy flanked on either side by identical twins Teddie and Babs, the symmetry of the performers is heightened by the matching posh frocks, handbags and hairdos. For the most part they simply stand and sing, but a sense of urgency is created by the way their bodies subtly bob up and down to the rhythm of the song. Every now and then, a line is enhanced by a carefully defined gesture which is performed sharply in triplicate. On the word 'wave', three right hands snap into a wave, the fingers waggling playfully. On the phrase 'hop hop hop', three heads tilt to their left then their right. Between the verses, the three sisters precisely mime taking lipstick out of their handbags, applying it, then putting it away again. All of these actions happen in near-perfect unison, and timed to the music – each stroke of the mimed lipstick is on the beat.[34]

Teddie Beverley explains how this style evolved: 'When we played all the theatres, there was one microphone, fixed into the floor ... and you couldn't move from it ... And so our movements were obviously restricted to that'.[35] An article in *The Stage* in 1952 noted that 'while some artists seem cramped and static with a microphone, others manage to suggest a sense of movement'.[36] The Beverley Sisters did this by using simple but precise gestures, with a consciously minimalist approach to choreography. Teddie Beverley recalls that, 'nothing was wasted, it was ... very rationed, we'd start off with a line with ten movements in, and cut it down to one. We liked economy of movement ... not too much flailing about and shuffling about.'[37]

Figure 8.1 The programme for the Regal, Hull in the week commencing Monday 3 March 1958, features a photo of the Beverley Sisters who topped the bill.

She gives the example of a song called 'The Sultan': '[A]s you do "harem", you just move the hips slightly. Now that is just suggestive – of a harem, see. We don't need to wobble all over the stage and stick your pelvis out and all that. Just that slight subtlety of the harem.'[38] Footage of a performance of that song from an early television appearance shows the three sets of hips begin to swing precisely on the word 'harem', and continue swinging in unison to the beat for the rest of the line. More than that, the footage shows how the Beverley Sisters managed to balance precise coordination with the projection of personality.

Because they use gestures sparingly, for much of the song they are simply standing and singing. While doing so, the individuality of each sister subtly announces itself. The angles of the heads and the expressions on the faces are slightly different. While one sister looks straight forward, another looks out to the side, and the third one looks down. One of the twins tends to widen her eyes, while the other tends to let her eyelids drop as she shyly casts her eyes downwards. The visual symmetry of the act and the coordination of the gestures mean that any deviation from strict uniformity becomes much more noticeable.[39]

This individuality was the key difference between the Beverley Sisters and the Tiller Girls. The Tillers were a phenomenon, with troupes working in the biggest theatres not just in Britain but also around Europe. To become a Tiller Girl was to become part of this phenomenon, but without any chance of standing out as an individual. The Tiller Girls were famous but each individual Girl was anonymous and therefore replaceable. On the other hand, each Beverley Sister was known by name – Joy, Babs and Teddie – and they were famous enough as individuals to have their private lives covered by the popular press.

The Tiller Girls appeared in top theatres, but always at the bottom of the bill. The Beverley Sisters also appeared in top theatres, but they were capable of topping the bill. The crucial difference was personality. The coordination seen in both acts required an impressive level of skill, but skill alone would not make a successful variety act. There had to be other elements surrounding it for it to please an audience.

The harder it looked, the louder the applause

While it was almost impossible for speciality acts to reach the top of the bill, it was perfectly possible for them to become well paid and well known. Joan Rhodes, for example, became a popular figure in variety after the Second World War. Her skill was spectacular strength, but it was the way the skill was presented that made the act unique. Young, slender and attractive, Rhodes heightened the unusualness of her strength by presenting herself glamorously: blonde hair, heels, basques, fishnet-stockinged legs.

With an image which flew in the face of the idea that she might be physically strong, she would go onstage and challenge the men in the audience to take her on in tests of strength. Men queued up in front of the stage and an usherette took the first four of them up onto the stage. She would bend a '5/8-inch bar of round bright steel' around her neck, and then ask the men to try to straighten it, which they could never do. Next she would challenge them to bend a six-inch nail, and when they had failed – 'very rarely one might kink it' – she would bend it backwards and forwards until it snapped. After bending a flat steel bar in her teeth, she would challenge the four men to a tug-of-war, holding a stirrup-handled rope in each hand, and asking two of them to pull at each of these. Finally, she would get them to examine a telephone directory, and when they had approved it, she would tear it in half, and sometimes quarters.[40]

The idea of challenging the audience in feats of skill was well established in variety, going back to at least as far as Houdini, and it was certainly a crucial part of what made Rhodes's act entertaining. Getting men up from the audience provided a context for her strength, proving just how difficult her accomplishments were. It was vital that she used men – to emphasize her femininity – and that they should be actual volunteers.

In April 1955, when she appeared at the Palladium in a bill topped by Dickie Valentine, she resisted the theatre management's attempts to subvert this idea: 'they said I couldn't have men up on the stage, and that they'd have to...plant four men. So I said, "No, I can't have that. They've got to volunteer to come up. And anyway, if they're the same men, people will notice that." '[41] Only genuine volunteers offered real authentication. It was important that they should examine the telephone directory, to demonstrate to the rest of the audience that there was no trickery involved, a suggestion that still rankled with Rhodes when I interviewed her in March 2010: 'They all said it was fixed – but it wasn't, I'm sorry.'

Working with volunteers also helped to establish a powerful connection with the audience. The element of challenge focused the idea of the audience sitting in judgement, and the fact that she always completed the challenges meant that they were effectively being invited to reward her with applause. Because the volunteers put themselves forward, there was an extent to which they represented the audience as a whole and were challenging her on behalf of them.

Sometimes they were genuinely set on beating her, and this meant they had to be handled with care. She had gags she could pull out to deal with difficult volunteers. Setting up the tug-of-war, she would instruct them to pull not jerk the rope, and if they did, she would say, 'You're a bit of a jerk', which would neutralize the threat by getting a laugh at the offender's expense. To the more general troublemaker she would say, 'Keep it up and you'll soon be a strong woman'.[42]

Taking on the volunteers in feats of strength could also make things difficult with the rest of the audience, who might want to see them succeed and symbolically triumph over her. A review of a show at the Chiswick Empire in August 1958 reads:

> Patrons are funny! There is dead silence as strong girl Joan Rhodes, using her hands, bends six-inch nails to angles of 90 degrees, but the applause almost lifts the roof when (as at Monday's first house) a husky male, using his feet and hands, succeeds in bending a nail about half a degree.[43]

On the whole, though, as she put it, 'I used to do quite well'.[44] Reading the detailed account of her act in her autobiography, it becomes clear that she had an acute awareness of audience response, and also realized that the things that got the best reactions were not necessarily the ones that demanded the most skill. Bending the nails, for example, was 'the hardest thing I did' but only got 'modest applause'. On the other hand, it was fine if she struggled to tear the telephone directory in two because 'the harder it looked the louder the applause'.[45] When I asked her if she ever made something look harder than it was to get more applause, Rhodes replied, 'I did in the end, but I didn't at the beginning because I didn't realize what was happening. I mean I used to make terrible faces.'[46]

She was not the only speciality act to realize that there was no direct correlation between the difficulty of a stunt and the amount of applause it got, and adjust the performance accordingly. A 1952 article in *The Stage* relates the following anecdote: 'Recently, when watching a juggler, we winced as he dropped a club, but his agent, sitting next to us, grinned. "That's just a trick to make it look more difficult", he whispered. "He drops it every night."'[47]

Kiddology

Chas McDevitt, who worked with many speciality acts, believes that they were all about 'kiddology':

> Well, half the time … like magic, it's not actually happening, you're kidding the audience to think that it's happening. And in the same way as doing a juggling act and that, the technique has to come with practice, but to make it an art, you know, you've got to kid them that it's absolutely fantastic …[48]

Similarly, Peter Prentice acknowledges that the success of El Granadas & Peter was due to more than just their skill:

> To be quite honest, all the rope spinning acts I've seen, and I've seen a lot of them now … [some of them] are brilliant rope-spinners, light years ahead of us, but they can't sell it … I always think we had the best western act in the country…they hadn't just got the polish and the finesse in that field that we had, I felt.

Achieving this polish and finesse meant getting the look of the act right, particularly their props and their satin cowboy costumes:

> My mother and father were great believers in cleanliness. Everything was washed and cleaned, ropes were washed twice a week, costumes were changed three or four times a week, different colours, beautiful diamantés. My mother, before the war, used to collect diamantés, and she brought some stuff from a man called Johnson in Birmingham. It was a big secret, we mustn't tell where we get the diamantés from.[49]

As with Joan Rhodes's telephone directory, part of 'selling' a skill – and making it look 'absolutely fantastic' – was to convince the audience that it was genuine and that nothing was being faked. Ronnie Ronalde's act featured not just his singing but his loud, melodic, bird-like whistling. His mentor, Steffani, realized that 'people did not believe I had no mechanical device in my mouth to whistle, especially my bird-calls, unless they could see my face clearly, so to "light my face" was vital to my act'.[50]

As well as being – or appearing to be – genuine, the skill also had to be conspicuous. Arthur Worsley was still a child when he started working as a ventriloquist in the 1930s, and by the 1950s, he was a big name in variety. Reviews talked of his 'quite phenomenal skill' and described him as 'an uncommonly good ventriloquist'.[51] His act was built on two brilliant ideas. The first was that, as one reviewer put it, 'he reverses the traditional roles of puppet and puppet master, and stands silent and shy while he is bullied'.[52]

Worsley's personality is intriguing in its own right, his face looking out to the audience with the kind of peculiar, endearing blankness of a Stan Laurel. He blinks placidly, looks crestfallen when the puppet shouts at him, and occasionally smiles and smirks with what genuinely looks like crushing shyness. Crucially, he also says almost nothing, leaving the talking to his manically bossy dummy, Charlie Brown.

The second brilliant idea was to build the act on the idea of openly demonstrating the hardest sounds for a ventriloquist to produce. In one routine, the dummy runs through the whole alphabet, emphasizing the difficult letters by stopping and reeling off a few alliterative phrases which use as many of them as possible. This reaches a climax at the letter W, when Worsley makes a rare interjection.

Worsley: And now the hardest letter
Charlie: W. I- is W the hardest letter? [Worsley nods] W? [Worsley nods] I always thought it was B. I always thought that the hardest thing for a ventriloquist to say was 'bread and butter'. You've never heard that done before, have you, 'bread and butter?'.

After rattling out some more B-laden phrases, Charlie turns malignly to Worsley and challenges him:

Say 'a bottle of beer' – without moving your mouth, son. Go on. Say 'a bottle of beer'! Without moving your mouth. SAY IT! [laughter] SAY IT! [laughter] How is it that when I shout, you spit in my face, how does that – ? [extended laughter] Say 'a bottle of beer' without moving your mouth, go on. Say a bottle of beer, a bottle of beer, a bottle of beer, a bottle of beer, a bottle of beer, a bottle of beer, a bottle of beer, a bottle of beer, a bottle of beer, a bottle of beer, a bottle of beer, a bottle of beer!53

By the ninth time the dummy has screeched the notoriously difficult phrase, the audience start to applaud Worsley's skill, and the applause lasts right through to the end of the sentence. The dialogue has been deftly constructed to make Worsley's ventriloquial skill as conspicuous as possible, and by doing so to cue the audience's applause. It also allows for some delicious comedy, playing on the very idea of what ventriloquism is. As the applause dies down, Charlie stares malevolently at Worsley and crows:

You can't do it, can you? [laughter]

Then his tone lightens:

> It never has been done. It's quite impossible – but I can do it, so watch me.

The dummy stares at the audience and its lips stay still as a voice – which is clearly 'Charlie's' and not Worsley's – says the magic words:

> A bottle of beer. [laughter]

Sometimes making skill look fantastic was more about exuberance than conspicuousness. The American harmonica player Larry Adler was a big name in variety from the mid-1930s, a highly skilled and distinctive musician with an instantly recognizable style. A review of a show at the Holborn Empire in August 1937 mentions his 'enthralling' virtuosity and the 'richly assorted music' which issued from his harmonica.[54] However, he was also a showman who had learned to make his musical skill look as flashy as possible by moving his whole body with a kind of insane energy when he played.

He discovered this trick by accident while playing Ravel's *Bolero* at Grauman's Chinese Theatre in Hollywood. Losing his place and worrying that he had got out of time with the orchestra, he covered up his mistakes by waving his arm 'like a crazed semaphore operator', and finishing the piece 'with a flourish and a swoop up the mouth organ'. After such a technical disaster, he was surprised by the audience's reaction: 'I couldn't believe what happened next. A roar of applause, shouts, cheers – the number was a big hit.' The next show, he played the number straight and made no mistakes, but got nothing like the same kind of reaction. The theatre manager told him to 'put back the showmanship', so he put the 'corny *stürm und drang* with the arms' back in, producing just as much enthusiasm: 'the audiences didn't know or care if *Bolero* was played correctly; they were impressed by the way I chopped an invisible tree'.[55]

Footage of his act from the 1937 film *Calling All Stars* shows him in action.[56] Given that the harmonica is a small instrument which can be played with small, inconspicuous movements of the hands, the frenzied animation of Adler's performance is extraordinary. He walks on quite calmly, and taps the side of his harmonica with his hand twice, in time with the cymbal. Suddenly, as he starts playing, everything is moving. His eyes widen and he hitches his eyebrows up as far as they can go. His torso rotates, emphasizing the twists and turns of the tune.

His hands are as long-fingered and articulate as Danny Kaye's, making big, precise movements as if he were moulding the music with them out of the air around him. Sometimes the left hand goes off on its own, as he takes it right away from the instrument and waves it in time. The climax of the song is clearly signalled as he bends his torso right back, his left elbow stuck out at right angles from his body, hand curved backwards, fingers splayed, eyes rolling back in his skull. A sustained note ends sharply, and he snaps forward into a shallow bow. It is an unmistakable invitation to applaud.

Beauty no less than thrills

One of the most successful speciality acts in the history of variety was the Ganjou Brothers & Juanita. (See Illustration 8.2.) The brothers were born in Poland, but the act started in American vaudeville when Bob Ganjou teamed up with Juanita Richards. By the time it came to England in 1933, brothers George and Serge had joined the act, and in 1934, Richards was replaced by Joy Marlowe, who became 'Juanita' until the act disbanded in around 1956.[57]

Figure 8.2 The programme for a revue called *Skylights* at the Hackney Empire in 1946 includes a photo of one of its star acts, the Ganjou Brothers & Juanita.

Their success was based on their ability to make an impact with audiences. Towards the end of his life, Serge Ganjou spoke of the 'gasps and the cheers from the audiences as we performed all those feats'.[58] Reviewers talk about audiences giving them 'one of those enthusiastic greetings that tells emphatically of success', or even 'holding up the show with applause'.[59] They played the Royal Variety Performance as early as 1933, were reputedly one of the highest paid acts in variety, and were important enough to present their own road show, *Rise and Shine*, in 1941.[60]

What they presented was an adagio act, a kind of acrobatic dance made up of a series of poses, balances, throws and catches. In this respect, it was nothing special. There were any number of acts based on what the *Manchester Guardian* called 'the old music hall game of throwing the girl about'.[61] There were adagio duos like the Diamondos or Gaston & Andree, although these tended to involve posing and balancing more than throwing girls around.[62] Much closer to the Ganjous were the Dehl Trio and the Bega Four, both of which performed a very similar sequence of stunts.[63]

Then there were the apache dancers, like Alexis & Dorrano or Karina & Company, who presented similarly dexterous throw-and-catch acrobatics, but in the dramatic setting of a sleazy bar fight with stylized misogynistic violence.[64] This was also the setting adopted by the Dior Dancers, the adagio troupe trained by Bob Ganjou and launched in 1957, adopting much of the choreography and many of the feats from their mentor's famous act.[65] Given that the basic moves which the Ganjous showed off in their act were not particularly unusual, what was it that made them stand out from other similar acts and enjoy such conspicuous success?

To start with, the sheer level of the skill was probably the highest. As a 1943 review in *The Stage* put it, 'Rarely has a young woman been thrown so far and so daringly as in this act, which achieves beauty no less than thrills.'[66] The same year, footage of their most famous routine, 'A Romance in Porcelain', was included in the film *Variety Jubilee*,[67] and the throws it shows are indeed both daring and thrilling.

In one move, Juanita dangles between two of the brothers, one holding her hands and one her feet, her body curved belly-down to form a U-shape. Swinging her back, they then launch her across the stage, sending her spinning in an arc that takes her up at least 12 feet above the stage and at least as far across it, into the arms of the third brother. Later in the routine, a similar move sends her across the stage, where a brother catches her by her right leg, holding her above his head in a neat, balletic position, and as he does so takes at least five steps backwards to pick up the momentum of the throw. By doing so, she seems to have flown across almost the entire width of the proscenium.

Some of the thrills come from sheer danger – the feeling that serious injury is not much more than a hair's breadth away. Juanita is standing upright when two of the brothers throw her up through a 180-degree curve, and when the third brothers catches her by the legs she is practically upside down, her arms crossed across her chest, her head perilously close to the floor. As *The Stage* suggested, the throws are indeed longer and more spectacular than those seen in similar acts.

That review was also right in asserting that the Ganjous achieved 'beauty no less than thrills'. The skills were vital, but so was the way they were presented. As Serge Ganjou explained, 'We were a sort of refined circus act. We were acrobats and then again we were dancers. It was all supposed to be very "tasteful" ... People took us terribly seriously.'[68] In 1937, Beswick Goodgame wrote in *The Era* that the act 'combines so effectively the thrill of modern adagio dancing with the old-world charm of Dresden china'.[69] This was a reference to the staging of the act, which was expensively distinctive. At the centre of the stage was a gigantic ornate mantelpiece clock, lavishly decorated with swirls and curlicues, and the act began with Juanita daintily draped down the swinging pendulum.

The costumes were just as unusual. Adagio and apache dancers tended to perform in very revealing costumes, which emphasized the strength and sexuality of young, fit bodies. Gaston & Andree, for example, wore trunks and a bikini respectively, and the Diamondos wore much the same but also had their entire bodies covered with dark body paint speckled with glittering sparkles. By contrast, the Ganjou Brothers dressed in Georgian costumes – powdered wigs, tunics, tights, white blouses with billowing bishop sleeves – which suggested they were ornamental figures from the giant clock. While Juanita's legs were very much on show, her frilled leotard and spangled headdress was modest compared with the bikinis that similar dancers tended to opt for.[70]

All of this gave the feeling of refinement they were aiming at, which was also emphasized by the choice of music. Rather than using something fast-paced or dramatic, they performed the routine filmed for *Variety Jubilee* to the graceful waltz rhythms of 'The Blue Danube'. The music had to be played just right, and this was so important that they took their own musical director – George's wife Adele Ganjou – on tour with them, to conduct the pit orchestra while they performed the act.[71] At the end, she would take her applause just as they would.

If the thrills were provided by the stunts, the beauty was achieved by the finesse with which they performed them. Reviewers praised their 'customary grace' and talked about Juanita sailing 'through space with the ease of a bird'.[72] The footage shows movements which are as detailed as they are fluid. Heads are angled, feet are pointed and arms are outstretched to create the maximum possible impact for each move. There are moments of precise coordination, when all three brothers adopt the same pose or take the same, controlled step in near-perfect unison. The rhythms of the movement always match those of the music, and every major stunt is timed to coincide exactly with the end of a significant phrase in the tune. Serge recalled, 'We were the first act to do adagio work like a ballet, where every movement was done to music.'[73]

In spite of Teddie Beverley's view that speciality acts were 'just visual', the Ganjous' performance clearly shows that they were aware of having to forge a strong rapport with the audience. Juanita is the focus of this, spending much of the routine looking straight out at the audience, her face radiating a charming, beaming smile even as she is manhandled, flung about, and held high over the brothers' heads. More importantly, the moves are structured to invite the audience to respond. At the end of most of the major stunts, the music pauses for a beat, and all four performers strike a still pose, arms stretched upwards or outwards, the gesture suggesting that the feat is being offered up for the audience's approval.

The climax of the act is even more pointed. They strike three dramatic poses, outwards, inwards and outwards again. First, Juanita is held aloft, arms stretched upwards, two of the brothers stretching their arms outwards. Second, Juanita sits on the centre brother's knee, face turned to stare into his eyes, while the brothers on either side hold her outstretched hands. Third, the same pose but with all arms stretched outwards and all faces turned to the audience and smiling. These poses are struck sharply and precisely, and perfectly timed to three notes from the orchestra, the first two staccato, the third extended until the curtain has swirled down in front of them. The moment is structured like a classic three-part joke, in which the third item in a list deviates from the first two, creating a sense of completion.[74] The audience is left in no doubt that this is the end of the act and that they are being cued to generously applaud the extraordinary display they have just witnessed.

All of this suggests that the Ganjou Brothers and Juanita owed their success not just to the superiority of their skill, but also to the superior way they framed it. To avoid being at the bottom of the variety hierarchy and having to fill the worst positions on the bill, speciality acts had to frame their skills properly, presenting them to the audience in such a way as to make them as conspicuously thrilling and entertaining as possible. It is the precarious tilt of Gintaro's tower of bricks that gets an audible 'oo' from the audience, not simply the fact he can balance it. It is the way Sereno & June sit up to hold their arms out smile at the audience that signals that they have successfully completed their epic head-to-head balance and would now like to be rewarded with some applause. It is the kimonos, the cod-oriental music and the giant screen emblazoned with a Chinese dragon that gives the Five Lai Founs' act its tone of exotic wonder.

Framing turned the skills on display into what Marinetti called 'elements of astonishment', but it also served another important function: to make an act distinctive. The distinctiveness of the Ganjous undoubtedly contributed to their success. As Serge Ganjou put it, 'we were different. You couldn't exactly put us in a slot.'[75] Being different was desirable because after personality, rapport and skill, novelty was the fourth great element of variety performance.

9

Novelty

The constant quest

According to a review of a show at the Manchester Hippodrome in January 1906, 'Novelty is the constant quest of the present-day manager of the variety theatre.'[1] Over 40 years later, in *The Stage Year Book 1949*, W. J. Bishop wrote that, 'Novelty seems to be one of the big demands for variety today.'[2] The word crops up in reviews of variety theatre almost as frequently as 'personality'.

'Novelty' suggests newness, freshness, innovation, and theatre managers were 'constantly conducting an international search' for these qualities.[3] This was partly because the format of variety tended to be rigid and standardized. Morris Aza's parents were important variety agents and would sometimes take him to the theatres with them. Even as a child he found himself thinking, 'I don't know what they mean by variety. Every show's exactly the same.' Cissie Williams 'had this format for every theatre in the country' and 'every week it was the same'.[4] According to Billy Marsh, who managed Bernard Delfont's variety department, it was vital 'to offer variety which is variety in the fullest sense of the word'. This meant 'offering the public a novelty and a new name' so as to 'attract audiences who seldom visit music halls and even draw in entirely new patrons'.[5]

Novelty was partly about maintaining the turnover of acts, finding fresh new faces to shovel onto the stage, but it was also about more than that. The *Oxford English Dictionary*'s various definitions of 'novelty' use adjectives such as 'unusual', 'unfamiliar' and 'original'. More pejoratively, the *OED* also uses words like 'useless' and 'trivial', and defines one meaning of novelty as 'a style of music or entertainment designed to have a frivolous or nonsensical appeal'. In variety, there was no shame in an act being useless, trivial, frivolous or nonsensical as long as it had appeal, and it boasted an extraordinary array of acts that fitted this description. A few examples will give an idea of the range of peculiarities on offer.

The legendary Henri Vadden's act climaxed with a heavy wooden cartwheel clanging down onto his head, cleverly caught on his spiked helmet. The 'protean actor' Owen McGiverney performed a scene from *Oliver Twist*, playing all the characters himself thanks to a series of lightning-fast costume changes. Charles 'Think a Drink' Hoffman poured water into apparently empty vessels to produce any drink an audience member requested. Professor Sparks demonstrated how his wife Thelmina could produce electricity from her body by attaching light bulbs to her, and persuaded audience member to try to bath a metal baby which gave them electric shocks. The Betty Hobbs Globe Girls walked about in unison atop giant white balls.[6]

Larry Adler attributed his success in variety to the fact that, 'In 1931 the mouth-organ was a novelty, good for cowboy tunes or in comedy acts but nobody had tried to play music *qua* music on it; I tried. It got results.'[7] Taking a novel instrument seriously was a novelty in itself and thus made a great act. Another approach was to have lots of people playing the same novelty instrument. Both Borrah Minevitch & his Harmonica Rascals and the Morton Fraser Harmonica Gang had multiple mouth organists playing up-tempo jazz numbers, and both featured midget musicians who provided a focus for physical comedy. The small musician in Minevitch's group was Johnny Puleo, an extremely gifted visual comedian with an extraordinarily expressive face, who went on to lead his own troupe of Harmonica Rascals. A less slapstick approach was taken by Troise & his Mandoliers, who filled the stage with men playing mandolins of various sizes including an enormous bass one, and then repeated the same format with banjos with his Banjoliers.

America's 'Monoped' dancer

The quest for novelty meant that physical peculiarity could be a positive advantage for variety acts. Carlton the Human Hairpin played on his excessive skinniness, adopting the bill matter 'The Thinnest Conjuror Extant'.[8] At the other end of the scale were obese performers such as the relentlessly cheery singer and banjulele player 'Two Ton' Tessie O'Shea, and the 'outsize girls' who made up the dance troupe Dawn White & her Glamazons, described as 'Robust, vigorous and romantic'.[9]

The American act Lowe, Hite & Stanley, which played at the Palladium in the late 1930s, was built on an extraordinary mismatch of bodies. Hite was well over 7 feet tall, Lowe was average-sized, and Stanley was tiny, less than half of Hite's height. They dressed alike in dinner suits and Canadian Mountie hats, and the physical coordination emphasized the difference in heights. While keeping the same small distance apart, the level of their heads formed a straight line at a remarkably steep angle – a peculiar visual novelty. There was also comedy to be had from the height difference, much of it centred on Stanley, who kept falling out of step or simply falling over. At one point, he accidentally bumps into Hite, his head around the level of the bigger man's crotch. Hite swipes him around the face and Stanley retaliates by biting his leg.[10]

One of the most successful acts to make use of physical peculiarity was Peg Leg Bates, the African-American tap-dancer who worked in British variety theatres through much of the 1930s and continued to appear in them into the early 1950s. Bates once said, 'Well, I'm into rhythm and I'm into novelty ... I'm into doing things that it looks almost impossible to do'.[11] The novelty in the act was that – as his stage name suggests – he only had one leg, the other being a wooden leg with a tip made of rubber and leather to allow him to tap with it. Surprisingly, Clayton Bates was not a regular two-legged tap-dancer who lost a leg and decided to continue – he had lost the bottom half of his left leg in his childhood and only took up tap-dancing afterwards.

The act was not played for laughs but for amazement. Bates dressed stylishly, rather than clownishly, and his tap technique was uniquely impressive. His right foot created fast, complex tap rhythms all by itself, while the wooden leg on the left was used more sparingly, underpinning the beats with more occasional, deeper-toned beats. Effectively, the wooden leg was the bass drum, and the right foot was the snare. To add to the excitement, Bates would sometimes balance and hop on the wooden leg. One stunt saw him quickly leaping from one leg to the other, his upper torso leaning forward and his free leg stuck straight out behind so that he was almost parallel with the floor, perfectly in time with the music.[12]

Footage from the *Ed Sullivan Show* demonstrates that he was an expert at cuing the audience to applaud, using a series of gestures, tempo shifts and finger clicks. In one particularly obvious cue, after punctuating the rhythm of his feet with handclaps, he stops dancing, stands straight, and his rhythmic claps change to simple applause.

He is not so much applauding himself as challenging the audience to applaud him. His face is stern and he actively moves his gaze around the audience as if checking they are all joining in the applause in fair recompense for the amazing stunts he has been treating them to.[13]

While the name Peg Leg Bates might sound disrespectful, there is no doubt that this extraordinary dancer's disability was the novelty that made him stand out from other dancers for whom it was near impossible to climb up the bill and gain individual recognition. In the mid-twentieth century, attitudes towards the disabled were callous by today's standards, and to an extent this was reflected in variety. In 1939, St John Ervine saw a show at an unnamed London variety theatre and wrote about it for *The Observer*, noting the way the comedians mocked 'the frail and the infirm, the mutilated and the deformed'.[14]

On the other hand, Bates's success shows that variety audiences could also see disability much more positively, readily accepting him as a star like any other. One reviewer described the 'extraordinary energy and spirit' of 'America's "Monoped" dancer', while a review of a show at the Manchester Hippodrome in 1939 argued that, 'The success of Peg-Leg Bates depends to some extent on the natural sympathy felt for a man doing his work against a considerable obstacle – in fact, for a tap-dancer, the loss of a leg would seem to be an insuperable obstacle – and succeeding without needing any sympathy'.[15]

This was a symptom of a wider egalitarianism in variety. While women, gay people, Jews and the disabled could be the butt of fairly frequent jokes, occasionally rather savage ones, these same groups could find escape from the prejudice of everyday life on the variety stage, and were as capable of winning applause as any other act. Black performers such as Bates were applauded for their talents rather than being ridiculed for their race. Indeed, black singers such as Turner Layton and Hutch were attractive, urbane and sophisticated, aspirational figures to be looked up to and admired.

It seems that this egalitarian spirit, decades ahead of its time, also extended to the backstage world, where the only hierarchy that mattered was the position on the bill and the size of the lettering on the poster. As Roy Hudd puts it, 'Performers always accepted anybody who was good at the job. That's what performers accepted, and the powers-that-be … only respected people who put bums on the seats.'[16] There are plenty of examples to support this. Beryl Reid went out with a black musician from the Norman Thomas Trio while working as a variety comic. She later wrote: 'I didn't see why this was wrong, but everybody in the world but me seemed to think it was, because he was black and I was white, and I hadn't learnt to

distinguish between the two colours.'[17] Similarly, Max Wall wrote
that 'homosexual people have always been a part and parcel of our
gorgeous world of rogues and vagabonds and always will be'.[18] He
thought of black performers as his 'brothers' (while carefully adding
that sisters are also included) and argued that, 'Colour prejudice
within the confines of the entertainment industry has usually been
conspicuous by its absence.'[19]

Back to the asylum

The essential novelty of Peg Leg Bates was the improbable contrast
between his skill and his physique, and physical peculiarity was often
made significant because of such contrasts. Teddy Brown's enormous girth, for example, contrasted pleasingly with the nature of
the instrument he played, as a *Times* reviewer pointed out in 1939:
'Unbounded, too, but in a Falstaffian sense, is Mr Teddy Brown,
whose mountainous person sets in sharp relief the mouse-like delicacy
of his touch upon that most horrid of instruments, the xylophone.'[20]
(See Illustration 9.1.)

Similarly, the novelty of Joan Rhodes's act was that her feats of
strength contrasted so beautifully with her glamour and exaggerated
femininity. As a review of a show at the Finsbury Park Empire in
July 1951 put it, 'Joan Rhodes upsets the popular conception of the
stronger sex by breaking six-inch nails with her fingers and tearing
telephone directories into four; but she pleasantly keeps her femi-
nineness.'[21] Many of the elements she included were designed to
heighten this contrast, from her use of male audience volunteers
to challenge her to the music she chose to come on to: 'Sweet and
Lovely'. As she explained:

> They wanted to do the toreador's thing, and I said, 'No, no – I want people
> to think I'm going to strip'. And I used to go on with that sort of outfit, or I
> had a big fan ... and [I would] go on as if I was going to do a fan dance.[22]

She also played the contrast between strength and glamour for laughs,
as in the song she wrote for herself, which she vampishly crooned, her
voice sexily husky:

> To look at me it's hard to see I live my life without love –
> The romance ends when the balcony bends; I'm an iron girl in a velvet
> glove.
> I meet a man, I shake his hand and my impression lingers –
> He screams with pain – I've done it again – look! No fingers![23]

Figure 9.1 A signed photograph of Teddy Brown, the World's 'Greatest' Xylophonist.

The contrasts which made for a great novelty act had the qualities of a joke, even when they were not comic. The idea of a one-legged tap-dancer sounds like gag, even though Peg Leg Bates's act was about breathtaking skill rather than comedy. One of the major theories of comedy states that incongruity lies at the heart of every joke, and in his book *The Act of Creation*, Arthur Koestler presents a detailed explanation of how this works. He argues that we perceive the world through various 'frames of reference', 'associative contexts' or 'universes of discourse'. When two frames of reference which are 'self-consistent but mutually incompatible' come together, perhaps through the double meaning of a word which can apply to both frames, a joke occurs. The term he uses to describe this is 'bisociation'.[24] Novelty works in much the same way. Joan Rhodes's act, for example, bisociated the frame of feminine glamour ('velvet glove') with the frame of extraordinary physical strength ('iron girl').

Novelty and comedy were closely connected, and many acts included novel elements framed with a kind of quirky, offbeat humour. In some cases, this involved a contrast between material and delivery. Reginald Gardiner was a straight actor who also appeared in major variety theatres like the Palladium and the Alhambra in the early 1930s, with an act based on impersonating train noises. He later made a record of the routine, which quickly became a children's favourite.[25] The charm of his performance was based on the contrast between the silliness of what he was doing and the seriousness with which he presented it. His RP accent, with excellent diction and a rather formal use of grammar and vocabulary, and his serious, aloof manner belied the fact that he was a grown man standing onstage making train noises:

> Well now we've unleashed this livid beast, we find it's still equally furious and it has a colossal argument with the rails it's running on. Like this – *buddle-a-der, giddle-a-dair, diddle-i-dee, diddle-i-der, giddle-a-der, diddle-a-dair, biddle-a-der, giddle-a-der* – and that goes on the entire journey.

At the end of the routine, dignified as ever, he announces:

> Well folks, that's all – back to the asylum.[26]

The magician Jasper Maskelyne used the opposite kind of contrast, presenting serious content with an air of silliness. In one routine he takes ten razor blades from a stand, places them on his tongue one by one, and apparently swallows them. He then swallows a length of cotton and washes it down with a mouthful of water. Finally, he leans his torso right back – turning sideways on to the audience – and pulls out the cotton revealing that the razor blades are now attached to it like washing on a line. This effect could easily be played for thrills, involving as it does that classic magical ingredient of apparently deadly peril. The idea of swallowing razor blades is horrific, and he demonstrates the danger by using one of the blades to cut a piece of card to shreds.

However, Maskelyne chooses to play the tricks for laughs. Rather than performing with the air of a man who risks slicing up the lining of his throat, he adopts a slightly flippant manner, somewhere between a jovial uncle and an upper-class twit. He swallows the razor blades with amused nonchalance, throwing in comments like, 'They're awfully nice when they're fresh, you know', or 'Don't you make me laugh, I shall cut me tonsils out'.[27] While in many ways he presents the classic image of the magician, dapper in his dinner suit and neatly slicked back hair, the silly way in which he presents the trick contrasts nicely with its grisly content, creating a pleasing air of novelty.

In some cases, the contrast between material and content was subtle, nuanced and complex, swapping one set of audience responses for another. The juggler Albert Rebla (usually known simply as 'Rebla') frequently appeared in variety in the 1920s and 1930s with an act in which, as one reviewer put it, 'skill is secondary to humour'.[28] His juggling skills were highly competent if not extraordinary,[29] and instead of presenting them for audience approval, with a series of climaxes and cues for applause, he played them purely for laughs, with what was described as 'a fascinating air of nonchalance'.[30]

Footage from 1935 shows him juggling three balls, sending them around fast in a tight circle right in front of his face. He adopts an expression of amazement – mouth tense, eyebrows raised, wide eyes following the path of the balls – but he does it in a mockingly half-hearted way, as if sending up the idea that what he does is amazing. He then straightens his arms, dropping his hands to waist level, his shoulders hunched and his wrists loose, as if he is finding the whole process tedious. His general manner, with hangdog face and loose, casual movement, suggests the kind of utter boredom of someone trapped in poorly paid casual labour, treating juggling as if it were stacking shelves, something that simply has to be got through.[31]

He even sends up the normal conventions of engaging with an audience. In one gag, after some business with a rubber ball, a top hat and a cane, he pops the ball under the hat and plops it onto his head, tucks the cane between his calves, and lazily raises his hands up, immediately letting them flop down again.[32] It is a hilariously cynical parody of the cue for applause. Even more daringly, at the end of the act, instead of gratefully accepting the audience's applause with a bow or upstretched arms, he would lazily turn away from them and wander off, dismissively flinging an arm up as if to say, 'To hell with the lot of it'.[33]

Cod acts

Rebla worked by presenting competent skill as if it was beneath his contempt, but another comically novel approach was to present apparent incompetence. Slim Rhyder was, as the name suggests, a comedy trick cyclist with a conspicuously skinny physique. Billed as 'The Elongated Chump', his appearance was thoroughly clownish: spats; baggy trousers which didn't quite reach down to his ankles; scruffy frock coat; toothbrush moustache; and a grey Cambridge bowler hat jammed onto his head. Throughout the act, he takes off more and more of his costume, ending up in a low-cut leotard, tights and large black underpants, as if to allow the audience to enjoy his emaciated figure to the best effect. The actual material of the act is a series of stunts in which he rides, messes about on, and falls off a series of scooters and bicycles of various sizes.

At one point, a 4-foot unicycle is brought on for him to ride. Holding the saddle in his hand, he stretches out his left leg, attempting and failing to get it up onto the pedal. Trying this a few times takes him over to the proscenium, which he uses to steady himself enough to actually mount the unicycle. Having done so, he goes to ride out onto the stage, but then thinks better of it and grabs the edge of the proscenium again for safety. Then he has another go, wobbling out across the stage in fits and starts, holding out his arms for the safety of the other side of the proscenium. When he reaches it, he gratefully grabs it and holds on tight, gurning at the audience to show his relief. The gag of pretending not to be able to ride a unicycle seems surprisingly modern – it is often used by street performers today – but Rhyder was doing it as early as 1943, when he appeared in the film *Variety Jubilee*.[34]

Such comic feigned incompetence was at the heart of what was known in variety as the 'cod acts', defined by Valantyne Napier as, 'A pretence or hoax act. E.g. A Cod Magic Act pretends to disclose the way the tricks are done.'[35] Cod acts were plentiful in variety. Tommy Cooper was a cod magician whose act outlived the variety era and became well known on television. Inspired by a bad ventriloquist he had booked for his road show, Sandy Powell developed a classic bad vent act in the guise of a decrepit Chelsea Pensioner entirely incapable of speaking without moving his lips or even keeping his dummy in one piece.[36] Gaston Palmer was a juggler whose cod masterpiece was a stunt in which he would attempt to get a number of spoons to land in a number of glasses. His repeated, increasingly desperate failure to do so would get laughs as well as building up expectation, and he would stretch the process out as long as he could. According to one source, at a show at the Holborn Empire in 1940, it took him an extraordinary 55 attempts before he successfully got 'All ze spoons in all ze glasses'.[37]

An exclamation from the audience

Another connection between novelty and comedy was the fact that, like a joke, a novel element could be brought to a head in a definite conclusion which invited audience response. Some acts only revealed the full extent of their novelty right at the end, creating a kind of punchline which invited amazement more than laughter. Valantyne Napier, for example, presented a human spider act. Clad in tight black costume which covered her entire head, she contorted herself into a flattened, spider-like pose and climbed onto a giant web at the back of the stage. However, it was only at the very end of this ornately creepy act that she revealed the full extent of its novelty: 'I came through the tabs to take my "call" and as I removed the hood of my costume there was always an exclamation from the audience as my long blonde hair fell down and they realized that the "spider" was a girl.'[38]

Bobbie Kimber's ventriloquist act ended with the opposite kind of gender surprise. Kimber's novelty was that as well as making dummies appear to talk, he did so while impersonating a woman. Offstage, he made no secret of his actual gender. In an article he wrote for *The Stage* in 1946 he openly admitted that he was a 'male presenting a "vent" act in the guise of a female impersonator'.[39] However, in the early part of his career he did not reveal to the audience that he was actually a man. A review of a show at the Chelsea Place in July 1947 suggests, 'There must be many in the audience who blissfully imagine they are watching a charming lady ventriloquist.'[40] A preview of the Royal Variety Show later that year put it even more strongly: 'Many people, including some of our leading critics, have been misled by his female impersonation.'[41] Indeed, it is possible to find reviews in which the critic has clearly been misled, talking of 'her technical ability and her gifts of informing her dummies with personalities as well as voices'.[42]

Things changed in December 1952, when the *Daily Mirror* did a front-page exposé after Kimber had appeared on the BBC's *Music-Hall*. It explained that 'Britain's TV audience' had been 'hoaxed', and used upper-case to heighten the shock as it revealed that,

'BOBBIE KIMBER IS A THIRTY-FOUR-YEAR-OLD MAN — MARRIED WITH A FOUR-
YEAR-OLD DAUGHTER'. Asked why he appeared as a woman, Kimber
replied, 'Just to be different. There aren't many women ventriloquists. I thought it would be a novelty.'[43] His secret revealed,
Kimber now had an even bigger novelty on his hands: even rarer
than a female ventriloquist, he could now play on being a cross-
dressing one.

Brian O'Gorman – son of Joe from the double act Dave and Joe
O'Gorman – has recalled seeing Kimber at around this time at the
Met, Edgware Road: 'The act was a clever response to the need of
variety comedians to present well-tried ideas in a novel way, putting a
new frame around old pictures. And he certainly succeeded, for when
he removed his wig at his curtain call, this onlooker at least, was surprised to see a man's head.'[44]

A less surprising but no less extraordinary curtain call reveal happened at the end of the Act Superb. This was a series of *tableaux viv-
ants* presented by a man, a woman, two dogs and a horse, all painted
white so as to look like statues. The curtains would swish apart to
reveal the performers striking a perfectly still pose, while a large
card was held up bearing the title of the scene in glittering letters.
After ten or 15 seconds, the curtains would close again, before opening to reveal the next static scene. At the end of the act, as the audience applaud, the performers suddenly break the pose. The man and
woman turn to the audience and throw up their hands to acknowledge
the applause, and the animals suddenly spring to life, moving about
naturally instead of standing stock still.

In itself, this cannot have been too much of a surprise. The *tab-
leau vivant* was an established genre, so the audience must have been
aware that the whole point of the act was that they were watching living beings pretending to be statues rather than actual statues. Having
said this, there might have been some novelty in the fact that the
animals as well as the humans were actually alive, given what was
demanded of them. In the scene 'The Rose of No-Man's Land', for
example, the horse had to bow its front half right down, kneeling on
its front legs and standing on its back ones. What is really extraordinary is the way in which the horse joins in the curtain calls, in a
bizarre twist on the normal conventions for acknowledging audience
response. As the curtains part again for the performers to take their
continuing applause, the horse bows its head in acknowledgement,
and even after the tabs closed, it sticks its head through them and
takes its final call by continuing to bow.[45]

A charm of manner

Like skill, novelty had to be framed and presented so as to win the maximum possible response from the audience. By itself, it had little value. For example, during a rather gruelling week at the Coventry Empire, Peter Sellers decided to abandon his usual act to try something different: he simply played the audience an EP of Christmas carols by the Wally Stott Orchestra, sitting onstage and humming along as the record played. After the first side, he announced, 'I knew you'd like it ... So let's hear the other side, shall we?'[46] This was certainly a novelty, but not an amusing one. As Harry Secombe put it, after the second half of the record had played through, 'This house was not very pleased'.[47]

A great novelty act was cleverly constructed so as to wring the maximum amount of humour and amazement from the basic incongruity on which it was built. Stanelli's act with his Hornchestra provides a good example of this. Stanelli was a skilled musician, who had trained at the Royal Academy of music, and he made his name in variety with a series of humorous double acts in which he played the violin.[48] In the 1930s, he introduced a new instrument of his own making which, as he explained in the act, consisted of 'a lot of motor horns – both electric ones, and bulb horns'.[49] They were arranged on a large frame, and because each horn had its own pitch, he could play tunes on them.

In 1934, a reviewer wrote, 'His act bristles with novel ideas, exploited with a charm of manner which is an asset to his work.'[50] This clearly suggests that Stanelli's success was built not just on the novelty itself, but also on the charming way he framed it. A studio recording of the act made two years later shows this to be the case. The appeal starts with Stanelli's engaging persona. He is well spoken and reasonably formal, but there is a raffish quality there, a kind of amused offhandedness. The act is stuffed with gags, starting at the beginning as he announces, 'And I would like to mention that I have been, er, playing this – instrument, oo, for the last decade or so, in fact – I've nearly got decayed playing it.' It seems like a weak gag, but it is actually a metajoke, playing on its own weakness. He emphasizes this by laughing exaggeratedly, breaking off suddenly – 'HA HA HA, uh!' – then apologizing – 'Oh I beg your pardon, so sorry'.

The actual business with the Hornchestra starts with a demonstration of how it works, which is an excuse for a series of sound gags. A blaring bulb horn is a cue for a fart joke ('Oh. I beg your pardon. I know I shouldn't have eaten that cucumber. Never does agree with me.'), while a particularly squeaky one is announced in a gently homophobic way as 'the Pansyphone'. Having thoroughly introduced his novelty, Stanelli is able to perform some more-developed musical gags. He plays a jaunty march to imitate a boy scouts' band, then shows the same band 'eighty seven and a half years later' by playing the same tune at a much deeper pitch and at a much slower, more knackered-sounding pace. He plays a snatch of Schubert's *Serenade*, his ridiculous instrument rendering it grotesquely comic. Finally, he demonstrates his skill, playing fast, flashy tunes on it such as 'Post Horn Gallop' and that favourite of variety big bands, 'Tiger Rag'.[51]

The Hornchestra is a striking, original novelty, but it is the careful step-by-step construction of the act that makes it so successful. Stanelli wrings the amusement out of his basic idea, using it as the excuse for a rich array of varied gags, and finishing by showing genuine – if ridiculous – musical talent, while presenting the whole thing with a distinctive personality.

An immense pale dignity

Probably the best example of how a carefully framed novelty could reap rich rewards is Wilson, Keppel & Betty. This troupe of eccentric sand-dancers was one of the most iconic acts in variety, and lives on today in the public imagination, still regularly cropping up as a reference in newspapers and inspiring any number of tribute acts, like the Egyptian-themed television advert for Go Compare in 2010.[52]

Englishman Jack Wilson and Irishman Joe Keppel were working in America when they started the act with Betty Knox in 1928, making their British debut at the Palladium in May 1932. They continued to work regularly in variety theatres for as long as they were there, and did not retire until 1962, during a summer season with Harry Secombe at Great Yarmouth.[53] If the sheer longevity of their career is an indication of the kind of success they enjoyed, so is the fact that they were invited to appear in the Royal Variety Performance three times, in 1933, 1945 and 1947.[54]

The act is built around a series of novelties. First there is the tongue-in-cheek Ancient Egyptian setting. Their painted backdrop shows sand dunes, palm trees, two ordinary pyramids and a third with a Sphinx's head improbably placed on top. Betty tends to dress like a belly dancer, perhaps wearing veils or a spangly headdress and bikini. Wilson and Keppel are cartoonish desert-dwellers in fezzes and long white robes or striped head-cloths and ludicrously short tunics.

Second, there is the sand-dancing. As the curtains part, Wilson and Keppel are revealed eccentrically shuffling across the stage, one of them pouring sand onto the stage from a brass tin. Then they shuffle back across the stage, one behind the other, striking a stereotypical Ancient Egyptian pose, right hand on hip with elbow sticking out behind, left arm crooked forward in a V-shape, hand flat, palm upwards. As they do so, the movement of their feet over the spilled sand makes a rhythmic, shuffling beat which perfectly coordinates with the up-tempo ersatz Middle Eastern music provided by the orchestra.[55]

Then there is the bizarreness of their appearance. There is a stark contrast between the exotically glamorous, sexually attractive Betty, and the grotesque Wilson and Keppel, who one critic described as 'one theme with variations'.[56] Both share the same stringy physique and emaciated, hollow-cheeked, beak-nosed faces, and their likeness is exaggerated by the matching black moustaches painted onto their faces.

The long-lived appeal of the act lay in the way these novelties were woven together, shaped and framed for maximum audience appeal. There was variety within their basic idea, because they had a number of routines they could pull out. There was a comic snake-charming bit with pipe and bongos and a ridiculous snake puppet which phallically extended its long tongue out towards Betty as she divested herself of her veils.[57] There was a manic, flapper-influenced routine with a staircase.[58] The different members of the act could appear in different routines, with (as *The Stage* put it), Wilson and Keppel 'causing great laughter with their comical appearances and clever dancing skits, and Betty showing great ability in more formal types of dancing'.[59]

The act both exploited and parodied sexual titillation. In one of Betty's solo routines, she flounces provocatively across the stage in a long, flowing black skirt and a black bra, the dirty glissando blasting out from the trombone leaving the audience in no doubt as to how she is appealing to them.[60] Elsewhere in the act, Betty's sexiness is sent up by the way that Wilson and Keppel are 'obviously at great pains to restrain unmusical desires'.[61] Even more preposterously, they would present themselves as objects of desire, lifting up one side of their tunics to reveal their scrawny upper thighs, their faces angled upwards in a hangdog, moustachioed version of coquettishness. Having showed first one leg, then the other, one of them raises his eyebrows suggestively.[62]

A 1959 article in the *Manchester Guardian* identifies what was probably the fundamental essence of their appeal: 'an immense pale dignity sustained in rather trying circumstances by two typically frail human beings of less than comely aspect'.[63] Wilson and Keppel look grotesquely goofy, and their choreography is equally silly. In one move, one of them faces the audience, hands placed under his chin, elbows horizontally out to the sides, hopping rightwards on his left leg while jerking his right knee upwards in time to the music. Meanwhile, the other bends over to grab his partner's right thigh and help its rhythmic jerking while hopping backwards himself. In another move, one stands far too close behind the other as they synchronies a fast two-footed shuffle across the stage.[64]

What makes such moves all the funnier is the seriousness and discipline with which they are carried out. Through all the silliness, their faces remain dolefully deadpan, leavened only by the moments when their eyes widen into a goggling stare. While their movements are not as mechanically identical as those of the Tiller Girls, they are well coordinated, and the rhythms of their shuffling are tightly in time. The sense of precision extended offstage, as they took the staging of the act very seriously. For example, they claimed to be particular about getting hold of the right sand to dance on, preferring Bedfordshire river sand because 'It is gritty but not too large, and will withstand dancing without dissolving too quickly into dust.'[65] As with Reginald Gardiner, the humour grew from seeing something ridiculous taken seriously.

A sandy cul-de-sac

Wilson, Keppel & Betty represent an essential contradiction in variety performance: they were a novelty act that became extremely familiar. In 1959, after playing British variety theatres for 27 years, they estimated they had done their act 15,000 times. It was important for Betty to remain young and attractive, so she had to be replaced by a new one every few years. The act lasted long enough to get through eight different Bettys. Asked whether he wearied of performing essentially the same act for so long, Joe Keppel replied simply, 'It's work, you know'.[66] By the late 1940s, reviewers started to fondly refer to unchanging familiarity of their routines. The act had 'long lost its novelty but not its fascination', it was 'a sandy cul-de-sac of perfection', greeted by the audience with 'the warm reception given to old friends'.[67] A particularly flowery review declared that, 'Their act, like the Sphinx itself, has deservedly stood the test of time and has the same power of fascination.'[68]

There may have been a constant quest for novelty, but it has often been pointed out that many performers would tour the same act around the variety circuit for years without changing it.[69] Some audiences even wanted acts to stay the same, enjoying the familiarity, as Ted Ray pointed out: 'Your music-hall patron unconsciously prided himself on knowing what was coming next. He liked it that way and felt a bit cheated if things were different.'[70] On the other hand, an angry letter to *The Stage* in 1939 complained about 'old, re-hashed material', and advised theatre managers to say to acts:

> Now look here, you have not only used that act on your previous visits here, but you have broadcast it, as well as made a film of it. For the future business of my hall I must give my patrons novelty and originality. If you cannot supply it, then I shall book others, even though they are amateurs.[71]

Stale or unoriginal acts were enough of a problem for there to be a jargon term for them: 'stereotyped acts'. The term is used in articles in the trade press from 1930 to the early 1960s.[72] Max Miller even used the word onstage, telling the audience at the Met, Edgware Road on 30 November 1957, 'I'm not a stereotype comedian, don't think that for one moment.'[73]

It was not just a question of performers sticking to the same old act; there was also widespread pilfering of material. Max Bygraves admitted, 'All our jokes came from books, magazines and "borrowing" from other comedians.'[74] Jimmy Jewel was equally open: 'Stealing or "knocking-off" material was common practice in show business. There is no copyright on routines.'[75]

It is not difficult to find examples of this. Ted Ray and Tommy Trinder both told the same gag about having been a female impersonator until 'a sailor chased me up an alley'.[76] Similarly, the different styles of the cheerfully wailing Cockney Suzette Tarri and the garrulous, violin-playing Austrian Vic Oliver cannot hide the fact that they are essentially telling the same gag:

Tarri:
I remember one day she went up to her room and found a man there – a strange man up in 'er room. You know she didn't want to be 'ard on 'im, she's very sorft-'earted. So she said, 'Now look 'ere – I'll give you 24 hours to get out.' [laughter][77]

Oliver:
Last night I came home and there was a strange blonde girl sitting in my room. Boy, was I cross? I was furious. Yeah, total stranger, too. I said to her, 'Listen, I don't know who you are but I'll just give you 48 hours to get out of my room.' [laughter]

Jokes were not the only things to be stolen. Tricks, stunts, ideas and whole routines could be taken from another act. It is impossible to say who originated the idea, but both Senor Wences and Bobbie Kimber presented a dummy in which the face was made from the back of their own hand decorated with lipstick, the mouth formed from the thumb and index finger.[78] Even the names of the dolls were similar: Wences' was called 'Johnnie', Kimber's 'Jenny'.[79] Moreover, Kimber's idea of presenting a cross-dressing ventriloquist act was not entirely original as he himself acknowledged, mentioning Lydia Dreams as a precursor.[80]

Some acts took precautions to protect their material. For example, an advert in a 1938 edition of *The Performer* shows a photo of a dachshund climbing a knotted rope next to an announcement: 'Mme. Christians with her Wonder Dogs including the original creation (which is fully protected) of a rope-climbing dog. This announcement is made for the purpose of preventing imitation of this particular trick, an illustration of which is here given.'[81] More straightforwardly, Nervo & Knox beat up a rival double act who stole their famous slow-motion wrestling routine.[82]

Even personality, that most individual quality of variety performance, was not safe from pilfering and plagiarism. Bob Monkhouse pointed out that the comics George Williams, Roy Barbour and Reg Dixon all adopted long-suffering stage personas at around the same time, and used strikingly similar catchphrases: 'I'm not well' (Williams) and 'I'm proper poorly' (both Barbour and Dixon).[83]

In late 1937, the Variety Artistes' Federation (VAF) realized that while the Lord Chamberlain could restrict the right to impersonate real people in stage plays, 'he does not intervene where ordinary variety work is concerned'. Their concern was that:

An artist can, at law, protect original material, in which he holds the copyright. But often he has no copyright in the material in which his personality expresses itself ... as a whole, the law is seriously defective in giving him the protection to which, in his artistic work, he is entitled. Variety artists are the chief sufferers.[84]

In July 1938, the VAF wrote to the Board of Trade, asking them to press for the ability to copyright personality at a convention to be held in Brussels the following year. The letter explained that variety performers wanted to be able to prevent 'unauthorised reproduction of their personalities constituted as self-expression and mannerisms, which entertaining value of personality is the greatest asset an entertainer possesses and is the basis of the goodwill on which he earns his livelihood'.[85]

Impersonating impersonators

The anxiety sprang as much from comic impersonation as outright theft of stage personas, with amateurs performing in talent nights in variety theatres and cinemas a particular target. Successful professional impersonators were seen as legitimate, particularly when they were as successful as Florence Desmond. She made her name with the hit record 'The Hollywood Party', released by HMV in 1932, featuring a solo sketch in which she performed all the film star guests attending an imaginary party hosted by Janet Gaynor.[86] Following the success of the record, she developed it as a highly influential stage act.

At around the same time another impersonator, Beryl Orde, was making a name for herself with a suspiciously similar repertoire to Desmond's. Four of the eight personalities Desmond imitated in 'The Hollywood Party' – Zasu Pitts, Jimmy Durante, Greta Garbo and Gracie Fields – also featured in Orde's act.[87] She may not have copied Desmond, but others copied both of them. An article in *The Times* in August 1934 explained how difficult it was for the BBC to find new material to fill the airwaves, and noted that:

> Each week the Audition Committee of the Variety Department listens to a dozen crooners offering a fairly accomplished imitation of Bing Crosby, and a dozen impersonators who follow Florence Desmond and Beryl Orde in impersonations of Mae West and Zasu Pitts (who are, in fact, so far removed from originality as to be impersonating impersonators!).[88]

The phenomenon of performers impersonating other impersonators shows just how stereotyped variety acts could be, and there is no doubt that many of them that were content to present something stale, unchanging, unoriginal or just plain stolen, probably contributing to the feeling Morris Aza had that it was the same thing every week. However, novelty was never far away, and there is perhaps no better example of the contradictory blend of the unoriginal and the genuinely bizarre than a particular moment from the act of Fred Roper & his Wonder Midgets, which boasted that, 'The tallest artiste is only 48 inches high'. A film of the act made for Pathé in 1936 shows a number of tiny performers singing and executing simple dance moves. In the middle of it all, a minute woman is led to the centre of the stage and announces, 'A slight impression of Florence Desmond's Hollywood Party', performing a cut-down version of the routine with Janet Gaynor introducing just two guests, Zasu Pitts and Greta Garbo, both of which sound impressively similar to Desmond's versions.[89] Plagiarized though it may be, an impersonation of another impersonator's impersonations by a member of a troupe of Wonder Midgets is a perfect example of variety's thirst for novelty.

Part Three

Variety Performance Today

10

Variety Now

The bastard side of the profession

While appearing in variety with his family's act El Granadas, Peter Prentice once found himself staying at a theatrical boarding house which also took in actors from the town's legitimate theatre. Going down to fill his hot water bottle, Prentice ran into the landlady, who introduced him to an actor staying at her establishment. Having announced that the actor was appearing at the Playhouse theatre and 'Mr Granada' – Prentice – was appearing at the Empire, she asked, 'Do you know each other?' The actor greeted the very idea that he would be familiar with anybody who worked in variety with contempt, replying, 'I don't know anyone on the bastard side of the profession.'[1]

With its penchant for novelty, sensationalism and scurrilous sexual innuendo – not to mention its brazen commercialism – variety has always been looked down upon. This kind of snobbery helps to explain why it has been so widely ignored by theatre historians and academics, and even written out of history. Variety is illegitimate theatre, a garish bastard sibling of the dramatic theatre, lacking the grit and authenticity of the music hall it grew out of, and unworthy of any kind of serious attention.

Having said that, while some have shunned or ignored it, there has also been a minority of intellectuals whose imaginations have been set ablaze by variety, fired up by the possibilities of the form. Marinetti was by no means the only writer who intellectualized the pleasures of variety by observing it from the outside. Throughout the twentieth century, key theatrical innovators looked to the variety theatre as source of inspiration for revitalizing their own side of the profession.

199

Vsevolod Meyerhold argued that 'although two-thirds of the acts in any of the better theatres of this type have no right to be called art, there is more art in the remaining third than in the so-called serious theatres which purvey "literary drama" '.[2] There is a hint of resentment in Antonin Artaud's argument, a feeling that variety and similar forms have stolen the legitimate theatre's thunder: 'Practically speaking, we want to bring back the idea of total theatre, where theatre will recapture from cinema, music-hall, the circus and life itself, those things that always belonged to it.'[3]

Reversing the logic of W. R. Titterton's comments about ballerinas, opera singers and other ambassadors of high culture being 'hordes of marauding savages' invading the variety stage, Edward Gordon Craig defended the actress Sarah Bernhardt when she did the same:

> In appearing in a London Music Hall Madame Bernhardt may be said to have returned to the true Theatre of today. The casual critic condemns what he wrongly supposes to be her 'desertion of the Theatre'. But consider for a moment what she 'deserts'. She leaves a worn out artificiality for a living artificiality ... what is her offence? She has been guilty of making one step in the right direction. The modern theatre is worn out; it never was so worn out as it is today. The music hall cherishing as it does so much creative talent of a somewhat exaggerated order is very much alive. Half, if not more, of the music hall 'turns' may be called 'creative' ... Madame Bernhardt does no creative work of this kind, but the fact of so celebrated a performer appearing on the music hall stage must be accepted as the 'legitimate' theatre's recognition of the force of what is known as the 'variety' stage.[4]

Legitimate theatre also recognized the force of the variety stage in casting its performers in straight plays. There is a long tradition of using variety comics as Shakespearean fools, from George Robey as Falstaff at His Majesty's Theatre in 1935 to Frankie Howerd as Bottom at the Old Vic in 1957 and Ken Dodd as Malvolio at the Liverpool Playhouse in 1971.[5] Samuel Beckett – whose writing echoes the absurdity of Wilson, Keppel & Betty or a Jimmy James sketch – cast Max Wall in *Krapp's Last Tape* in 1975, and the hangdog comic also appeared in a later production of *Waiting for Godot*.[6] John Osborne directed Wall as Archie Rice in a 1974 revival of his play *The Entertainer*, a play about an unsuccessful Max Miller-type comedian eking out a living in the latter days of the variety theatres.

More significantly, the alternative-theatre movement drew on variety not just for casting or the subject matter of plays, but as an aesthetic approach that offered a more exciting, direct link between performer and audience. This started with Theatre Workshop, the first British company which aimed to reconnect with a popular working-class audience by operating outside of the established theatre circuits. Ewan MacColl, who co-founded Theatre Workshop with Joan Littlewood and wrote many of their early shows, saw his childhood trips to the Salford Hippodrome as a much more important influence than the two straight plays he had seen, which 'enveloped' him in boredom 'like a thick, stultifying fog'.

Seeing 'some of the most notable comics of the English stage' at the Hippodrome was a totally different matter: 'It was the variety theatre which really made the most profound impression on me; the live music, the wandering limelights, the incredibly beautiful chorus girls, the grotesquely made-up comics and the dashing acrobats – these were indeed the stuff that dreams are made on!'[7] MacColl readily admitted 'borrowing from the technique' of variety in his Theatre Workshop plays. *Uranium 235* (1946) is a good example – in one scene Einstein is portrayed as a comedian, explaining his theories in the form of cross-talk patter with one of the other characters.[8]

The companies that followed in Theatre Workshop's footsteps drew just as heavily on variety's techniques. John McGrath of 7:84, for example, identified variety as one of the key features of popular theatre, arguing that: 'Most of the traditional forms of working-class entertainment that have grown up seem to possess this element. They seem to be able to switch from a singer to a comedian, to a juggler, to a band, to a chorus number, to a conjurer...with great ease.'[9]

Cherishing the jewels of the past

While variety might not have caught the attention of theatre historians and academics, its memory has refused to die in the popular imagination. Inspired by the final demise of the Metropolitan, Edgware Road, Ray Mackender and Gerry Glover established the British Music Hall Society (BMHS) in September 1963, declaring its mission in the motto: 'Cherishing the jewels of the past and actively supporting the interests of the future'. The BMHS is still very active today, staging shows, running a study group, publishing the magazine the *Call Boy*, and possessing an extraordinary archive of music hall and variety memorabilia.

Most of the theatres might have gone by the mid-1960s, but town halls and civic theatres continued to stage revival shows featuring authentic variety acts for the next two decades. For example, Battersea

Town Hall hosted a *Gala Battersea Music Hall* on 15 November 1974 (with acts such as Elsie & Doris Waters and Ted Durante & Hilda), and a week-long *Easter Variety Spectacular* ran at the Chesterfield Civic from Monday 12 to Saturday 17 April 1982 (with acts such as Ken Platt, Terri Carol and Jack Seaton).[10] The BMHS has run high-profile revivals of its own, like its *Silver Jubilee Gala Show* at the Palladium in September 1988.[11]

As variety slips further into the past, far from being forgotten, interest in it has grown, particularly in the last decade. In 2002 and 2004, the BMHS, the Somerset and West Music Hall Society, and the Grand Order of Water Rats organized the National Music Hall and Variety Festival in Weston-Super-Mare.[12] In 2005, the De La Warr Pavilion in Bexhill-on-Sea staged a season called Variety Now, presenting what was described as 'a repertoire of contemporary artworks that reflect new ideas whilst giving context to their histories'.[13] In January 2011, the BFI ran a series of screenings celebrating variety on television.[14] A few weeks later, BBC4 aired its own season of programmes on variety, the centrepiece being a new two-part documentary presented by Michael Grade.[15]

The BBC4 season was mostly made up of documentaries, but television also makes sporadic attempts to revive the TV variety show itself. *Britain's Got Talent* is by far the most successful recent example, but it is not the only one. In 2007, BBC1 ran a Graham Norton-fronted series called *When Will I Be Famous*, which presented 'the very best variety acts from the UK and around the world',[16] packaged with the celebrity panel and public voting which have become ubiquitous in recent television entertainment.

Perhaps most significantly, in 2005, an Equity taskforce led by performers such as Jo Brand, Jimmy Cricket and Tony Robinson announced that the Blackpool Grand would be designated the National Theatre of Variety, with a view 'to train younger generations in the arts and history of variety and to showcase them in festivals'.[17] This new centre, which was officially opened on 18 February 2006, was intended to tap into what *The Independent* described as 'a new-found public appetite for ... a more edgy kind of variety show'.[18]

Examples of this new 'edgy' style of variety include the Hoxton Bark, staged at the Hoxton Hall by producer Anne-Louise Rentell in 2002, and the company Medium Rare – the self-styled 'pioneer of Modern Variety in Britain' – which has run shows at venues like Hammersmith Working Men's Club and the Tabernacle, off Portobello Road since 2003.[19] Probably the most successful example of new-style variety is

La Clique, first mounted at the Edinburgh Fringe in 2004. According to its founder, Brett Haylock, 'It is a variety show, and what *La Clique* did was sped that up and kind of made it contemporary and sexy – and you know, an entire new generation...feel like they've discovered variety.'[20] The show, which tours internationally, puts on bills made up of balancers, jugglers, unicyclists, contortionists, puppeteers, trapeze artists, hoop manipulators, and strippers – an indication of the connections between this new kind of variety show and the current modish reinvention of burlesque. Following a run at the London Hippodrome in late 2009, *La Clique* won the Laurence Olivier Award for Best Entertainment.[21]

Best of British Variety is a very different kind of revival show, anything but edgy and unlikely to ever win any kind of theatre award. Touring since 2008, it has featured acts such as Frank Carson, Jimmy Cricket, the Krankies, Brotherhood of Man, Paul Daniels and Cannon & Ball, all of which have their origins in working-class entertainment and once regularly featured on prime-time television or the pop charts. This kind of line-up initially attracted big audiences, described rather snobbishly by one reviewer as either 'silver-haired' or 'thirty- or fortysomethings' who 'had tattoos and looked like they suck air out of car tyres each morning'.[22]

A relic of the Victorian age

Edgy or otherwise, there are important differences between revival shows and historical variety. In place of theatre chains contracting individual acts in bills which lasted for one week only, there are producers marketing a self-contained touring show. In place of the blocky typography of a variety bill designed to draw in audiences with the name of the act topping the bill, *La Clique*'s marketing draws more heavily on the graphic design associated with circus or artistic cabaret and it is the name of the show itself rather than the individual acts that pulls the punters in.

As for the entertainment itself, both *La Clique* and *Best of British Variety* favour a compère over historical variety's use of programmes and number boards to introduce the acts. The edgy revivals such as *La Clique* present bills entirely made up of speciality acts, which in the days of Moss Empires were merely the lowly warm-up acts booked to build up the energy for the singers, bands and comedians further up the bill. Then there is the striptease, which is far more glamorous and ironic than the more straightforward kind of exploitation seen in the low-budget touring nude revues that increasingly dominated the dying circuit of the 1950s.

The name *La Clique* is an interesting choice of title, suggesting a show aimed at a select audience of those in the know – a far cry from historical variety's populism. This connotation may be unintended, but there is a tangible whiff of elitism around Medium Rare's decision to charge £40 a ticket for shows they were staging in 2005, even if this price did include the sushi and sake which were served to the audience.[23]

On the face of it, *Best of British Variety* may seem more authentic, lacking any kind of elitism and featuring an older generation of working-class entertainer. The Krankies' Ian Tough claimed that 'We're the last of the line of the vaudeville performers',[24] but in fact, none of the performers have any connections with actual historical variety. Paul Daniels openly acknowledged this, saying, 'the reason I took this show is because I never did variety theatre in my day'.[25]

The press reaction to both kinds of revival show illustrates that the old snobbery continues to plague variety. 'No wonder variety died', concluded Veronica Lee in a damning review of *Best of British Variety*,[26] thus conflating the flaws in the show she saw with the entire historical form it was supposedly emulating. Many reviewers have rhapsodized about the merits of edgier revivals shows, but often do so by disparaging historical variety, describing it as a collection of 'ageing comics, ventriloquists and cack-handed magicians' or 'tinsel, totty and mother-in-law jokes'.[27] More colourfully, in an article on Medium Rare, Nick Curtis confessed, 'Previously I thought variety, like rickets and child labour, was a relic of the Victorian age we were well rid of.'[28]

Variety may be dead, but its legacy amounts to much more than TV documentaries, stylish but ersatz revival shows or *Britain's Got Talent*. Dave Russell has argued that variety 'held within it the seeds of many of the most successful elements of later twentieth-century popular culture'.[29] In spite of the snobbery that has either portrayed it as a sneer-worthy relic or entirely ignored it, the basic genetic code of variety runs through much of the popular entertainment that dominates today.

TV, summer seasons and panto

In order to trace variety's descendents we need to go back to the point where the theatres were closing and look at what happened to the acts that had once populated them. In 1960, *The Stage Year Book* put on optimistic spin on a dire situation by cheerily announcing that, 'Many artists find they can live very well on their Summer show and pantomime bookings, with perhaps an occasional television booking for in-between periods.'[30] TV might have helped to kill variety as a live form, but it also provided it with a lengthy afterlife.

Sunday Night at the London Palladium was just one of a series of successful television variety shows that continued well into the 1980s. ITV's *Live at Her Majesty's*, for example, was first broadcast as late as 1983, regularly attracting audiences of 13 or 14 million people.[31] Some variety performers, like Frankie Howerd, Tommy Cooper and Morecambe & Wise, were lucky enough be given their own shows on television, often built on a variety format.

The Morecambe & Wise Show is a particularly good example, because its set design deliberately echoed the features of a variety theatre, complete with wings and the curtains that Eric and Ernie appeared in front of while performing cross-talk routines or clowning around with their guest stars. Their producer John Ammonds recalled that this made things more difficult in terms of camera angles and setting and striking for each scene, but 'they wanted the studio to feel more like a theatre...it was all about trying to recapture that special kind of atmosphere that they'd had in their touring days'.[32]

There is an extent to which the very form of television itself echoes the structure of the variety show that filled the Empires and Hippodromes in the first half of the twentieth century. Michael Grade worked for the variety agency run by Billy Marsh before going on to enjoy a glittering career in TV management at LWT, the BBC and Channel 4. In his autobiography he recalled how his uncle, Lew Grade – who had worked as a dancer in variety before becoming one of its biggest impresarios – had told him that:

> Putting together variety bills as an agent had taught him the art of television scheduling when he took over ATV. And any aptitude I developed in turn for scheduling television programmes originated in Billy Marsh's office, where I gradually learned that there is only one correct running order for variety acts, and that the show will be a flop if this sequence isn't followed.[33]

As for live work, *The Stage Year Book* might have been misleadingly optimistic, but it was essentially right. Roy Hudd started his career in the very last days of the theatres, and he recalls where he went to find work once they shut down: 'When variety finished, that was the important jobs – get a nice good nine- or ten-week panto, and a nice good healthy summer season … if you had those two that was fine, and any little bits of work you picked up in between was a bonus.'[34]

These little bits of work picked up in between might have included a booking at one of the very few theatres that survived the great extinction of the late 1950s like the City Varieties in Leeds, the New Metropole in Glasgow or even the London Palladium, which continued to programme variety bills right through to the end of the 1970s, when they were elbowed out by big budget stage musicals. There was also the Coventry Theatre, which ran spring and autumn seasons.[35]

As for summer seasons and pantomime, these had always been important fixtures in the diaries of variety artistes, but when the theatres disappeared they became absolutely crucial. Summer seasons were staged in seaside theatres, often on piers, and ranged from small concert parties to big spectaculars starring well-known variety acts, running twice nightly. Michael Grade, who programmed summer seasons while working for Billy Marsh, describes how important they were:

> Where variety migrated to were what we called 'summer season shows' – Bournemouth, Yarmouth, Blackpool, Weymouth, Scarborough, Torquay, Painton. Variety was kept alive by sort of 16–18 weeks of summer seasons in all these venues around the country. That's where you found variety … They were revues, you know, they had production values … you'd have headliners, you'd have Morecambe & Wise, you'd have Bruce Forsyth, you'd have Cliff [Richard] & the Shadows, you'd have Frank Ifield, you'd have Frankie Vaughan … Max Bygraves, Tommy Cooper, Frankie Howerd, Des O'Connor, Harry Worth … Val Doonican, Ken Dodd, obviously. And that was where variety acts really made a living … Summer season and pantomime became variety, really. That's where the acts got their work from.[36]

As Grade suggests, pantomimes – in which variety performers played parts in the fairy tale narratives and often performed an excerpt from their regular act – could fill up another decent chunk of the calendar. Roy Hudd remembers looking forward to a 'nice good nine- or ten-week panto', and Wyn Calvin recalls working in pantomimes staged by Tom Arnold which ran until March, getting a late boost from the schools' half-term holidays.[37]

Clubs

Between the summer seasons and the pantos there were the clubs. In 1958, *The Stage Year Book* stated that:

> With the closure of so many of the Halls many professional artists have turned to the Clubs for their livelihood … In the Club field a large number of really solid performers derive a fairly steady income from an almost continuous demand. Some of the provincial Clubs possess concert halls with capacities varying from 300 to close upon 1,000 with very good stages, dressing rooms and lighting facilities.[38]

Ten years later, the transition from theatres to clubs was so complete that the same publication announced that 'one may read Clubland as synonymous with Variety'.[39] Working-men's clubs, and the bigger privately owned clubs like the Batley Variety Club and Bernard Manning's Embassy Club in Manchester, offered a good source of income for refugees from the collapsed theatre circuits.

Opinion was starkly divided as to what the clubs were actually like to perform in. Frankie Howerd, who started playing them in 1962, argued that, 'from an artiste's point of view they were a superb transference of the Music Hall (and with much better money than the old Sheffield Empire ever paid, even allowing for inflation), and in their fashion were a return to the very origins of Music Hall'.[40] Jimmy Jewel's assessment was much more blunt: 'We worked pubs and clubs – terrible bloody places'.[41]

The comparison with early music hall was very apt in terms of the audience, which was rowdier and less attentive than in the variety theatres. Morris Aza was an agent when the clubs were taking over, describing them as 'pretty hairy places' which were 'tough to work … because somehow you're constricted in a theatre, aren't you? You're sat where you are, you can't move, and there's something different about it. Those clubs, there's waiters walking about and this kind of thing, and banging and clanging, and it was much harder work.'[42] Max Bygraves argued that, 'They paid well but artistically it was not rewarding. The customers are lovely people but by the time they let you on to do the cabaret spot, which is usually about eleven pm, their brains are dulled by drink.'[43] Even Frankie Howerd acknowledged the unruliness of club audiences: 'The drunk and the heckler. In a theatre the lights go down, attention is focused upon you – and off you go. Clubs are not the same. The cabaret is only part of the night out; if you want to ignore it, you can.'[44]

Clubs were also demanding on performers in other ways, not least because they required them to perform for longer. Roy Hudd had been used to doing eight minutes with his double act in the variety theatres, but the clubs wanted him to go on for an hour. Then there were the staging problems. The layout of most clubs meant that, as Howerd put it, 'there are people literally within finger-tip touch, while others are at the back of a huge auditorium', and in some cases 'some members of the audience are sitting almost behind me when I perform'.[45]

This meant that using scenery was all but impossible, and one of Jimmy Jewel's gripes was that, 'We couldn't do production sketches in those venues'.[46] Many clubs were unsuitable for speciality acts, and Howerd recalled adagio dancers crashing into tables while working on stages too small to accommodate them. As a result, the quirkier, showier elements – dancers, sketches and the weird and wonderful selection of speciality acts – tended to disappear. All that was left were variety's true inheritors: singers, bands and stand-up comedians.

Stand-up comedy

Stand-up comedy is one of variety's most important contributions to today's popular entertainment. The line connecting Max Miller to modern comedians such as Michael McIntyre is by no means unbroken, but the fact is that the very form of stand-up evolved from music hall song, and started life as the front cloth comedy of variety.[47] From there, it moved into the clubs, which played host to both variety comedians and a younger generation of performers who started out in them. Club comedians such as Bernard Manning, Frank Carson and Charlie Williams took a more basic approach to stand-up than their variety predecessors, playing less on personality and presenting a string of unrelated packaged jokes.

The modern comedy club – from which most of today's stars have emerged – originated from the alternative comedy movement, which started in 1979 with the opening of the Comedy Store in London, and the founding of Tony Allen's Alternative Cabaret group. In the past 30 years, it has blossomed from a tiny, largely metropolitan scene peopled by radicals, eccentrics and crazy amateurs, to the highly commercialized national circuit of today.

The early stars of alternative comedy – performers such as Alexei Sayle, Jim Barclay, Pauline Melville, Tony Allen, Rik Mayall and French & Saunders – tended to come from left-wing theatre groups and student revue. They had no real roots in earlier stand-up traditions, and were actually partly motivated by contempt for older comics. Club comedians were seen as both bigoted and formulaic, and alternative comedy frequently ridiculed their stale old formulas. Meanwhile, Alexei Sayle sometimes got laughs out of the surprisingly sudden venom with which he ridiculed variety:

> Great time for variety acts, though, the fifties, and er, actually people are always going on about, erm, about the British music hall, you know, and how and why it died out. I'll tell you why it died out, 'cos it was *shite!* [laughter][48]

In spite of this, the early alternative comedians realized the historical roots of the form they were seeking to reinvent. Looking back to the early days of the Comedy Store on its tenth birthday in 1989, Pauline Melville admitted: 'It felt that we were clearing new ground, in fact we were probably just treading old music hall territory.'[49]

Others were more conscious of looking to the past to find the way forward. In the early days of the circuit, it was often referred to not as 'comedy' but as 'cabaret' to reflect the diversity of acts on show. Arthur Smith recalls that, 'The opening night at Jongleurs had a lassoist' and that Maria Kempinska, who ran the venue, would put on '20 minutes of a contemporary dance troupe or a heavy-metal band'.[50] Crystallizing the idea that the nascent scene was about more than just stand-up comedy, Roland and Claire Muldoon of the theatre company CAST (Cartoon Archetypical Slogan Theatre) founded New Variety.

CAST were a pioneering alternative theatre group who had producing left-wing theatre shows since the 1960s, but by the early 1980s they were living under the shadow of impending cuts to their funding from the Thatcher government. Warren Lakin, who was CAST's administrator at the time, recalls: 'Roland came up with the brilliant idea that we should diversify – and work up another avenue of income just in case our wages went down the toilet, basically.' In January 1982, they started mounting New Variety shows at the Old White Horse pub on Brixton Road, and as Lakin puts it, 'suddenly... we were putting on lots of performers and we had a cash flow'.

There were artistic as well as practical reasons for adopting variety as the form for their new venture. Lakin argues that they were trying to influence the direction of the whole scene:

> It was quite obvious that there were two flags being planted in the ground here. There were those people that were very serious about it being a night

for all kinds of art forms, and then there were those that were definitely saying, 'Well the bias is towards comedy. If you wanna give people a good night out then it's got to be funny-funny all the way.' Well CAST stuck to its guns and said, 'No, we like mixing all kinds of comedy, stand-up, sketch comedy, with performance poetry, the ranting poets, we'll have a band in there, we'll have music, we'll have some juggling, the whole bloody lot really'...so Roland and Claire dubbed it New Variety.[51]

For Roland Muldoon, the label 'variety' was important: 'I objected to the word "cabaret" because you might be surprised I'm a bit of a nationalist when it comes to culture in a sense, you know. Variety is a British idea, I don't like any of the other stuff really.' Variety was exciting because he had always seen direct address as 'my big turn-on', and he cheerfully admits that 'quite honestly, I find theatre totally boring... In variety, 20 minutes is a long time... And in theatre, three hours is a short time.'[52]

The New Variety shows at the Old White Horse were an immediate success, and CAST started expanding their operation. With the help of a Greater London Council grant of around £25,000, they established eight venues across London and put on a New Variety tour across 32 London boroughs. Towards the end of 1982, Warren Lakin left CAST, and with the permission of the Muldoons, he started running his own New Variety nights in Sheffield, with shows in pubs such as the George IV opposite Kelvin Flats and the Royal in Heeley, where the stand-up comedian Linda Smith performed some of her earliest routines.

Roland Muldoon saw that there was a 'broken line' between historic variety and what he was doing, and in 1986 this connection became very tangible when CAST acquired the Hackney Empire. Since being a prominent London variety theatre, the Hackney Empire had been a TV studio and a bingo hall, but by the mid-1980s Mecca were looking to get rid of it, because they wanted to shed the responsibility of maintaining a historic building. Muldoon recalls:

> They couldn't get rid of it, because it had domes... after a year or so we'd talked our way in, and we got it for very little money, with the responsibility of putting the domes back on. But what we saw was the possibility of paying for our survival by having a big audience. And at that point in time, nobody had done that in the alternative world.[53]

When they took it over, they found it to be, 'A brilliant place. Falling apart, dog-eared. Seats falling apart, you know.'[54] Nonetheless, they brought it back to life, putting on fully-fledged variety shows for the first time since the 1950s, when the theatre had closed like so many others. As well using the kind of acts they knew from their smaller, pub-based New Variety venues, they also brought in authentic variety performers. This was not always easy. According to Muldoon, a visit to the theatre by a small-time variety comedian ended badly when he made an ill-judged racist quip to the black stage manager. However, they had a happier experience with some other veterans of the historical variety circuit, notably the extraordinary paper-tearer, Terri Carol, who had first appeared as a solo act as early as 1930.[55] Carol's performances in New Variety saw a late revival in her career, leading to appearances on TV, and she only retired in the mid-1990s at the age of 80.

The other venues in the New Variety circuit eventually disappeared, and even the Hackney Empire moved away from variety, putting on shows across a wide range of theatrical genres – solo stand-up, music, dance, Shakespeare, Caribbean farce. The theatre had to attract private finance as well as money from the Arts Council and the National Lottery, and with this came an increasingly managerial atmosphere. By 2004, the Muldoons felt they had been marginalized in the theatre they had brought back to life, and moved on to other ventures.

One of these has been the revival of New Variety. On 9 September 2010, they put on the first of a series of shows at the Barbican, under the banner *New Variety Lives*, with a bill that included the comedy balancing act Michael Pearse, the cod magician Otis Cannelloni, and the singing poet John Hegley, alongside some varied stand-up comics. The previous year, Warren Lakin had mounted his own revival, *Variety Lives*, with a touring show and a residency at the Brighton Komedia.

New Variety left its mark on the comedy circuit, by ensuring that it was about more than just straight stand-up. In the 1990s, I compèred and co-ran Sheffield's Last Laugh Comedy Club for five years, and there was a wide variety of acts in the bills we put on there. Alongside the stand-ups, there were poets (Hovis Presley), impressionists (Alistair McGowan, Ronni Ancona), jugglers (Pierre Hollins, and even a very young Ross Noble), comic singers (Earl Okin, Steve Gribbin), double acts (Big Fun Club), character comedians (Al Murray, Johnny Vegas, Matt Lucas as Sir Bernard Chumley), and magicians (Ian Keable). Such acts might have become less important but they persist even today, as Barry Cryer points out: 'Variety is not dead because this current generation, if you go to a gig and there's several people on the bill, you'll very likely see a ventriloquist and a juggler and a magician.'[56]

Pop music

The rock gig has a more direct line of descent from variety than stand-up comedy. Its origins can be traced to the 1950s, when shows starring skiffle musicians or rock 'n' roll singers were rare examples of commercial success in the dying variety theatres. Soon the theatres themselves had disappeared, but the pop concert continued to thrive in other venues. *The Stage Year Book* of 1962 records this transformation:

> The proof that we are not really without Variety is the fact that in most of the places where once an Empire or a Royal stood, the local cinema or some suitable hall is now staging one-night stands, shows with an emphasis on trad and modern, beat and rock, and all that jazz, and other shows which appeal to youth. Many of these shows carry their own comedians, youngsters with a flair for comedy, or sometimes, established professionals who fit in with the new type of show which has gradually grown up over the years.[57]

What is being described here is clearly a rock 'n' roll package tour with a comedian as compère, a good example of which would be the 1958 UK tour by Buddy Holly and the Crickets for the Grade organization. Described by Holly biographer Philip Norman as 'a variety bill which could just as well have taken the road in the late forties', the show played twice nightly at cinemas like the Gaumont State in Kilburn, the Ritz, Wigan, and Trocadero, Elephant and Castle.[58] Supporting Holly on the bill were musical acts of various styles, and the show was compèred by the young comedian Des O'Connor. This was clearly the moment that the rock gig left the womb of variety, but significantly *The Stage Year Book* explicitly saw it as continuation of – and not a break with – the variety tradition

Just as the modern comedy circuit was founded partly on a conscious attempt to revive variety, so a number of key pop and rock artists have looked to their theatrical past for inspiration. Ray Davies encountered variety indirectly – through records, films and his father's memories of seeing it in the theatres[59] – but however tenuous the connection, he acknowledged it as a key source of inspiration for the songs he wrote for his iconic band the Kinks in the 1960s:

> For years and years, I denied it...I think that's because music hall is, in rock and roll terms, quite an uncool thing to be associated with...But music hall was undeniably an important influence. And I'd put someone like ... George Formby right up there with ... [the celebrated blues musician]

Bill Broonzy...Some of the acoustic guitar stuff I do resonates with the George Formby style.[60]

There is a distinct music hall feel to 'Dedicated Follower of Fashion', a song which sends up the style-obsessed dandies of 1960s youth culture, recalling the sharp-eyed observation of social types featured in so many comic songs of the late nineteenth century.[61] 'All of My Friends Were There' – which tells the tale of a performer getting jeered by the audience after drinking too much beer before going onstage – sounds even more music hall.[62] Over a jaunty, oom-pah rhythm, Davies wistfully spills out fast-paced strings of words in an accentuated Cockney accent, his speedy diction echoing the delivery of Harry Champion. 'The Village Green Preservation Society', directly references 'vaudeville and variety' in its list of disappearing icons of Englishness.[63]

Variety was also there in the stage performance. As Kinks bassist John Dalton put it, 'Ray was an actor on stage; he was acting...That was music hall, old-fashioned music hall is all it is'.[64] As if to advertise the connection, during their 1970s *20th Century Man* tour, Davies had the lobbies of some of the venues they played decorated with photos of Max Miller, Billy Cotton, Max Wall, Dan Leno, Herbert Campbell and Johnny Danvers.[65]

Another variety aficionado, Ian Dury, had fallen in love with the form having been taken to see it in the theatre by his mother when he was a child. Dury emerged from the London pub rock scene of the early 1970s, rising to fame with his band the Blockheads alongside the first wave of punk bands. A 1978 article in the *Sunday Times* noted that, 'On stage, Ian Dury mixes music hall and comedy with hard-driving music. He plays with the microphone like a manic Gene Vincent and clowns with scarf, cane and undies like Norman Wisdom gone mad.'[66]

As with Ray Davies, the influence showed in both songs and performance. 'Billy Bentley' and 'Billericay Dickie' not only sound like music hall songs, their lyrics – telling tales of working-class leisure pursuits – are also firmly in the same tradition. The first conjures up a day trip to London by a suburban teenager by recording the phrases he hears and the places he passes through: 'Move along, there'; 'Nice time, ducky?'; 'Hyde Park Corner'; 'Ealing Broadway'; 'Fucking Ada'.[67]

In the second, Dury takes on the character of a working-class Casanova to recall a series of sexual encounters in places such as Thanet, Shoeburyness and Burnham-on-Crouch with women like

Nina, who turns into 'a seasoned-up hyena' when he gets her 'in the back of my Cortina'.[68] Dury had his own song praising icons of Englishness – 'England's Glory' – which includes a whole series of music hall and variety references: Frankie Howerd; the Gertie Gitana song, 'Nellie Dean'; Gracie Fields; Max Miller; Vera Lynn; George Formby; Little Tich; Richard Hearne's slapstick character Mr Pastry; and Billy Cotton's catchphrase, 'Wakey, wakey!'.[69]

Dury's stage performances were full of touches drawn from variety comedians and magicians. He would sometimes don a Tommy Cooper fez onstage, and pull cross-eyed, gurning faces while singing. During instrumental solos, he would do bits of business with plastic toys or water pistols, pulling silk scarves from his sleeves or stuffing them in his mouth. His catchphrase, 'Oi, oi!' was adapted from Jimmy Wheeler's ('Aye, aye!'), and he would use it as a form of call-and-response, barking it out to the audience to goad them into yelling it back at them.[70] Nearing the end of his life, Dury played a concert on a Sunday night at the London Palladium, openly referencing the history of the venue by announcing, 'Danny Kaye is listening, Bing is listening'.[71]

Even more significantly, in 1978, at the height of his success, Dury chose Max Wall as one of his support acts for a big show at the Hammersmith Odeon. Wall had recorded his own version of Dury's song 'England's Glory' for Stiff Records in 1977,[72] and he had toured with another rock band – Mott the Hoople – a few years earlier. According to Wall's autobiography, this had gone reasonably well: 'I went down well in nine or ten places out of about fourteen dates. The fact that my old material went over well to a young generation was pleasing to me, and in some venues ... I "did a bomb" as they say nowadays.'[73]

Playing to a punk crowd was a different matter, as Blockheads' keyboard player Mick Gallagher recalled: 'Ian always had a smattering of music hall in his delivery and Max was one of his heroes, but I think it was maybe a bit adventurous to put him on in front of that punk audience who didn't really have a clue who he was.'[74] The show was widely reviewed in the music press, and although reports vary in detail, they all agree on the basic events. The account in the *New Musical Express* reads:

> The grand old stand-up comic, jaunty titfer, insouciant cig, had to wait out a storm of abuse before he could begin. 'You're excited, I know that. If you want THE WALK, I'll do it and get off.' He finally got to do it, and they

loved it – the mandrill's bum and the mannequin's wobbly hauteur, the comic dose of ridicule and dreams, shake once and reflect. 'You bastards – that's the best fucking geezer at wot 'e does in the world, and you've upset 'im!' yelled Dury...Back came Max and sung Buster Keaton's come-back number after a decade of alcoholism and madness 'gotta make 'em laugh, I wanna cry'. If there was anyone present who wanted to know where Ian Dury's creativity was coming from, Max Wall spilled out a bibful.[75]

Having been heckled and abused by what another reviewer described as 'a tiny but mindless section',[76] Wall was rescued by Dury's interjection and his own funny walk routine, emerging from the ordeal triumphant. When the *New Musical Express* journalist asked him about the audience, he replied cheerfully, 'They were worse when I went on with Mott the Hoople...I died like a louse in a Russian's beard'.[77]

Dury was not the only punk-generation performer to claim artistic ancestry in variety. John Lydon has explained how he drew on a number of variety comedians to create his Johnny Rotten stage persona:

I die of nerves before I go onstage 'cos I don't know what I'm gonna do. And because of that, I'd have to just pull things out from deep down inside. Look, there's Arthur Askey in there, there's Ken Dodd, 'We are the Diddymen, we come from Knotty Ash!'. There's even [Norman Wisdom].[78]

He has argued that, 'What England didn't understand about the Sex Pistols is that we are music hall! There was always a sense of piss-take and fun to it.'[79]

Following Dury's lead, Madness took the variety influence into the pop charts of the 1980s. Lead singer Suggs has claimed that, 'Tommy Cooper was a big factor in Madness', and argued that, 'Music hall was the precursor to rock'n'roll!'[80] Again variety echoes through their repertoire, the cheery tunes and cartoonish, innuendo-laden lyrics of early hits like 'Baggy Trousers' and 'House of Fun' recalling the kind of numbers that George Formby or Max Miller used to sing.[81]

After splitting up and reforming, Madness continue to record and perform, and the title song of their recent album *The Liberty of Norton Folgate* references music hall and Dan Leno in the lyrics. In May 2009, they presented a stage show based on the record at the Hackney Empire. As with Dury's London Palladium show, the history of the venue was directly referred to, with Suggs announcing, 'Welcome one and all to the Hackney Empire – the scene of many crazed working-class entertaining evenings.'

To evoke an imagined version of music hall, the audience was seeded with people dressed in cod Victorian costumes, shouting colourful heckles. Around the auditorium, jugglers, balancers and ventriloquists entertained small sections of the crowd. Tommy Cooper-style fezzes were on sale, and a number of punters were wearing them. Film of Little Tich's big boot dance was projected behind the band, and the between-song banter was peppered with variety references: 'Can you hear me, mum?' an adaptation of Sandy Powell's catchphrase; and again, the Billy Cotton catchphrase, 'Wakey, wakey!'.[82]

A similar show was staged by Damon Albarn's band the Good, the Bad and the Queen at Wilton's Music Hall in December 2006. Compèred by comedian Harry Enfield, in the guise of a cod music hall chairman, the first half of the show featured an hour of turns by sand-dancers, contortionists and escapologists.[83] This pseudo variety-show format might have seemed slightly at odds with the spacey, melancholy tone of the music, but like Ray Davies, Ian Dury and Suggs before him, Albarn also consciously drew on music hall influences with his earlier and more famous band, Blur. In 1993, he described their second album, *Modern Life Is Rubbish*, as 'futuristic music hall',[84] although the influence did not become particularly audible until their next two records, on songs like 'Parklife' and 'Country House'.[85] The verses of 'Parklife' are made up of what is effectively a character monologue performed by the actor Phil Daniels, described by Suggs as 'an impression of me doing an impression of Max Miller'.[86]

Playing to the crowd

In some ways, the Madness show at the Hackney Empire and Albarn's show at Wilton's are not much different from fashionable reinvented variety shows like *La Clique*. What makes them more significant is that although they consciously draw on the past, in doing so they acknowledge an actual historical connection. The rock gig and stand-up are both firmly rooted in variety, and more importantly both share variety's most essential qualities.

This starts with the way the entertainment is produced. Like a variety bill, a touring rock show is made up of separate items, each band being effectively an individual production, and this structure is essentially the same as the one-night stand tours that followed the closing of the theatres. In much the same way, the shows which take place in today's comedy clubs – from the Comedy Store down to the humblest open-mike night – are not a single theatrical production, but a collection of acts, each booked individually.

The performance itself also shows its historical roots. Like variety artistes, rock singers and stand-up comedians project their personalities, lacking a clear division between onstage and offstage selves. As in variety, they play directly to the crowd, lacking any notion of a fourth wall. In both rock gigs and stand-up shows, the audience play an active role, laughing or applauding if they are enjoying themselves, heckling or throwing things if they are not. Conspicuous skill – whether in the form of a flashy instrumental solo or a particularly clever or audacious joke – is rewarded with applause. There is even an element of novelty in rock and stand-up, in their penchant for the catchy, the quirky and the bizarre, manifesting itself in anything from Ian Dury's stage tomfoolery to Harry Hill's outsize collars and beetle-crusher shoes.

Of course, there are also important differences. Unlike the front cloth comics of variety, modern stand-ups tend to write their own material, are free to talk openly about sex and other unseemly matters, and rarely end their act on a song. Rock gigs are generally much less formal than a night of variety, and it is pop's general tendency for frenzy that made it sit so uneasily in the theatre bills of the 1950s.

In spite of this, though, the essential performance dynamics are the same: personality, participation, skill and novelty. Variety's honest pursuit of delight and direct appeal to the audience made it a completely different beast from the narrative plays of legitimate theatre. It may have been the bastard side of the professional, but it was an exciting bastard, full of energy and vibrancy. For such an openly commercial form of theatre, lacking higher artistic motivations, it has left behind a surprisingly long-lived nostalgia, and inspired a truly diverse set of artists, playwrights, theatre directors, comedians, musicians and revivalists of every kind. Beyond all that, variety's legacy is still very much alive in the popular entertainment of today, its lifeblood flowing through its descendents stand-up comedy and the rock gig half a century after it passed into history.

Notes

1 Britain's Got Talent

1. Jerome Taylor, 'Struggling ITV clears schedules for talent show: *Britain's Got Talent* grabs 50 per cent of Saturday peak-time viewing audience', *The Independent*, 26 May 2009, p. 10.
2. *Britain's Got Talent Live Tour 2009 Programme*, p. 3
3. E. Jane Dickson, 'The best of British', *Radio Times*, 30 May–5 June 2009, pp. 14–18 (p. 18) [Piers Morgan]; Jane Fryer, 'THE OLD ONES ARE THE BEST ... at least that's what Paul Daniels keeps telling me!; They're even more ancient than their gags. So why do these geriatric jokers still play to sell-out crowds? *Daily Mail*, 6 September 2008, p. 60; Liane Jones, 'The impressionist's got form, but Britain's really got talent', *Independent on Sunday*, 17 June 2007.
4. Tanya Gold, 'It wasn't singer Susan Boyle who was ugly on *Britain's Got Talent* so much as our reaction to her', *The Guardian* (G2 Section), 16 April 2009, p. 5.
5. Leigh Holmwood, 'Saturday: A dream come true: Unknown Scottish singleton Susan Boyle became one of the most talked-about people in the world this week after a brief TV appearance. How?', *The Guardian*, 18 April 2009, p. 24
6. Mark Lawson, 'National: *Britain's Got Talent*: Winners and losers: The price of overnight fame – from Amy Winehouse to Susan Boyle', *The Guardian*, 2 June 2009, p. 11.
7. Leigh Holmwood, 'National: *Britain's Got Talent*: ITV in the spotlight after "exhausted" Susan Boyle enters private clinic: Psychiatrist queries stress load put on reality TV stars: Talent show runner-up needs to rest, says brother', *The Guardian*, 2 June 2009, p. 11.
8. Clive Barker, 'The "image" in show business', *Theatre Quarterly*, 8(29) (spring 1978), pp. 7–11, 8.
9. Michael Hogan, '*Britain's Got Talent*; the variety show with no variety; The weekend on television', *Daily Telegraph*, 7 June 2010, p. 30.

2 The Variety Bill

1. Max Wall, *The Fool on the Hill*, London: Quartet, 1975, p. 33.
2. Brooks McNamara, 'The scenography of popular entertainment', in Joel Schechter (ed.), *Popular Theatre: A Sourcebook*, London and New York: Routledge, 2003, p. 12.

3. For example, see Hunter Davies, *The Grades: The First Family of British Entertainment*, London: Weidenfeld & Nicolson, 1981, p. 70; Roger Wilmut, *Kindly Leave the Stage: The Story of Variety 1919–1960*, London: Methuen, 1985, pp. 84–86; Valantyne Napier, *Act as Known: Australian Speciality Acts on the World Vaudeville/Variety Circuits from 1900 to 1960*, Brunswick, Victoria: Globe, pp. 21–23; Norman Wisdom (with William Hall), *My Turn*, London: Random House, 2002, p. 103.

4. Interview with Michael Grade, by telephone, 28 April 2011.

5. Diana Howard, *London Theatres and Music Halls 1850–1950*, London: Library Association, 1970, pp. 135–37. Images of the Lewisham Hippodrome can be found at: www.theatrestrust.org.uk/resources/images/show/81-faade-of-lewisham-hippodrome-london and www.age-exchange.org.uk/projects/past/libraryofexperience/heartoflewisham/leisure/index.html

6. 'Lewisham Hippodrome', *Lewisham Borough News*, 9 April 1946, p. 5.

7. These were tunes chosen by Sydney Kaplan when he was the Musical Director for the Finsbury Park Empire in the 1950s (see programmes for the Finsbury Park Empire, 7 June 1954 and 5 July 1954 respectively).

8. This description is from a review of another show in which Bartlett & Massey appeared at around this time ('Finsbury Park Empire', *The Performer*, 7 October 1948, p. 11).

9. Patrick Pilton, *Every Night at the London Palladium*, London: Robson, 1976, p. 38.

10. Guy R. Bullar and Len Evans (eds.), *The Performer: Who's Who in Variety*, London: Performer, 1950, p. 68.

11. Ian Bevan, *Top of the Bill: The Story of the London Palladium*, London: Frederick Muller, 1952, p. 206.

12. 'Lively variety at the Hippodrome', *Manchester Guardian*, 22 August 1939, p. 11.

13. See photo reproduced in Roy Hudd (with Philip Hindin), *Roy Hudd's Cavalcade of Variety Acts: A Who Was Who of Light Entertainment 1945–60*, London: Robson, 1998, p. 1.

14. 'The Palace: Billy Cotton and variety', *Manchester Guardian*, 29 October 1940, p. 6.

15. As suggested by a *Times* review which says they 'mingle conversation on economics with neatly contrived acrobatics' ('The Coliseum: London police witness "Garrison Theatre"', *The Times*, 4 November 1941, p. 6).

16. 'WHAT THE PUBLIC WANTS! REEL 3 OF 4' (1911.15), 1933, www.britishpathe.com/record.php?id=77255, 6/7/09.

17. 'FREDDIE BAMBERGER' (1654.25), 1936, www.britishpathe.com/record.php?id=28678, 6/7/09.

18. Herbert Smith (dir.), *British Lion Variety no. 17*, GB, British Lion, 1936.

19. *The Golden Years of British Comedy*, Universal, 2005, DVD 8235253–11, disc 1.
20. 'TONIGHT IN BRITAIN – reel 2' (1323.04), 1953, www.britishpathe.com/record.php?id=74961, 6/7/09.
21. Interview with Michael Grade, by telephone, 28 April 2011.
22. See footage of Turner Layton in Herbert Smith (dir.), *Soft Lights and Sweet Music*, GB, British Lion, 1936 (in which he sings 'My SOS to You'); Herbert Smith (dir.), *Calling All Stars*, GB, British Lion, 1937 (in which he sings 'East of the Sun').
23. The Lewisham Hippodrome programme does not list the tunes played during the interval for this show, but these examples are taken from Kaplan's stint at the Finsbury Park Empire in the 1950s (see programmes for the Finsbury Park Empire, 19 April 1954, and 7 June 1954 respectively).
24. See photo available at www.adelphifilms.com/stills-detail.asp?film=A+Ray+of+Sunshine&CurrentPage=3
25. The cartoon backdrop can be seen in Adrian Brunel (dir.), *Elstree Calling*, UK: British International Pictures, 1930.
26. 'Manchester stage and screen: The Hippodrome', *Manchester Guardian*, 16 April 1946, p. 3.
27. Brown performs this stunt in various films, one example being Brunel, *Elstree Calling*.
28. Eric Midwinter, *Make 'Em Laugh: Famous Comedians and their Worlds*, London: George Allen & Unwin, 1979, p. 74.
29. See clip shown on *Heroes of Comedy*, Channel 4, 31 January 1992.
30. Oswald Mitchell and Challis Sanderson (dirs.), *Stars on Parade*, UK: Butcher's Film Service, 1936.
31. 'The Day Hostilities Terminated', on Robb Wilton's War, Flapper/Pavilion Records, 2001, PAST CD 7854.
32. 'Henry Hall and variety', *Manchester Guardian*, 30 August 1938, p. 11.
33. Pilton suggests that this pattern only lasted until 'almost until the Second World War' (*Every Night*, p. 64), but a programme from the Finsbury Park Empire for the week commencing 7 June 1954 shows bill toppers the Beverley Sisters being followed by the obscure Alex & Nico, described as 'Continental Comedy Clowns'.
34. 'Round the halls', *The Stage*, 6 February 1947, p. 5.
35. Napier, *Act as Known*, p. 23; Wilmut, *Kindly Leave the Stage*, p. 86.
36. Interview with Peter Prentice, by telephone, 28 October 2010.
37. *Ibid*.
38. 'The art of the music hall – A manager's secrets – £500 a week for a star', *The Observer*, 2 August 1936, p. 3.
39. 'Impresario in music-hall', *The Times*, 23 August 1951, p. 2.
40. Beryl Reid, *So Much Love*, London: Arrow, 1984, p. 45.
41. Interview with Jack Seaton, by telephone, 2 February 2010.
42. Interview with Ken Joy, by telephone, 15 October 2010.

43. See Richard Anthony Baker, 'Variety's Iron Lady – Cissie Williams', *The Stage*, 21 January 2005 (www.thestage.co.uk/features/feature. php/6188, 2/7/09); Davies, *The Grades*, pp. 99, 120; Pilton, *Every Night*, p. 52; Wilmut, *Kindly Leave the Stage*, p. 84; interview with Jack Seaton, by telephone, 2 February 2010.
44. Wilmut, *Kindly Leave the Stage*, p. 84.
45. A full Moss Empires contract dating from 1949 is reproduced in Napier, *Act as Known*, pp. 148–49.
46. Ted Ray, *Raising the Laughs*, London: Werner Laurie, 1952, p. 91.
47. Pilton, *Every Night*, p. 52.
48. G. J. Mellor, *The Northern Music Hall*, Newcastle upon Tyne: Frank Graham, 1970, p. 145.
49. Interview with Teddie Beverley, by telephone, 3 September 2008.
50. Napier, *Act as Known*, p. 41.
51. Valantyne Napier, *Glossary of Terms Used in Variety, Vaudeville, Revue & Pantomime*, Westbury, Wiltshire: Badger Press, 1996, p. 50.
52. *Ibid.*, p. 18; John East, *Max Miller: The Cheeky Chappie*, London: Robson, 1993, p. 72; Chris Woodward, *The London Palladium: The Story of the Theatre and Its Stars*, Huddersfield: Northern Heritage/ Jeremy Mills, 2009, p. 88.
53. Bevan, *Top of the Bill*, p. 235.
54. Interview with Peter Prentice, by telephone, 28 October 2010.
55. Jimmy Jewel, *Three Times Lucky*, London: Enigma, 1982, pp. 73–74.
56. Interview with Wyn Calvin, by telephone, 22 January 2010.
57. Interview with Arthur Smith, Canterbury city centre, 23 May 2009.
58. *Ibid.*
59. Interview with Wyn Calvin, by telephone, 22 January 2010.
60. A collection of 4,065 record cards kept by Lawson Trout was donated to the British Music Hall Society by his daughter, Betty Flute, in 1994. In 1999, the information from the cards was typed up by S. S. Berenzweig (who incorrectly attributed them to 'Lawrence Trout').
61. 'As "The Performer" see it: Bill matter', *The Performer*, 10 November 1938, p. 2. The 'Federation' refers to the Variety Artistes' Federation.
62. Joe Collins, *A Touch of Collins*, London: Headline, 1987, p. 33.
63. Norman Hoskins, 'The terror of Cranbourn Mansions', *Call Boy*, 46(3) (autumn 2009), pp. 6–7; 6.
64. Dame Vera Lynn, *Some Sunny Day*, London: HarperCollins, 2009, p. 43.
65. Interview with Ronnie Ronalde, by telephone, 28 August 2009.
66. Ray, *Raising the Laughs*, p. 78.
67. Interview with Teddie Beverley, by telephone, 3 September 2008.
68. Interview with Peter Prentice, by telephone, 28 October 2010.
69. Eric Morecambe, Ernie Wise and Dennis Holman, *Eric and Ernie: The Autobiography of Morecambe & Wise*, London: Star Books/WH Allen, 1974, p. 64.

70. Napier, *Act as Known*, pp. 139–40.
71. Interview with Morris Aza, Golders Green, 19 April 2010.
72. See Davies, *The Grades*; Collins, *Touch of Collins*, pp. 60–76.
73. Programme from the Regal Theatre, Hull, for week commencing 3 March 1958.
74. See Napier, *Act as Known*, p. 137; Wilmut, *Kindly Leave the Stage*, pp. 82–83.
75. Barry Took, *Star Turns: The Life and Times of Benny Hill & Frankie Howerd*, London: Weidenfeld & Nicolson, 1992, p. 33.
76. Interview with Dame Vera Lynn, Ditchling, East Sussex, 12 April 2011.
77. Napier, *Act as Known*, p. 170.
78. Interview with Joan Rhodes, Belsize Park, 30 March 2010.
79. Interview with Teddie Beverley, by telephone, 3 September 2008.
80. Interview with Joan Rhodes, Belsize Park, 30 March 2010.
81. Bob Monkhouse, *Crying with Laughter*, London: Arrow, 1994, pp. 55–56.
82. Frank Bruce, 'The new comedy materialist', in Frank Bruce and Archie Foley (eds.), *More Variety Days: Fairs, Fit-ups, Music Hall, Variety Theatre, Clubs, Cruises and Cabaret*, Edinburgh: Tod, 2000, pp. 141, 135.
83. Robert Orben, *One-Liners*, New York: D. Robbins, 1951; Robert Orben, *The Encyclopedia of Patter*, New York: Louis Tannen, 1946; Lewis and Faye Copeland, *10,000 Jokes, Toasts and Stories*, Garden City, New York: Garden City Books, 1939.
84. Wall, *Fool on the Hill*, p. 148.
85. Interview with Dame Vera Lynn, Ditchling, East Sussex, 12 April 2011.
86. Interview with Teddie Beverley, by telephone, 3 September 2008.
87. Interview with Dame Vera Lynn, Ditchling, East Sussex, 12 April 2011.
88. 'Evening shadows in the music-hall', *The Times*, 3 July 1961, p. 17.
89. *Ibid.*
90. Interview with Barry Cryer, by telephone, 20 January 2010.
91. Interview with Barry Cryer, by telephone, 16 October 2009.
92. See Arthur Askey, *Before Your Very Eyes*, London: Woburn, 1975, pp. 99–100; Roy Hudd, *A Fart in a Colander*, London: Michael O'Mara, 2009, p. 74; Harry Secombe, *Arias and Raspberries*, London: Robson, 1989, p. 183.
93. Bevan, *Top of the Bill*, p. 16.
94. Napier, *Act as Known*, p. 164. See www.vam.ac.uk/images/image/44056-popup.html for an image of a Music Hall Artistes' Railway Association membership card.
95. Interview with Peter Prentice, by telephone, 28 October 2010.
96. Florence Desmond, *Florence Desmond by Herself*, London: George G. Harrap, 1953, p. 31.
97. Interview with Ken Joy, by telephone, 15 October 2010.

98. Bruce Forsyth, *Bruce: The Autobiography*, London: Sidgwick & Jackson, 2001, p. 92; Ronnie Ronalde, *Around the World on a Whistle*, Ormeau, Australia: Blackbird, 1998, p. 59.

99. Morecambe *et al.*, *Eric and Ernie*, p. 108.

3 Music Hall Becomes Variety, 1890–1927

1. 'Music hall and variety', *The New Encyclopaedia Britannica*, Micropaedia, vol. 8, 5th edn, Chicago and London: Encyclopaedia Britannica, 1992, p. 444.

2. Dave Russell, 'Varieties of life: The making of the Edwardian music hall', in Michael R. Booth and Joel H. Kaplan (eds.), *The Edwardian Theatre*, Cambridge: Cambridge University Press, 1996, p. 81.

3. W. R. Titterton, *From Theatre to Music Hall*, London: Stephen Swift, 1912, pp. 116, 123.

4. Maurice Willson Disher, *Winkles and Champagne: Comedies and Tragedies of the Music Hall*, London: Batsford, 1938, p. 137.

5. Russell, 'Varieties of life', p. 63.

6. Benny Green, *The Last Empires: A Music Hall Companion*, London: Pavilion/Michael Joseph, 1986, p. 1.

7. *Ibid.*, p. 7.

8. However, there are rival claims. Mellor, for example, argues that the Star Music Hall in Bolton, established in 1832, was 'one of, if not *the* first true "Music Halls" in the country' (*Northern Music Hall*, p. 17).

9. *Ibid.*, pp. 121–39.

10. Green, *Last Empires*, p. 183.

11. Asa Briggs, *The History of Broadcasting in the United Kingdom*, *Volume II: The Golden Age of Wireless*, London: Oxford University Press, 1965, p. 76. Similarly, Andy Medhurst wrote, 'The development of the music-hall institution is especially instructive in that it demonstrates the growth of the first entertainment *industry*. The music-hall marks the first instance of the transformation of hitherto unregulated patterns of recreation into the profitable commodity of leisure' ('Music hall and British cinema', in Charles Barr (ed.), *All Our Yesterdays: 90 Years of British Cinema*, London: BFI, 1986, p. 169).

12. 'Home truths', *The Performer*, 22 January 1942, p. 5.

13. See Green, *Last Empires*, pp. 64–68.

14. Mellor, *Northern Music Hall*, p. 17.

15. Russell, 'Varieties of life', p. 62.

16. Mellor, *Northern Music Hall*, p. 183.

17. Titterton, *From Theatre to Music Hall*, pp. 115–16.

18. Mellor, *Northern Music Hall*, p. 125.

19. Napier, *Act as Known*, p. 112.

20. Bevan, *Top of the Bill*, p. 33.

21. Titterton, *From Theatre to Music Hall*, p. 121.
22. 'Royalty in the music hall: The "Command" Performance at the Palace', *Manchester Guardian*, 2 July 1912, p. 9.
23. W. MacQueen-Pope, *The Melodies Linger On: The Story of Music Hall*, London, WH Allen, 1950, p. 434. However, as Dave Russell has pointed out, the 1912 Royal Command show was the culmination of a long process not only of the refinement of music hall, but also in the democratization of the Royal family ('Varieties of life', pp. 65–66).
24. Quoted in D. F. Cheshire, *Music Hall in Britain*, Newton Abbot: David & Charles, 1974, pp. 52–53.
25. Titterton, *From Theatre to Music Hall*, p. 121.
26. Mellor, *Northern Music Hall*, p. 186.
27. Various artists, *A Night at the Music Hall*, JSP Records, 2007, JSP 1903, disc B.
28. Mellor, *Northern Music Hall*, p. 143.
29. *Ibid.*, p.157.
30. *Ibid.*, pp. 129, 145–46.
31. Programme for the Oxford, week ending 24 July 1897, from the private collection of Max Tyler.
32. Programme for the New Cross Empire, week commencing 21 November 1904, from the private collection of Max Tyler.
33. See Green, *Last Empires*, pp.156–63.
34. J. B. Booth, 'Fifty years: The old music hall – A national product', *The Times*, 18 March 1932, p. 15.
35. Green, *Last Empires*, p. 180.
36. Quoted *ibid.*, p. 45.
37. Quoted *ibid.*, pp. 299–300.
38. See Mellor, *Northern Music Hall*, p. 136; Russell, 'Varieties of life', pp. 68–69.
39. Cheshire, *Music Hall in Britain*, pp. 57–58.
40. Macqueen-Pope, *Melodies Linger On*, p. 426; Disher, *Winkles and Champagne*, p. 138.
41. Ray, *Raising the Laughs*, pp. 43–44.
42. See Raymond Mander and Joe Mitchenson, *British Music Hall: A Story in Pictures*, London: Studio Vista, 1965, p. 36.
43. Russell, 'Varieties of life', p. 65.
44. Bevan, *Top of the Bill*, p. 48.
45. Wall, *Fool on the Hill*, p. 55.
46. Desmond, *Florence Desmond*, p. 29.
47. 'Closing of the Tivoli', *The Times*, 26 January 1914, p. 6; 'Variety gossip', *The Stage*, 13 September 1923, p. 13.
48. 'Variety gossip – Licensing: The Middlesex', *The Stage*, 7 November 1918, p. 8.
49. 'Mr C. B. Cochran's affairs: A discharge granted', *The Times*, 23 April 1925, p. 5.

50. 'The end of "The Empire": Home of English ballet', *The Times*, 21 January 1927, p. 17.
51. H. M. Walbrook, 'Alhambra memories', *The Stage*, 20 July 1933, p. 11; 'Variety gossip', *The Stage*, 22 March 1934, p. 12.
52. Bevan, *Top of the Bill*, p. 45.
53. Agate, James, *Immoment Toys: A Survey of Light Entertainment on the London Stage, 1920–1943*, London: Jonathan Cape, pp. 181–82.
54. Beswick Goodgame, 'Swinging it at Finsbury Park', *The Era*, 13 January 1937, p. 5.
55. Programme for the Finsbury Park Empire, week commencing 11 January 1937.
56. Lynn, *Sunny Day*, p. 128.
57. Desmond, *Florence Desmond*, p. 73.
58. Macqueen-Pope, *Melodies Linger On*, p. 426.
59. Various artists, *A Night at the Music Hall*, disc A.
60. Interview with Jack Seaton, by telephone, 2 February 2010.
61. Russell, 'Varieties of life', p. 68.
62. Briggs, *History of Broadcasting, Volume I*, pp. 343–44.
63. *Ibid.*, *Volume II: The Golden Age of Wireless*, p. 77.
64. Arthur Woods (dir.), *Radio Parade of 1935*, GB: British International Pictures, 1934.
65. Various artists, *A Night at the Music Hall*, disc C.
66. 'Death of Mr. George Formby: A comedian of the old school', *The Times*, 9 February 1921, p. 8.
67. Recorded 11 June 1926, and included on George Formby, *England's Famed Clown Prince of Song*, JSP Records, 2004, JSP 1901, disc A. David Bret notes that on these recordings, Formby sounds so much like his father that 'it is often difficult to tell them apart' and that 'the few fans who bought them were again only interested in the artist whose work was being covered, and some critics found them in very poor taste' (David Bret, *George Formby: A Troubled Genius*, London: Robson, 2001, p. 22).
68. Formby, *England's Famed Clown Prince of Song*, disc A.
69. *Ibid.*, disc E. Having said he sings it relatively straight, the slightly forced 'Hee hee!' and 'Ho ho!' sandwiched between the refrain of 'Where's that tiger?' does bring out some of the comic potential of the song.
70. *Ibid.*, disc C.

4 The Golden Age of Variety, 1928–52

1. 'The Palladium: Variety's come-back', *The Era*, 5 September 1928, p. 13; 'The music-hall rally', *Manchester Guardian*, 5 September 1928, p. 8.
2. 'Palladium: Variety's come-back', p. 13.
3. Bevan, *Top of the Bill*, p. 74.

4. 'Revival of the variety performance: The popular single "turn"', *The Times*, 4 June 1926, p. 12.

5. 'Palladium: Variety's come-back', p. 13; 'The music-hall rally', *Manchester Guardian*, 5 September 1928, p. 8; 'The variety stage', *The Stage*, 6 September 1928, p. 11.

6. 'Palladium: Dick Henderson', *The Observer*, 9 September 1928, p. 14.

7. 'Music-hall rally', p. 8.

8. Bevan, *Top of the Bill*, p. 87.

9. *Ibid.*, pp. 61–67.

10. *Ibid.*, p. 78; 'Death of Mr George Black', *The Performer*, 8 March 1945, p. 5. The latter source claims that Black's first chain actually included 14 cinemas.

11. 'George Black', *The Performer*, 10 November 1938, p. 19.

12. Bevan, *Top of the Bill*, p. 69.

13. 'Death of Mr George Black', *The Performer*, 8 March 1945, p. 5.

14. 'Palladium: Dick Henderson', *The Observer*, 9 September 1928, p. 14.

15. Wall, *Fool on the Hill*, p. 34. Also see pp. 33–34.

16. Trav S. D, *No Applause Just Throw Money: The Book that Made Vaudeville Famous*, New York: Faber, 2005, p. 86; Harry Stanley (with Sandy Powell), *'Can You Hear Me, Mother?' Sandy Powell's Lifetime of Music-Hall*, London: Jupiter, 1975, p. 109; Mellor, *Northern Music Hall*, p. 52.

17. Brian O'Gorman, *Laughter in the Roar*, Westbury, Wiltshire: Badger, 1998, p. 33.

18. Bevan, *Top of the Bill*, p. 208.

19. *Ibid.*, pp. 88–89, 73.

20. Interview with Jack Seaton, by telephone, 2 February 2010.

21. Bevan, *Top of the Bill*, p. 86.

22. Jewel, *Three Times Lucky*, p. 97.

23. 'Death of Mr George Black', *The Performer*, 8 March 1945, p. 5.

24. Charles W. Stein (ed.), *American Vaudeville as Seen by Its Contemporaries*, New York: Knopf, 1984, pp. 4–5, 109–10, 335–37.

25. Davies, *The Grades*, p. 48; programme for the London Pavilion, 25 July 1932.

26. A. W. Tolmie (ed.), *The Stage Year Book 1949*, London: Carson & Comerford, p. 51.

27. Interview with Dame Vera Lynn, Ditchling, East Sussex, 12 April 2011.

28. Frank Woolf, 'Variety's invasion of the cinemas: Great increase in running time', *The Era*, 18 March 1937, p. 5.

29. 'How the cinemas have helped variety', *The Era*, 16 October 1931, p. 3.

30. W. J. Bishop, 'Thrills between films: Circus in a cinema', *The Era*, 13 January 1937, p. 5.

31. Fred Russell, 'Home truths', *The Performer*, 22 January 1942, p. 5.

32. Wall, *Fool on the Hill*, p. 160.

33. 'More cinemas over to variety', *The Era*, 25 March 1937, p. 1; 'Variety at cinema prices: Changes in Manchester district', *The Era*, 17 February 1937, p. 13.
34. A programme from The Empress, Brixton, week commencing 17 August 1942 advertises 'The FINEST cinema entertainment in South London', with a showing of Joan Crawford in *A Woman's Face* and Wallace Beery in *Two-Gun Cupid* starting at 3 p.m.
35. 'The Alhambra and variety', *The Era*, 12 February 1930, p. 11.
36. Briggs, *History of Broadcasting in the United Kingdom, Volume II*, p. 78.
37. Interview with Dame Vera Lynn, Ditchling, East Sussex, 12 April 2011.
38. Briggs, *History of Broadcasting in the United Kingdom, Volume II*, p. 84.
39. Lynn, *Sunny Day*, p. 67; Jewel, *Three Times Lucky*, p. 113.
40. See Louis Barfe, *Turned Out Nice Again: The Story of British Light Entertainment*, London: Atlantics, 2008, p. 21; Briggs, *History of Broadcasting in the United Kingdom, Volume II*, pp. 105, 115.
41. Unnamed writer from 1934, quoted in Briggs, *History of Broadcasting in the United Kingdom, Volume II*, p. 75.
42. *Ibid.*, pp. 271–72.
43. 'Wireless ban developments – Miss Gracie Fields decides to obey prohibitive clause' – Mr Norman Long sticks to the BBC', *Manchester Guardian*, 29 December 1932, p. 7.
44. East, *Max Miller*, p. 134.
45. Gracie Fields, *Sing as We Go*, London: Frederick Muller, 1960, pp. 96, 56.
46. 'The vaudeville campaign', *The Era*, 29 January 1930, p. 9.
47. Bevan, *Top of the Bill*, p. 94.
48. 'The "times" and the halls', *The Performer*, 6 January 1938, p. 9.
49. 'Biggest variety boom for years. Will there be a famine?', *The Era*, 21 July 1938, p. 1.
50. Programme for *Variety Comes Back to the London Palladium*, October 1943.
51. Woodward, *London Palladium*, pp. 142, 147.
52. Davies, *The Grades*, p. 120.
53. 'As "The Performer" sees it', *The Performer*, 22 January 1942, p. 2.
54. Mellor, *Northern Music Hall*, p. 40 [the Argyle Theatre]; *The Stage Year Book 1950*, London: Carson & Comerford, pp. 263–65. [London variety theatres]
55. 'The art of the music hall – A manager's secrets – £500 a week for a star', *The Observer*, 2 August 1936, p. 3. *Apple-Sauce!* would later be restaged at the Palladium.
56. Interview with Dame Vera Lynn, Ditchling, East Sussex, 12 April 2011.
57. 'General Theatre Corporation. Substantial improvement', *Manchester Guardian*, 16 December 1942, p. 2.

58. 'Death of Mr George Black', and W. J. Bishop, 'George Black', *The Stage*, 8 March 1945, p. 3.
59. Woodward, *London Palladium*, pp. 151–52.
60. Interview with Michael Grade, by telephone, 28 April 2011.
61. Programme from the London Casino, dated 5 April to 1 May 1948.
62. 'Our London correspondence', *Manchester Guardian*, 11 June 1947, p. 4.
63. 'Variety gossip', *The Stage*, 12 June 1947, p. 3.
64. Davies, *The Grades*, pp. 133–34.
65. 'The variety stage', *The Stage*, 12 August 1948, p. 3.
66. 'The Palladium: Mr Danny Kaye', *The Times*, 4 February 1948, p. 2.
67. Martin Gottfried, *Nobody's Fool: The Lives of Danny Kaye*, New York: Simon & Schuster, 1994, p. 135.
68. *Ibid.*, p. 143; Bevan, *Top of the Bill*, p. 168.
69. Bevan, *Top of the Bill*, p. 159.
70. Kurt Singer, *The Danny Kaye Saga*, London: John Spencer/Badger, 1959, p. 96.
71. *Ibid.*, p. 102.
72. 'The niceness of Mr Kaye: "Better me than Hitler–"', *Manchester Guardian*, 13 June 1949, p. 3.
73. Pilton, *Every Night*, pp. 35–36.
74. Interview with Michael Grade, by telephone, 28 April 2011.
75. Bevan, *Top of the Bill*, p. 9.
76. 'The Palladium' can be heard on Lenny Bruce, *The Lenny Bruce Originals Volume 2*, Fantasy Records, 1991, CDFA 526. One of the things that makes this routine interesting is the references it uses. Both Bruce and his audience have a surprising awareness of British show business. Val Parnell is mentioned by name – albeit being described as 'the house booker', a demotion that would no doubt have appalled him – and is a major character in the routine. There is also a reference to the Scots music hall star Sir Harry Lauder, whose career had started over 60 years before 'The Palladium' was recorded.
77. 'Criticism of variety bills by the national dailies has caused considerable amounts of unfavourable comment by the profession generally during the past few weeks, mainly on account of notices of the International Variety season at the Casino ... The fault seems to lie in the fact that critics are sent from some newspapers who have little knowledge and little love of the music hall, and are unduly prejudiced in their notices by this' ('Variety gossip', *The Stage*, 24 July 1947, p. 3).
78. Booth, 'Fifty years', 18 March 1932, p. 15.
79. MacQueen-Pope, *Melodies Linger On*, p. 436.
80. Harry Foster, 'Free Trade in Foreign Artists: Harry Foster Explains the Case for the Agents', *The Era*, 16 October 1931, p. 3.
81. 'Too many foreign acts: Disclosures at VAF meeting', *The Era*, 10 March 1937, p. 3; 'VAF and foreign acts: Protest meeting to be called', *The Era*, 3 February 1937, p. 3.

82. Napier, *Act as Known*, p. 20.
83. *Ibid.*, pp. 44–45, 55–57, 83.
84. Interview with Joan Rhodes, Belsize Park, 30 March 2010.
85. Six British acts in next Palladium bill', *The Stage*, 31 March 1955, p. 3; 'Two British youngsters triumph', *The Stage*, 14 April 1955, p. 7.
86. *Stage Year Book 1950*, pp. 36–37.
87. Max Bygraves, *I Wanna Tell You a Story*, London: Star/WH Allen, 1976, p. 97.
88. Interview with Ronnie Ronalde, by telephone, 28 August 2009.
89. Foster, 'Free Trade in Foreign Artists', *The Era*, 16 October 1931, p. 3.
90. 'Round the halls', *The Stage*, 26 August 1948, p. 5.
91. East, *Max Miller*, p. 151. The precise sum quoted by Miller in his riposte to Parnell varies depending on who is telling the anecdote, but the basic point remains the same.
92. 'Four West End appearances', *The Performer*, 7 February 1952, p. 3.
93. *The Stage Year Book 1951*, London: Carson & Comerford, p. 50.
94. Mellor, *Northern Music Hall*, pp. 200–2.
95. Bevan, *Top of the Bill*, pp. 215–16.

5   Variety Falls Apart, 1953–65

1. *The Stage Year Book 1961*, London: Carson & Comerford, p. 14.
2. *The Stage Year Book 1956*, London: Carson & Comerford, p. 17.
3. 'What we think: National Trust for variety theatres?', *The Stage*, 20 February 1958, p. 3.
4. John Betjeman, 'Architecture for entertainment', *Daily Telegraph*, 16 November 1959, p. 13.
5. 'Evening shadows in the music-hall, *The Times*, 3 July 1961, p. 17.
6. Interview with Roy Hudd, Concert Artistes' Association, London, 12 March 2010.
7. *Stage Year Book 1961*, p. 22.
8. Based on listings of 'London Music Halls', in *Stage Year Book 1951*, pp. 195–96. I calculated this based on the audience capacities and number of shows per week as listed here. The theatres listed are: Brixton Empress; Camberwell Palace; Chelsea Palace; Chiswick Empire; Clapham Junction Grand; Collins' Music Hall; East Ham Palace; Finsbury Park Empire; Golders Green Hippodrome; Hackney Empire; Lewisham Hippodrome; the Metropolitan; New Cross Empire; the Palladium; the Queen's, Poplar; King's Cross Regent; Shepherd's Bush Empire; Victoria Palace; Walthamstow Palace; Wood Green Empire; Woolwich Empire.
9. Based on listings of 'London and suburban theatres', in *The Stage Year Book 1960*, London: Carson & Comerford, pp. 247–49. Unsurprisingly, variety theatres are no longer listed separately at this point, and it is worth noting that each theatre's listed capacity has fallen, in one case rather dramatically – the Met's auditorium, which used to hold 1,682 now

only holds 1,076. The figures given here yield a total weekly capacity of 83,616 on the assumption that each theatre operates a twice nightly policy – this may no longer have been the case, making this a liberal estimate.

10. 'No Glasgow Empire re-development yet', *The Stage*, 14 September 1961, p. 1.
11. 'Glasgow Empire's farewell show', *The Stage*, 7 February 1963, p. 3.
12. John Alexander, *Tearing Tickets Twice Nightly*, London: Arcady, 2002, p. 18 (also see pp. 16–18).
13. *Ibid.*, p. 53.
14. 'Farewell to the Met', *The Stage*, 3 January 1963, p. 4.
15. Norman Shrapnel, 'The Met's final night', *The Guardian*, 13 April 1963, p. 4; Alexander, *Tearing Tickets*, p. 59.
16. W. J. Bishop, 'Variety of the year', in Tolmie, *Stage Year Book 1949*, p. 49.
17. Barfe, *Turned Out Nice Again*, p. 79.
18. 'Hackney Empire not to close', *The Stage*, 20 January 1955, p. 1.
19. 'Another music hall to close', *Manchester Guardian*, 19 January, 1956, p. 5.
20. 'Tax menace analysed: Memorandum prepared for chancellor', *The Performer*, 25 November 1954, pp. 1, 11.
21. Ross Wade, 'TV is killing itself – By murdering variety', *The Stage*, 10 October 1957, p. 6.
22. A. W. McKinty, 'Wyn takes a step', *The Stage*, 16 January 1958, p. 6.
23. Napier, *Act as Known*, p. 99.
24. Barfe, *Turned Out Nice Again*, p. 65.
25. 'Variety theatres: The Coliseum', *The Times*, 5 August 1930, p. 8; *Turns*, BBC1, 30 August 1984, 11 p.m.
26. 'Televariety', *The Performer*, 7 February 1952, p. 10.
27. Interview with Teddie Beverley, 3 September 2008, by telephone.
28. *The Stage Year Book 1955*, London: Carson & Comerford, pp. 21–22.
29. 'Overture', *The Performer*, 25 November 1954, p. 2.
30. Interview with Teddie Beverley, 3 September 2008, by telephone.
31. 'TV is killing itself – By murdering variety'.
32. Interview with Wyn Calvin, by telephone, 22 January 2010.
33. *Stage Year Book 1955*, p. 22.
34. Pilton, *Every Night*, p. 93.
35. *Ibid.*
36. Forsyth, *Bruce*, p. 111.
37. Interview with Roy Hudd, Concert Artistes' Association, London, 12 March 2010.
38. Interview with Don Smoothey, Ham, 9 October 2009.
39. 'TV is killing itself – By murdering variety'.
40. 'Shepherd's Bush Empire closure', *The Stage*, 24 September 1953, p. 3; Barfe, *Turned Out Nice Again*, pp. 72–73.

41. 'More theatres to close', *The Stage*, 18 November 1954, p. 1; 'Walham Green Granville to close again', *The Stage*, 16 August 1956, p. 12.

42. 'Transformation of Wood Green Empire', *The Stage*, 14 July 1955, p. 11.

43. 'ATV take lease on Hackney Empire', *The Stage*, 2 February 1956, p. 9; Louis Barfe, 'London belongs to television', www.transdiffusion.org/emc/studioone/london.php, 9/3/2010.

44. 'The Met's final night', *The Guardian*, 13 April 1963, p. 4.

45. Betjeman, 'Architecture for entertainment', p. 13; Andrew Gray 'TV will have to subsidise theatres', *The Stage Year Book 1957*, London: Carson & Comerford, pp. 28–30.

46. 'The curtain falls on a famous music hall: End of the Glasgow Empire', *The Stage*, 28 March 1963, p. 5.

47. *Ibid*.

48. *Ibid*., p. 3.

49. Interview with Don Smoothey, Ham, 9 October 2009.

50. Mollie Ellis, 'In the property business?', *Stage Year Book 1961*, pp. 21–23; p. 21.

51. *The Stage Year Book 1962*, London: Carson & Comerford, p. 24.

52. Interview with Wyn Calvin, by telephone, 22 January 2010.

53. Wall, *Fool on the Hill*, p. 213.

54. Bevan, *Top of the Bill*, p. 86.

55. 'Bury the words music hall – Says an agent', *The Stage*, 13 January 1955, p. 3.

56. 'Scottish flavour: Let's drive these variety pessimists out of town!', *The Stage*, 6 December 1956, p. 4.

57. Reg Barlow, 'Mr Sellers and variety', *The Stage*, 20 August 1959, p. 4.

58. *Stage Year Book 1956*, p. 17.

59. Sidney Vauncez, 'Killing the golden (variety) goose', in Anthony Merryn (ed.), *The Stage Year Book 1966*, London: Carson & Comerford, p. 17.

60. Article repr. in Richard Anthony Baker, *British Music Hall: An Illustrated History*, Stroud: Sutton, 2005, p. 286. A similarly vivid account, written by *Daily Mail* critic Robert Muller can be found in Mellor, *Northern Music Hall*, pp. 214–16.

61. John Earl in the introduction to Alexander, *Tearing Tickets* p. 6.

62. Clarkson Rose, *Red Plush and Greasepaint*, London: Museum, 1964, p. 67.

63. Barry Cryer, *You Won't Believe This But…* , London: Virgin, 1996, p. 32.

64. Interview with Roy Hudd, Concert Artistes' Association, London, 12 March 2010.

65. Sydney W. Carroll, 'Nudity is crudity: Away with all flesh', *The Era*, 6 May 1937, p. 1.

66. W. J. Rickets, 'Nudity and obscenity: The remedy', *The Era*, 14 May 1937, p. 7.

67. Frank Woolf, 'Comic strip tease: Hullaboloney at Victoria', *The Era*, 8 April 1947, p. 5.

68. Interview with Barry Cryer, by telephone, 20 January 2010.
69. Interview with Roy Hudd, Concert Artistes' Association, London, 12 March 2010.
70. Andrew Gray, 'Variety', *Stage Year Book 1956*, pp. 17–19; p. 17.
71. Interview with Roy Hudd, Concert Artistes' Association, London, 12 March 2010.
72. Advert for the People's Palace in Dundee, owned by the Livermore Brothers, quoted in Mellor, *Northern Music Hall*, p. 28.
73. Hudd, *Fart in a Colander*, p. 70.
74. *Stage Year Book 1955*, p. 21.
75. Interview with Chas McDevitt, by telephone, 25 January 2010.
76. *Ibid*.
77. Chas McDevitt, *Skiffle: The Definitive Inside Story*, London: Robson, 1997, p. 116.
78. *Stage Year Book 1957*, p. 23.
79. 'Finsbury Park Empire', *The Stage*, 4 September 1958, p. 4.
80. Interview with Chas McDevitt, by telephone, 25 January 2010.
81. 'Metropolitan: Skiffle show', *The Stage*, 24 January 1957, p. 5.
82. Interview with Chas McDevitt, by telephone, 25 January 2010.
83. 'Chiswick Empire', *The Stage*, 6 March 1958, p. 4.
84. Interview with Chas McDevitt, by telephone, 25 January 2010.
85. McDevitt, *Skiffle*, p. 67.
86. 'Tit Bits' can be heard on various artists, *The Best of British Comedy*, Disky, 2002, cat. no. CB 795122, disc 1.
87. Interview with Chas McDevitt, by telephone, 25 January 2010.
88. 'Mr Sellers and variety'.
89. 'Chiswick Empire', *The Stage*, 27 November 1958, p. 7.
90. Interview with Roy Hudd, Concert Artistes' Association, London, 12 March 2010.
91. Des O'Connor, *Bananas Can't Fly!*, London: Headline, 2001, pp. 111–16.
92. Interview with Arthur Smith, 23 May 2009, Canterbury city centre.
93. 'What we think: Horror comics', *The Stage*, 28 November 1957, p. 3.
94. Interview with Barry Cryer, by telephone, 20 January 2010.
95. Ronalde, *Around the World*, p. 173.
96. *Stage Year Book 1956*, p. 17.
97. Interview with Don Smoothey, Ham, 9 October 2009.
98. Jimmy Jewel, *Three Times Lucky*, London: Enigma Books, 1982, p. 168.
99. See 'TV is killing itself – By murdering variety'; *The Stage Year Book 1957*, London: Carson & Comerford, p. 28; *Turned Out Nice Again: The Story of British Light Entertainment*, p. 85.
100. Mollie Ellis, 'Variety has a Year of Changes', *The Stage Year Book 1958*, London: Carson & Comerford, pp. 17–18; Mollie Ellis, 'Good omens for variety', *The Stage Year Book 1959*, London: Carson & Comerford,

pp. 23–25; Mollie Ellis 'A pep-pill for the provinces', *The Stage Year Book 1960*, London: Carson & Comerford, pp. 27–29; Mollie Ellis, 'What next in variety?', *Stage Year Book 1962*, pp. 24–25; Mollie Ellis, 'The decline of humour', *The Stage Year Book 1963*, London: Carson & Comerford, pp. 20–21.

101. Mollie Ellis, 'Good Omens for Variety', p. 25.
102. GJ Mellor, *The Northern Music Hall*, Newcastle-Upon-Tyne: Frank Graham, 1970, p. 212.
103. *Bruce: The Autobiography*, p. 158.
104. *The Stage Year Book 1955*, London: Carson & Comerford, p. 21.
105. 'Variety Records Broken at the Globe, Stockton', *The Stage*, 8 July 1954, p. 3.
106. *Stage Year Book 1956*, p. 18.
107. *Ibid.*; 'Variety gossip', *The Stage*, 20 January 1955, p. 3.
108. East, *Max Miller*, pp. 155–56.
109. Interview with Jack Seaton, by telephone, 2 February 2010.
110. Bevan, *Top of the Bill*, p. 86.
111. Napier, *Act as Known*, p. 160.
112. 'Half a century of service', *The Performer*, 26 September 1957, p. 1.
113. Interview with Michael Grade, by telephone, 28 April 2011.
114. *Ibid.*

6 Personality

1. F. T. Marinetti, 'The variety theatre 1913', in Umbro Apollonio (ed.), *Futurist Manifestos*, London: Thames & Hudson, 1973, p. 126.
2. Bevan, *Top of the Bill*, p. 79.
3. Interview with Teddie Beverley, by telephone, 16 September 2008.
4. Interview with Peter Prentice, by telephone, 28 October 2010.
5. O'Gorman, *Laughter in the Roar*, p. 3.
6. Hudd, *Fart in a Colander*, p. 30.
7. Reginald Barlow, 'Variety of 1952', *The Stage Year Book 1953*, London: Carson & Comerford, p. 17.
8. See 'Leicester', *The Stage*, 19 December 1936, p. 6 [Harry Roy]; 'Holborn Empire', *The Times*, 2 March 1937, p. 14 [Max Miller].
9. 'Miss Gracie Fields: Last night at the London Palladium', *Manchester Guardian*, 22 July 1936, p. 10.
10. 'What the variety stage wants – Miss Gracie Fields explains – Personality', *The Observer*, 30 July 1933, p. 17.
11. 'Leicester', *The Stage*, 19 December 1936, p. 6.
12. 'Harry Roy's New Stage Show' on Harry Roy, *The Cream of Harry Roy*, Flapper/Pavilion Records, 1991, PAST CD 9741.
13. D. E. Britten, 'Harry Roy at the "Bush"', *The Era*, 3 March 1937, p. 5.
14. 'Harry Roy's New Stage Show', on Harry Roy, *The Cream of Harry Roy*, Flapper/Pavilion Records, 1991, PAST CD 9741.

15. 'Gracie Fields at the Holborn Empire', on various artists, *Variety –
    "Live!"*, Windyridge Records, 2005, WINDYVAR14. Two recordings
    exist of this same show, which dates from 11 October 1933 – presum-
    ably Fields was recorded at both houses. The repertoire covered is
    identical, but the patter between songs subtly differs in both substance
    and delivery.

16. 'Gracie at the Holborn Empire', on Fields, *Sing as We Go*. This is the
    other recording from the Holborn Empire on 11 October 1933.

17. Lawson Trout files.

18. 'Gracie Fields at the Holborn Empire', on *Variety – "Live!"*.

19. Interview with Roy Hudd, Concert Artistes' Association, London,
    12 March 2010.

20. 'Max Miller at the Holborn Empire First House October 7th 1938',
    on Max Miller, *Max Miller*, EMI Comedy, 2000, 7243 5 28599 2 4.
    'Luxemburg' is a reference to Radio Luxemburg, the radio station on
    which he broadcast particularly when he was banned by the BBC.

21. 'Metropolitan', *The Stage*, 17 April, 1958, p. 4.

22. A. Crooks Ripley, 'Is Max Behavin' Iself?', *Vaudeville Pattern*, London:
    Brownlee, 1947, pp. 35–38; 37.

23. 'Holborn Empire', *The Times*, 11 April 1939, p. 8.

24. 'Max Miller at the Holborn Empire First House October 7th 1938', on
    Max Miller.

25. 'Variety stage', *The Stage*, 19 September 1952, p. 3.

26. 'The incomparable Max Miller', *The Stage*, 21 February 1952, pp. 1, 5.

27. Quoted in O'Gorman, *Laughter in the Roar*, p. 1. There is an important
    connection with Max Miller here, as the character of Archie Rice was
    consciously based on a kind of failed version of Miller.

28. 'Little Stick of Blackpool Rock', on George Formby, *'V' for Victory*,
    Redrock Records, 1995, RKD23 PPL.

29. 'Imagine Me on the Maginot Line' (*ibid.*).

30. Interview with Joan Rhodes, Belsize Park, 30 March 2010.

31. Interview with Dame Vera Lynn, Ditchling, East Sussex, 12 April 2011.

32. Forsyth, *Bruce*, p. 86.

33. Interview with Barry Cryer, by telephone, 16 October 2009.

34. 'More Chestnut Corner', *Great Radio Stars Volume Two*, Pavilion
    Records, 1991, PAST CD 9728.

35. 'Tommy Trinder at the Embassy Theatre, Peterborough', on
    Variety – Live!.

36. Interview with Roy Hudd, Concert Artistes' Association, London,
    12 March 2010.

37. Interview with Joan Rhodes, Belsize Park, 30 March 2010.

38. Programme from the London Palladium, week commencing 19
    September 1932.

39. 'Band conductor put in prison – unpaid income tax – nobody to accept
    last-minute payment', *Manchester Guardian*, 20 June 1927, p. 10.

40. 'Round the variety halls: Wood Green Empire', *The Stage*, 2 April 1953, p. 5.
41. Interview with Teddie Beverley, by telephone, 3 September 2008.
42. 'Round the halls: The Palladium', *The Stage*, 11 March 1954, p. 5.
43. 'Review: Autumn spectacular at the Palace Theatre, Manchester', *The Guardian*, 19 October 1963, p. 6.
44. Interview with Teddie Beverley, by telephone, 16 September 2008.
45. 'We Have to Be So Careful', on the Beverley Sisters, *The Biggest Hits*, Rex Recordings, 2007, REXX 113.
46. Interview with Teddie Beverley, by telephone, 16 September 2008.
47. *Ibid.*
48. *Ibid.*
49. *Ibid.*
50. Barker, '"Image" in show business', p. 8.
51. Joan Rhodes, *Coming on Strong*, Darlington: Serendipity, 2007, p. 82.
52. Interview with Barry Cryer, by telephone, 20 January 2010.
53. Desmond, *Florence Desmond*, p. 207.
54. Quoted in East, *Max Miller*, p. 16. I have qualified this sentence ('is supposed to have said') because John East is believed by some people with a good knowledge of variety to be a less than reliable source, and this quote is taken from a personal anecdote.
55. R. B. Marriott, 'Farewell to Max Miller', *The Stage*, 16 May 1963, p. 6.
56. Lynn, *Sunny Day*, pp. 140–41.
57. Interview with Jack Seaton, by telephone, 2 February 2010.
58. Interview with Peter Prentice, by telephone, 28 October 2010.
59. East, *Max Miller*, p. 73.
60. Interview with Barry Cryer, by telephone, 20 January 2010.
61. See East, *Max Miller*, pp. 10–11, 33–34.
62. Interview with Peter Prentice, by telephone, 28 October 2010.
63. Singer, *Danny Kaye Saga*, p. 6.
64. Interview with Don Smoothey, Ham, 9 October 2009.
65. *Ibid.*
66. Interview with Jack Seaton, by telephone, 2 February 2010.
67. Interview with Morris Aza, Golders Green, 19 April 2010.
68. 'What the variety stage wants', p. 17.
69. Gracie Fields, *Sing as We Go*, London: Frederick Muller, 1960, p. 67.
70. *Ibid.*, p. 132.
71. See Bevan, *Top of the Bill*, p. 78; Pilton, *Every Night*, pp. 15, 122.
72. Alexander, *Tearing Tickets*, p. 35.
73. Lynn, *Sunny Day*, p. 299.
74. Ted Kavanagh, *Tommy Handley*, London: Hodder & Stoughton, 1949, p. 12.
75. William Cook, *Morecambe & Wise Untold*, London: HarperCollins, 2007, pp. 154, 164.
76. Interview with Don Smoothey, Ham, 9 October 2009.

77. Interview with Morris Aza, Golders Green, 19 April 2010.

78. Secombe, *Arias*, p. 179.

79. Richard Fawkes, *Fighting for a Laugh: Entertaining the British and American Armed Forces 1939–46*, London: Macdonald and Jane's, 1978, p. 145. ENSA stands for Entertainments National Service Association.

80. Trav S. D., *No Applause*, p. 141.

81. Quoted in Michael Billington, *How Tickled I Am*, London: Elm Tree, 1977, p. 24. The golliwog refers to the former trademark of Robertson's Marmalade.

82. Interview with Wyn Calvin, by telephone, 22 January 2010.

83. Interview with Joan Rhodes, Belsize Park, 30 March 2010.

84. Ronalde, *Around the World*, pp. 134–35.

85. Eddie Gray booklet, author's collection.

86. Pilton, *Every Night*, pp. 40–41. Another source puts the number of posters at a dozen (Bevan, *Top of the Bill*, p. 132).

87. Interview with Morris Aza, Golders Green, 19 April 2010.

88. 'Tommy Trinder at the Embassy Theatre, Peterborough', on *Variety – Live!*.

89. 'The Western Brothers', on various artists, *Great Radio Comedians*, BBC Records, 1973, MONO REC151M, side 2.

90. Stanley (with Powell), '*Can You Hear Me, Mother?*, pp. 62–64.

91. 'Gracie at the Holborn Empire', on Fields, *Sing as We Go*.

92. Reproduced in Green, *Last Empires*, p. 82.

93. Interview with Wyn Calvin, by telephone, 22 January 2010.

94. Interview with Roy Hudd, Concert Artistes' Association, London, 12 March 2010.

95. Ivor Brown, 'Theatre and life', *The Observer*, 29 August 1943, p. 2.

96. Interview with Don Smoothey, Ham, 9 October 2009.

97. Interview with Roy Hudd, Concert Artistes' Association, London, 12 March 2010.

98. Hence the use of gender-specific language – funny *man* and straight *man* – used in the previous paragraph.

99. Interview with Don Smoothey, Ham, 9 October 2009.

100. Interview with Jack Seaton, by telephone, 2 February 2010; Ray, *Raising the Laughs*, p. 105.

101. Collins, *Touch of Collins*, p. 122.

102. Interview with Peter Prentice, by telephone, 28 October 2010.

103. 'The importance of being yourself: The humour of Max Bygraves', *The Stage*, 10 August 1950, p. 1.

104. Fields, *Sing as We Go*, p. 61.

105. Interview with Morris Aza, Golders Green, 19 April 2010.

106. Fields, *Sing as We Go*, p. 105.

107. 'Absent friends – Do they matter?', *Daily Mirror*, 29 July 1940, p. 4.

108. David Bret, *The Real Gracie Fields: The Authorised Biography*, London: JR Books, 2010, p. 91; 'Variety gossip', *The Stage*, 8 August 1940, p. 3.

109. 'Variety gossip', *The Stage*, 8 August 1940, p. 3.

110. Bret, *Real Gracie Fields*, p. 110.

111. Desmond, *Florence Desmond*, p. 285.

112. Interview with Morris Aza, Golders Green, 19 April 2010.

113. 'London Palladium: Miss Gracie Fields', *The Times*, 5 October 1948, p. 7.

114. 'London Palladium', *The Performer*, 7 October 1948, p. 11.

115. Smith, *Calling All Stars*.

116. Hudd (with Hindin), *Roy Hudd's Cavalcade*, p. 146.

117. 'Whitehall Theatre: Peek-a-boo again', *The Times*, 18 July 1945, p. 6.

118. Beryl Reid, *So Much Love*, London: Arrow, 1984, pp. 216–17.

119. 'Chiswick Empire: Ronnie's fans', *The Stage*, 28 March 1957, p. 4.

120. Interview with Ronnie Ronalde, by telephone, 28 August 2009.

121. Ray, *Raising the Laughs*, p. 66. The name Nedlo was a reversal of Ray's actual surname, Olden. Hugh Neek was a slightly tortuous pun on the word 'unique'.

122. 'Fiddling and fooling', *Great Radio Stars Volume Two*.

123. Frankie Howerd, *On the Way I Lost it*, London: Star, 1977, p. 67.

124. *Ibid*. p. 69.

125. *Fifty Years of Radio Comedy*, BBC Records, 1972, MONO REC 138M.

126. Bevan, *Top of the Bill*, p. 147. Similar accounts can be found in Singer, *Danny Kaye Saga*, p. 95; Pilton, *Every Night*, p. 35.

127. 'London Palladium', *The Performer*, 5 February 1948, p. 9.

128. Singer, *Danny Kaye Saga*, p. 97.

129. Gottfried, *Nobody's Fool*, p. 188. As a child, my father's second wife was taken to see Danny Kaye on one of his tours of provincial variety theatres, and the one thing she could remember about it was the moment when he sat on the edge of the stage and chatted to the audience.

130. See Singer, *Danny Kaye Saga*, pp. 95–96.

131. 'Round the halls', *The Stage*, 5 February 1948, p. 3.

7 Participation

1. *The Era*, 18 March 1937, p. 6.

2. Disher, *Winkles and Champagne*, p. 141.

3. Macqueen-Pope, *Melodies Linger On*, p. 438.

4. 'Variety stage', *The Stage*, 13 November 1952, p. 3.

5. *Ibid.*, p. 3.

6. Quoted in Green, *Last Empires*, p. 154.

7. Wilmut, *Kindly Leave the Stage*, p. 68.

8. Quoted in Jim Steinmeyer, *Hiding the Elephant: How Magicians Invented the Impossible*, London: Arrow, 2005, p. 150.
9. Interview with Dame Vera Lynn, Ditchling, East Sussex, 12 April 2011.
10. Gottfried, *Nobody's Fool*, pp. 74–75.
11. DANNY KAYE 6 (ROYAL COMMAND PERFORMANCE) video newsreel film, www.britishpathe.com/record.php?id=81650, 20/7/10.
12. Interview with Jack Seaton, by telephone, 2 February 2010.
13. Interview with Teddie Beverley, 16 September 2008, by telephone.
14. Constantin Stanislavski, *An Actor Prepares*, London: Methuen, 1980, p. 72.
15. Antonin Artaud, *The Theatre and Its Double*, London: John Calder, 1977, p. 64.
16. Lynn, *Sunny Day*, p. 215.
17. Cook, *Morecambe & Wise Untold*, p. 16.
18. Forsyth, *Bruce*, p. 125.
19. Interview with Wyn Calvin, by telephone, 22 January 2010.
20. Iain Mackintosh, *Architecture, Actor and Audience*, London and New York: Routledge, 1993, p. 172.
21. *Ibid.*, p. 128.
22. *Ibid.*, p. 121.
23. Howerd, *On the Way*, p. 67.
24. Smith, *Calling All Stars*. Bennett's use of eye contact is much the same in another Herbert Smith film from the same time, *Soft Lights and Sweet Music*.
25. Cook, *Morecambe & Wise Untold*, p. 171.
26. This clip is included in the documentary *The Story of Light Entertainment* (Part 1: Double acts), BBC2, 22 July 2006.
27. From the foreword to Clarkson Rose, *Red Plush and Greasepaint*, London: Museums, 1964, p. 5.
28. Greg Palmer (dir.), *Vaudeville*, Thirteen/WNET, KCTS/9 Television and Palmer/Fenster 1997.
29. St John Ervine, 'At the play: Music hall', *The Observer*, 19 February 1939, p. 14.
30. Russell, 'Varieties of life', pp. 61–82; p. 71.
31. Green, *Last Empires*, p. 166.
32. *Ibid.*, p. 45.
33. *Ibid.*, p. 135.
34. *Ibid.*, p. 41.
35. Askey, *Before Your Very Eyes*, pp. 98–99.
36. Interview with Wyn Calvin, by telephone, 22 January 2010.
37. Ray, *Raising the Laughs*, p. 123.
38. Collins, *Touch of Collins*, p. 76.
39. See Bygraves, *Tell You a Story*, pp. 186–87; Secombe, *Arias*, p. 193.
40. Interview with Roy Hudd, Concert Artistes' Association, London, 12 March 2010.

41. Forsyth, *Bruce*, p. 93.
42. See Reid, *So Much Love*, p. 19; Ronalde, *Around the World*, p. 57.
43. Interview with Don Smoothey, Ham, 9 October 2009. Smoothey also gave an account of this interview in *The Stage*, where he added that, 'They ended up cheering and giving us an ovation' (Patrick Newley, 'King of the bill', *The Stage*, 11 October 2001, p. 12).
44. Roy Hudd, *Roy Hudd's Book of Music-Hall, Variety and Showbiz Anecdotes*, London: Robson, 1993, p. 82.
45. Wisdom (with Hall), *My Turn*, p. 107.
46. 'Scottish flavour', *The Stage*, 24 October 1957, p. 5.
47. Interview with Don Smoothey, Ham, 9 October 2009.
48. Interview with Wyn Calvin, by telephone, 22 January 2010.
49. Interview with Roy Hudd, Concert Artistes' Association, London, 12 March 2010.
50. Reproduced in Napier, *Act as Known*, p. 149.
51. Interview with Don Smoothey, Ham, 9 October 2009.
52. Interview with Jack Seaton, by telephone, 2 February 2010.
53. Cook, *Morecambe & Wise Untold*, p. 103.
54. O'Connor, *Bananas*, pp. 79–80.
55. Interview with Ken Joy, by telephone, 15 October 2010.
56. Secombe, *Arias*.
57. Interview with Don Smoothey, Ham, 9 October 2009.
58. Interview with Roy Hudd, Concert Artistes' Association, London, 12 March 2010.
59. 'Variety theatres: The reopening of the Palladium', *The Times*, 5 September 1928, p. 10.
60. Interview with Wyn Calvin, by telephone, 22 January 2010.
61. 'Royalty in the music hall: The "Command" performance at the Palace', *Manchester Guardian*, 2 July 1912, p. 9.
62. Howerd, *On the Way*, p. 93.
63. Secombe, *Arias*, p. 210.
64. Marinetti, 'Variety theatre', pp. 126–31; p. 127.
65. Interview with Roy Hudd, Concert Artistes' Association, London, 12 March 2010.
66. Interview with Teddie Beverley, 16 September 2008, by telephone.
67. Napier, *Act as Known*, p. 42.
68. Bygraves, *Tell You a Story*, p. 114.
69. Bret, *George Formby*, p. 74.
70. Eric Midwinter, *Make 'Em Laugh: Famous Comedians and their Worlds*, London: George Allen & Unwin, 1979, p. 202.
71. Billington, *How Tickled*, pp. 25–28.
72. *Great Radio Comedians*, BBC Records, 1973, MONO REC 151M.
73. 'On Behalf of the Working Classes' (track 12), *Robb Wilton's War*, Pavilion Records, 2001, PAST CD 7854. Recorded at the Argyle Theatre, Birkenhead, 13 November 1939.

74. Bygraves, *Tell You a Story*, p. 98.
75. 'London Palladium', *The Performer*, 5 February 1948, p. 9.
76. Singer, *Danny Kaye Saga*, p. 99.
77. 'Profile: Danny Kaye', *The Observer*, 15 May 1949, p. 2.
78. Singer, *Danny Kaye Saga*, p. 99.
79. Gottfried, *Nobody's Fool*, p. 217.
80. Philip Auslander, *Liveness: Performance in a Mediatized Culture*, London and New York: Routledge, 1999, p. 2. To be fair, Auslander has the grace to qualify his cynicism, acknowledging that, 'concepts such as these do have value for performers and partisans of live performance'.
81. Interview with Dame Vera Lynn, Ditchling, East Sussex, 12 April 2011.
82. Secombe, *Arias*, p. 149.
83. Singer, *Danny Kaye Saga*, p. 107.
84. Interview with Wyn Calvin, by telephone, 22 January 2010.
85. Interview with Peter Prentice, by telephone, 28 October 2010.
86. Interview with Jack Seaton, by telephone, 2 February 2010.
87. Napier, *Glossary*, 1996, p. 16.
88. See Forsyth, *Bruce*, p. 52; Wall, *Fool on the Hill*, p. 31.
89. Maclean Rogers (dir.), *Variety Jubilee* (GB: Butcher's Film Service, 1943).
90. Interview with Jack Seaton, by telephone, 2 February 2010.
91. Interview with Dame Vera Lynn, Ditchling, East Sussex, 12 April 2011.
92. 'Joe Loss Stage Show', on various artists, *Stars of Variety*, Music Collection International, 1994, cat. no. GAGDMC002, cassette 1, side 2.
93. Oswald Mitchell (dir.), *The Dummy Talks*, GB: British National Films, 1943.
94. Interview with Ken Joy, by telephone, 15 October 2010.
95. 'The music-hall: Modern influences', *The Times*, 26 October 1938, p. 12.
96. Interview with Dame Vera Lynn, Ditchling, East Sussex, 12 April 2011.
97. Interview with Peter Prentice, by telephone, 28 October 2010.
98. Interview with Roy Hudd, Concert Artistes' Association, London, 12 March 2010.
99. Singer, *Danny Kaye Saga*, p. 42.
100. Interview with Teddie Beverley, 3 September 2008, by telephone.
101. Harry Secombe, *Twice Brightly*, London: Robson Books, 1974, p. 53.
102. Interview with Wyn Calvin, by telephone, 22 January 2010.
103. Interview with Dame Vera Lynn, Ditchling, East Sussex, 12 April 2011.
104. Napier, *Act as Known*, p. 131.

105. 'The music-hall: Modern influences', *The Times*, 26 October 1938, p. 12.
106. Interview with Joan Rhodes, Belsize Park, 30 March 2010.
107. Secombe, *Arias*, p. 146.
108. Interview with Roy Hudd, Concert Artistes' Association, London, 12 March 2010.
109. Bygraves, *Tell You a Story*, p. 43.
110. Interview with Ronnie Ronalde, by telephone, 28 August 2009.
111. Pilton, *Every Night*, p. 167.
112. 'Tommy Trinder at the Embassy Theatre, Peterborough', on *Variety – Live!*.
113. Interview with Don Smoothey, Ham, 9 October 2009.
114. 'Max at the Finsbury Park Empire October 12th 1942' on *Max Miller*.
115. 'Max at the Met', recorded 30 November 1957, on Max Miller, *There'll Never Be Another*, Pulse/Castle Communications, 1998, PLS CD 268.
116. 'Tommy Trinder at the Embassy Theatre, Peterborough', on *Variety – Live!*.
117. *Ibid*. The technique of giving voice to what the comedian imagines the audience are thinking ('Huh-huh, he's got a car!') is very common today, and is discussed in my book Oliver Double, *Getting the Joke: The Inner Workings of Stand-up Comedy*, London: Methuen, 2005, p. 225.
118. DANNY KAYE 7 (ROYAL COMMAND PERFORMANCE) video newsreel film, www.britishpathe.com/record.php?id=81651, 23/7/10.
119. *Ibid*.
120. *Ibid*.

8 Skill

1. PICCADILLY THEATRE OF VARIETIES video newsreel film, www.britishpathe.com/record.php?id=28682, 27/07/10.
2. *Turns*, BBC1, 14 August 1989, 11.05 p.m.
3. Mitchell, *The Dummy Talks*.
4. See photos and caption, Napier, *Act as Known*, p. 91.
5. *Turns*, BBC1, 24 July 1989, 10.55 p.m.
6. Marinetti, 'Variety theatre', pp. 126–31; p. 126.
7. See Woodward, *London Palladium*, pp. 103, 133, 148.
8. Cook, *Morecambe & Wise Untold*, p. 111.
9. 'Evening shadows in the music-hall', *The Times*, 3 July 1961, p. 17.
10. Betty Clarkson, 'George Clarkson and Gail Leslie – The essence of versatility', in Bruce *et al.*, *Those Variety Days*, pp. 57–69; esp. pp. 57–60.
11. Clive Barker, 'What training – For what theatre?', *New Theatre Quarterly*, 11(42) (May 1995), pp. 99–108; p. 99.
12. Lupino Lane, *How to Become a Comedian*, London: Frederick Muller, 1945, pp. 55–56.

13. Interview with Peter Prentice, by telephone, 28 October 2010.
14. Interview with Roy Hudd, Concert Artistes' Association, London, 12 March 2010.
15. Jewel, *Three Times Lucky*, pp. 21, 34.
16. Chris Dell, 'The Dehl Trio', *Call Boy*, 47(1) (spring 2010), pp. 14–15; p. 14.
17. Marinetti, 'Variety theatre', pp. 126–31; p. 128.
18. Ernest W. Low, 'Acrobats and how they are trained', *Strand Magazine*, 10 (Jul.–Dec. 1895), repr. in Charlie Holland, *Strange Feats & Clever Turns*, London: Holland & Palmer, 1998, pp. 52–59; p. 52.
19. 'Music-hall thrill: Motor-cyclist's fall when looping loop', *Manchester Guardian*, 26 February 1931, p. 9.
20. Interview with Chas McDevitt, by telephone, 25 January 2010.
21. Interview with Peter Prentice, by telephone, 28 October 2010.
22. O'Gorman, *Laughter in the Roar*, p. 43.
23. Versions of this can be found in 'Variety stage', *The Stage*, 19 September 1952, p. 3 [Billy Bennett]; Wilmut, *Kindly Leave the Stage*, p. 10 [Robb Wilton]; East, *Max Miller*, p. 142 [Max Miller].
24. O'Gorman, *Laughter in the Roar*, p. 3.
25. Interview with Teddie Beverley, by telephone, 16 September 2008.
26. Quoted in Peter Jelavich, *Berlin Cabaret*, Cambridge, MA and London: Harvard University Press, 1996, p. 180.
27. TONIGHT IN BRITAIN – reel 1, video newsreel film, www.british-pathe.com/record.php?id=74960, 27/7/10
28. DANNY KAYE 7 (ROYAL COMMAND PERFORMANCE).
29. Quoted in Jelavich, *Berlin Cabaret*, p. 180.
30. Tiller Girls choreographer Barbara Aitken, quoted in Pilton, *Every Night*, p. 115.
31. *Ibid.*
32. *Ibid.*
33. 'Round the variety halls', *The Stage*, 2 April 1953, p. 5.
34. Footage from an edition of the *Beverley Sisters Show*, *c.*1950s, from a privately produced DVD of archive footage sent to me by the Beverley Sisters.
35. Interview with Teddie Beverley, by telephone, 3 September 2008.
36. 'Variety stage', *The Stage*, 13 November 1952, p. 3.
37. Interview with Teddie Beverley, by telephone, 16 September 2008.
38. *Ibid.*
39. Again, this footage is from the privately produced DVD of archive footage sent to me by the Beverley Sisters.
40. Joan Rhodes, *Coming on Strong*, Darlington: Serendipity, 2007, pp. 82–83.
41. Interview with Joan Rhodes, Belsize Park, 30 March 2010.
42. Rhodes, *Coming on Strong*, p. 83.
43. 'Chiswick Empire', *The Stage*, 21 August 1958, p. 4.

44. Interview with Joan Rhodes, Belsize Park, 30 March 2010.

45. Rhodes, *Coming on Strong*, p. 83.

46. Interview with Joan Rhodes, Belsize Park, 30 March 2010.

47. 'Variety stage', *The Stage*, 19 September 1952, p. 3.

48. Interview with Chas McDevitt, by telephone, 25 January 2010.

49. Interview with Peter Prentice, by telephone, 28 October 2010.

50. Ronalde, *Around the World* p. 68.

51. 'Prince of Wales Theatre: A contrast in styles', *The Times*, 9 October 1956, p. 3; 'Victoria Palace: Off the record', *The Times*, 3 November 1954, p. 6.

52. 'London Hippodrome: Shirley Bassey in variety', *The Times*, 23 July 1957, p. 5.

53. Arthur Worsley's act, as filmed for the *Ed Sullivan Show*, 6 January 1957. This is available on the DVD box set *Elvis: The Ed Sullivan Shows*, Image Entertainment/Sony BMG, 2006, cat. no. 88697 00669 9, disc 3.

54. 'Holborn Empire: The boys from Manchester', *The Times*, 10 August 1937, p. 8.

55. Larry Adler, *It's Ain't Necessarily So*, Glasgow: Fontana/Collins, 1985, p. 53.

56. Smith, *Calling All Stars*.

57. The date is given as 1956 in 'Obituaries: Serge Ganjou', *The Stage*, 26 November 1998, p. 33, although it is given as 1957 in Wilmut, *Kindly Leave the Stage*, p. 94.

58. Patrick Newley, 'Nothing less than poetry in motion', *The Stage*, 21 July 1994, p. 19.

59. 'The Royal Performance', *The Stage*, 25 May 1933, p. 4; 'The Princes "magic carpet" ', *The Stage*, 3 June 1943, p. 4.

60. 'Phoenix', *The Stage*, 30 October 1941, p. 4.

61. 'Hippodrome', *Manchester Guardian*, 4 June 1946, p. 3.

62. Footage of these acts was included in *Turns*, BBC1, 10 July 1989, 10.55 p.m. (the Diamondos); *Turns*, BBC1, 7 August 1989, 11.05 p.m. (Gaston & Andree).

63. Footage of the Dehl Trio: THE DEHL TRIO (issue title – STREAM-LANED) video newsreel film, www.britishpathe.com/record.php?id= 36608, 30 July 2010. Footage of the Bega Four: Smith, *Calling All Stars*.

64. Footage of these acts was included in *Turns*, BBC1, 31 July 1989, 10.55 p.m. (Alexis & Dorrano); Herbert Smith, *Soft Lights and Sweet Music* (Karina and Company).

65. 'Bob Ganjou's new act', *The Stage*, 28 March 1957, p. 4; 'Meet Merian', *The Stage*, 27 June 1957, p. 4. Footage of the Dior Dancers' act from *Sunday Night at the London Palladium*, ITV, 17 April 1960, can be found on DVD box set *Sunday Night at the London Palladium*, Network, 2010, cat. no. 7952806, disc 1.

66. 'Princes "magic carpet" ', p. 4.

67. Rogers, *Variety Jubilee*.

68. Newley, 'Poetry in motion', p. 19.
69. Beswick Goodgame, 'Larry Adler's "Tune Inn" at Holborn', *The Era*, 14 May 1937, p. 8.
70. To qualify this point slightly, the Ganjou Brothers and Juanita also wore other costumes, and as Serge Ganjou put it, 'photographers always wanted to take pictures of us half naked' (Newley, 'Poetry in motion', p. 19).
71. 'Obituary: Ganjou', *The Stage*, 20 January 1977, p. 9.
72. 'Royal Performance', *The Stage*, p. 4; 'Finsbury Park', *The Stage*, 19 September 1946, p. 3.
73. Wilmut, *Kindly Leave the Stage*, p. 94.
74. For a more detailed explanation of this, see Double, *Getting the Joke*, pp. 207–8.
75. Newley, 'Poetry in motion', p. 19.

9 Novelty

1. 'Variety theatres', *Manchester Guardian*, 30 January 1906, p. 8.
2. 'Variety of the year', pp. 49–52; p. 49.
3. 'The theatres: The theatre of varieties', *The Times*, 24 January 1910, p. 4.
4. Interview with Morris Aza, Golders Green, 19 April 2010.
5. 'Variations in variety', *The Stage*, 25 March 1948, p. 5.
6. For more on these acts, see Hudd (with Hindin), *Roy Hudd's Cavalcade*, pp. 82, 117, 172, 185; Woodward, *London Palladium*, pp. 67, 215, 223, 225. Footage of Professor Sparks and Thelmina: '(ELECTRIC WOMAN) video newsreel film', www.britishpathe.com/record.php?id=16639, 24/8/10. Footage of Charles 'Think a Drink' Hoffman: www.youtube.com/watch?v=okGBeX-BTD8, 24/8/10.
7. Adler, *Ain't Necessarily So*, p. 47.
8. Woodward, *London Palladium*, p. 201.
9. 'Shepherd's Bush Empire closure', p. 3.
10. 'Vaudeville act: Lowe, Hite and Stanley', www.youtube.com/watch?v=SA6wYvVnq4g, 25/8/10. There is some confusion as to whether Lowe or Stanley was the smallest member of the act, but as it was originally a double act, Lowe and Hite, made up of Henry Hite and the average-sized Lowe, I assume that Stanley was the little person.
11. Quoted in Edward Helmore, 'Obituary: Peg Leg Bates', *The Independent*, 11 December 1998, p. 7.
12. 'PEG LEG BATES COMPILATION Vintage African American Historical', www.youtube.com/watch?v=2icYxQazgI0, 25/8/10.
13. 'Clayton "PegLeg" Bates – Tap', www.youtube.com/watch?v= 9EFLY ETrWpc, 25/8/10.
14. St John Ervine, 'At the play: Music hall', *The Observer*, 19 February 1939, p. 14.

15. 'Manchester stage and screen: Robey at the New Hippodrome', *Manchester Guardian*, 13 July 1937, p. 13; 'Lively variety at the Hippodrome', *Manchester Guardian*, 22 August 1939, p. 11.

16. Interview with Roy Hudd, Concert Artistes' Association, London, 12 March 2010.

17. Reid, *So Much Love*, p. 34.

18. Wall, *Fool on the Hill*, p. 68.

19. *Ibid.*, p. 88.

20. 'Holborn Empire', *The Times*, 21 February 1939, p. 12.

21. 'Round the halls', *The Stage*, 5 July 1951, p. 5.

22. Interview with Joan Rhodes, Belsize Park, 30 March 2010.

23. Quoted in Rhodes, *Coming on Strong*, p. 82. Footage of Rhodes's act can be found at http://video.google.com/videoplay?docid=-278737049 3823940699# (accessed 25/8/10), where she sings this song, although I should point out that her performance here is quite different from what she would have presented in her variety act. Pretty much all of the stunts which would have filled an act that would last at least ten minutes are thrown into this two-minute number, and they are thrown away without the proper build-up – patter, male audience volunteers, drum rolls, cues for applause, etc.

24. See Arthur Koestler, *The Act of Creation* (rev. Danube edn), London: Pan Books, 1970, pp. 32–42, esp. pp. 35, 38.

25. The 78RPM record was issued by Decca, serial no. F5278. See 'Gramophone records for children: Favourites old and new', *The Times*, 17 December 1937, p. 21.

26. Reginald Gardiner, 'Trains', on various artists, *Great Radio Stars*. RP stands for received pronunciation.

27. 'JASPER MASKELYNE video newsreel film', www.britishpathe.com/ record.php?id=10853, 25/8/10.

28. 'Variety theatres: The Alhambra', *The Times*, 15 August 1928, p. 10.

29. I sent footage of his act to Tim Roberts, course director at Circus Space in London and a juggler himself, who commented: 'Technically all his stuff is what most people learn in their first year ... One or two of his hat moves at the beginning were interesting, but not technically difficult. But his ball stuff is pretty standard' (personal email, 19/7/10).

30. 'Variety theatres: Mr Herb Williams at the Coliseum', *The Times*, 4 December 1928, p. 14.

31. *Turns*, BBC2, 14 August 1982, 10.15 p.m.

32. This move is included in two Pathé clips: 'REVELER (JUGGLER) (aka REBLA) video newsreel film', www.britishpathe.com/record. php?id=36937, 26/8/10; 'THE FAMOUS COMEDY JUGGLER video newsreel film', www.britishpathe.com/record.php?id=10826, 26/8/10.

33. Again, he can be seen doing this in the Pathé clips: 'REVELER (JUG-GLER) (aka REBLA) video newsreel film'; 'THE FAMOUS COM-EDY JUGGLER video newsreel film'.

34. Rogers, *Variety Jubilee*.
35. Napier, *Glossary*, p. 19.
36. The origins of this act are described in Stanley (with Powell), '*Can You Hear Me, Mother?*, p. 175; footage of it can be found on *Golden Years of British Comedy*, disc 1.
37. See O'Gorman, *Laughter in the Roar*, pp. 37–39.
38. Napier, *Act as Known*, p. 95.
39. Bobbie Kimber, 'Impersonation', *The Stage*, 5 December 1946, p. 5.
40. 'Round the halls: Chelsea Palace', *The Stage*, 31 July, 1947, p. 5.
41. 'Who's who in Royal Variety: Pen pictures of the artists', *The Stage*, 6 November 1947, p. 1.
42. 'Prince of Wales Theatre: A variety programme', *The Times*, 14 August 1945, p. 2.
43. Clifford Davis, 'The biggest BBC hoax is out...', *Daily Mirror*, 15 December 1952, p. 1.
44. O'Gorman, *Laughter in the Roar*, p. 51.
45. Oswald Mitchell and Challis Sanderson (dirs.), *Stars on Parade*, GB: Butcher's Film Service, 1936.
46. Secombe, *Arias*, p. 189.
47. Harry Secombe, *Strawberries and Cheam*, London: Robson, 1996, p. 14.
48. He toured the Moss circuit in about 1914 with Stanelli & Carrodus. By 1919 he was appearing as Stanelli & Edgar, and in 1922 as Stanelli & Douglas. In the early 1930s, he was back as Stanelli & Edgar, being filmed by Pathé in this act. Later he went solo, and also appeared with his own show, *Stanelli's Bachelor Party*.
49. 'Stanelli and his Hornchestra', *Great Radio Stars*.
50. 'The variety stage: Streatham Hill', *The Stage*, 5 July 1934, p. 3.
51. 'Stanelli and his Hornchestra', *Great Radio Stars*.
52. D. J. Taylor, 'Social mobility's a dance that goes round in circles. Best not Go Compare', *Independent on Sunday*, 17 October 2010, p. 98.
53. Richard Anthony Baker, 'Cleopatra's nightmare', *Music Hall Studies*, 4 (winter 2009/10), pp. 140–46.
54. Lord Delfont, *Curtain Up! The Story of the Royal Variety Performance*, London: Robson, 1989, pp. 48, 67, 75.
55. Rogers, *Variety Jubilee*.
56. 'The Hippodrome', *Manchester Guardian*, 23 August 1932, p. 11.
57. 'Wilson, Keppel & Betty ride again', www.youtube.com/watch?v=OMZJf5x6QKs, 27/8/10. Frustratingly, YouTube gives no indication of where this footage comes from (film title, date, etc.).
58. 'LONDON CLUBS AND CABARETS – TROCADERO RESTAURANT video newsreel film', www.britishpathe.com/record.php?id=9390, 27/8/10.
59. 'The variety stage', *The Stage*, 6 May 1937, p. 3.
60. 'Wilson Keppel & Betty (Patsy) 1940s', www.youtube.com/watch?v=Bj7bOxpXf-o, 27/8/10.

61. '40 years on, and happy as sand-dancers: W. & K'.s resounding tinkle', *Manchester Guardian*, 26 June 1959, p. 7.
62. Rogers, *Variety Jubilee*.
63. '40 years on', p. 7.
64. Rogers, *Variety Jubilee*.
65. '40 years on', p. 7.
66. *Ibid*.
67. These quotes taken respectively from: 'Round the halls', *The Stage*, 8 February 1951, p. 5; 'Max Bygraves: Salesmanship at the Palace Theatre', *Manchester Guardian*, 2 October 1956, p. 5; 'Round the halls', *The Stage*, 10 March 1949, p. 5.
68. 'The Metropolitan', *The Stage*, 6 April 1950, p. 4.
69. For example, see Ray, *Raising the Laughs*, p. 120; Rose, *Red Plush and Greasepaint*, London: Museum Press, 1964, pp. 65–66; Stanley (with Powell), *'Can You Hear Me, Mother?*, p. 102.
70. Ray, *Raising the Laughs*, p. 120.
71. B. Gray, 'Variety material', *The Stage*, 29 June 1939, p. 4.
72. For example, see: 'The vaudeville campaign', *The Era*, 29 January 1930, p. 9; Frank Woolf, 'Limit reached in foreign acts? New problem', *The Era*, 17 February 1937, p. 5; Kimber, 'Impersonation', p. 5; 'Curtain falls on a famous music hall', p. 5. As early as 1899, an act appearing in variety in Bristol was praised for avoiding 'stereotype stock phrases' ('Fred W. Millis in Bristol: Palace of Varieties', *The Era*, 12 August 1899, p. 19).
73. 'Max at the Met' on Miller, *There'll Never Be Another*.
74. Bygraves, *Tell You a Story*, p. 189.
75. Jewel, *Three Times Lucky*, p. 99.
76. Ted Ray, 'Fiddling and Fooling', *Great Radio Stars Volume Two*; Tommy Trinder, 'Tommy Trinder at the Embassy Theatre, Peterborough', on *Variety – Live!*.
77. Suzette Tarri, 'My Daughter's Wedding Day' on various artists, *They Played the Empire*, Decca, 1982, RFLD 23 MONO [recorded at the Argyle Theatre, Birkenhead, probably on 23 October 1939]; Vic Oliver, 'Joins the Army' on various artists, *Those Wonderful Comedians*, Memoir Records, 2001, CDMOIR 556 [recorded at a Forces concert in around March 1941].
78. The earliest reference I have found to Wences' hand dummy is 1937 ('The Palladium: Mr Harry Richman in popular songs', *The Times*, 6 July 1937, p. 14); while the earliest reference to Kimber's hand dummy is 1945 ('Prince of Wales Theatre: A variety programme', *The Times*, 14 August 1945, p. 2). However, the origin of the idea remains inconclusive, and indeed it could have been thought up by yet another performer.
79. See 'Welcome return of Senor Wences', *The Stage*, 4 May 1961, p. 7; 'East Ham Granada: Single, double', *The Stage*, 15 September 1955, p. 5.
80. Kimber, 'Impersonation', p. 5.

81. *The Performer*, 10 November 1938, p. 31.
82. Jewel, *Three Times Lucky*, p. 100.
83. Bob Monkhouse, *Over the Limit: My Secret Diaries 1993–8*, London: Century, 1998, p. 189.
84. 'Personality: Protective steps', *The Stage*, 14 October 1937, p. 10.
85. 'Copyright in personality: VAF and Brussels Convention', *The Era*, 21 July 1938, p. 1.
86. Wilmut, *Kindly Leave the Stage*, p. 28.
87. Florence Desmond's 'The Hollywood Party' appears on: various artists, *Music Hall to Variety: Volume Three, Second House*, EMI/World Records, no date, SH150; a film of the routine appears in 'RADIO PARADE reel 6 video newsreel film' available at www.britishpathe.com/record.php?id=76255. Beryl Orde impersonates Greta Garbo and Jimmy Durante in Arthur Woods (dir.), *Radio Parade of 1935*, GB: British International Pictures, 1934; Zasu Pitts and Gracie Fields in 'BERYL ORDE AND EDDIE POLA video newsreel film', www.britishpathe.com/record.php?id=28184, 27/8/10.
88. 'Search for talent. Lack of new material: Public and private auditions', *The Times*, 14 August 1934, p. xvii.
89. 'FRED ROPER AND HIS WONDER MIDGETS video newsreel film', www.britishpathe.com/record.php?id=27646, 27/8/10.

10   Variety Now

1. Interview with Peter Prentice, by telephone, 28 October 2010.
2. Edward Braun (ed.), *Meyerhold on Theatre*, London: Methuen, 1969, p. 136, fn.
3. Artaud, *Theatre*, p. 66.
4. Edward Gordon Craig, 'Madame Bernhardt and variety', *The Mask*, 3(7–9) (January 1911), p. 145.
5. See James Harding, *George Robey & the Music Hall*, London: Hodder & Stoughton, 1990, pp. 156–60; Howerd, *On the Way* pp. 128–33; Charles Lewsen, 'Twelfth night: Liverpool Playhouse', *The Times*, 12 November 1971, p. 10.
6. 'Max Wall in *Krapp's Last Tape*', *The Times*, 8 November 1975, p. 9.
7. Howard Goorney and Ewan MacColl (eds.), *Agit-prop to Theatre Workshop: Political Playscripts 1930–50*, Manchester: Manchester University Press, 1986, p. xv.
8. Ewan MacColl, *Journeyman: An Autobiography*, London: Sidgwick & Jackson, 1990, p. 213. For this scene from *Uranium 235*, see Goorney and MacColl, *Agit-prop*, pp. 107–8.
9. John McGrath, *A Good Night Out*, London & New York: Methuen, 1981, p. 56.

10. Posters for these events were on show at the British Music Hall Society's exhibition at Sands Studios, London in May 2009.
11. Woodward, *London Palladium*, p. 277.
12. Patrick Newley, 'Getting vocal about variety', *The Stage*, 19 February 2004, p. 51.
13. 'Variety acts at the De La Warr Pavilion', www.thisisliveart.co.uk/projects/variety/variety.html, 9/3/10.
14. 'Variety', www.bfi.org.uk/whatson/bfi_southbank/exhibitions/mezzanine_and_beyond/previous_atrium_displays/variety, 18/04/11.
15. *The Story of Variety with Michael Grade*, BBC4. Part 1, 'After the War', first aired 28 February 2011 and part 2 first aired 7 March 2011.
16. 'About the show', www.bbc.co.uk/whenwillibefamous/about/about_show.shtml, 18/4/11.
17. Louise Jury, 'Ladies! Gentlemen! "The good old days" return. A new National Theatre of Variety marks the rebirth of a classic form of entertainment', *The Independent*, 21 March 2005, p. 7.
18. Ian Herbert, 'Old-time variety returns to Blackpool, with a new face', *The Independent*, 18 February 2006, p. 9.
19. 'About us', www.mediumrare.tv/mrare.html, 8/10/10.
20. *The Culture Show*, BBC2, 19 August 2008.
21. Andrew Johnson, 'Variety the spice of life; Let's give a big hand to … trad acts with a sexy twist though the costumes are still gaudy, the corny gags and old-hat magic have vanished as entertainment from the old school returns', *Independent on Sunday*, 16 May 2010, p. 24.
22. Veronica Lee, 'Best of British Variety Tour, Embassy Theatre, Skegness, *The Observer* (*Review* section), 10 August 2008, p. 16.
23. Nick Curtis, 'The freak show that's seducing the A-list', *Evening Standard*, 21 September 2005, p. 32.
24. Jane Fryer, 'THE OLD ONES ARE THE BEST … at least that's what Paul Daniels keeps telling me!; They're even more ancient than their gags. So why do these geriatric jokers still play to sell-out crowds?, *Daily Mail*, 6 September 2008, p. 60.
25. *Ibid*.
26. Veronica Lee, 'Let's not do the time warp: MORE THEATRE: Best of British Variety Tour Embassy Theatre, Skegness', *The Observer* (*Review* section), 10 August 2008, p. 16.
27. Jessica Lack, 'Exhibitions: Variety: Bexhill-on-Sea', *The Guardian* (*Guide*), 29 October 2005, p. 37; Amy Lame, 'A whole new song and dance', *The Times* (*The Knowledge*), 15 October 2005, p. 20.
28. Curtis, 'Freak show', p. 32.
29. Russell, 'Varieties of life', pp. 61–82; p. 61.
30. *Stage Year Book 1961*, p. 14.
31. Barfe, *Turned Out Nice Again*, p. 308.

32. Graham McCann, *Morecambe & Wise*, London: Fourth Estate, 1999, p. 199.

33. Michael Grade, *It Seemed Like a Good Idea at the Time*, London, Basingstoke and Oxford: Macmillan, 1999, p. 66.

34. Interview with Roy Hudd, Concert Artistes' Association, London, 12 March 2010.

35. Interview with Michael Grade, by telephone, 28 April 2011.

36. *Ibid.*

37. Interview with Roy Hudd, Concert Artistes' Association, London, 12 March 2010; interview with Wyn Calvin, by telephone, 22 January 2010.

38. George Le Roy, 'Engagements in clubs', *Stage Year Book 1959*, pp. 27–28; p. 27.

39. Sidney Vauncez, 'Will it be bingo-variety?', in Merryn, *Stage Year Book 1969*, 33–34; p. 33.

40. Howerd, *On the Way*, p. 245. Howerd was by no means the only one who argued that the clubs were like a return to the origins of music hall.

41. Jewel, *Three Times Lucky*, p. 144.

42. Interview with Morris Aza, Golders Green, 19 April 2010.

43. Bygraves, *Tell You a Story*, pp. 167–68.

44. Howerd, *On the Way*, p. 249.

45. *Ibid.*, p. 246.

46. Jewel, *Three Times Lucky*, p. 144.

47. For a more detailed account of this, see Oliver Double, *Stand-Up! On Being a Comedian*, London: Methuen, 1997, pp. 21–88; Double, *Getting the Joke*, pp. 29–36.

48. Alexei Sayle at Theatre Royal, Nottingham, October 1983 (bootleg cassette recording).

49. John Connor, 'Laughs in store', *City Limits*, 4–11 May 1989, pp. 16–17; p. 17.

50. Interview with Arthur Smith, Canterbury city centre, 23 May 2009.

51. Interview with Warren Lakin, by telephone, 7 September 2010.

52. Interview with Roland Muldoon, Barbican Centre, 10 September 2010.

53. *Ibid.*

54. *Ibid.*

55. Patrick Newley, 'Obituaries: Terri Carol', *The Stage*, 14 February 2002, p. 13.

56. Interview with Barry Cryer, by telephone, 20 January 2010.

57. Ellis, 'What next in variety?', pp. 24–25

58. Philip Norman, *Buddy: The Biography*, London and Basingstoke: Macmillan, 1996, p. 221.

59. Denise Sullivan, *Rip It Up! Rock & Roll Rulebreakers*, San Francisco: Backbeat, 2001, p. 40.

60. Thomas M. Kitts, *Ray Davies: Not Like Everybody Else*, New York: Routledge, 2008, p. 65. This kind of point continues to be made by

rock singers even today. Billy Bragg, for example, recently declared, 'Speaking personally, I sometimes feel more of an affinity with Gus Elen than I do with Elvis Presley' (*The Good Old Days?* Radio 3, 29 November 2009).

61. Originally released on a single in 1966, now available on The Kinks, *You Really Got Me*, Select Records, 2000, SELCD560.

62. Available on The Kinks, *The Kinks Are the Village Green Preservation Society*, Sanctuary Records, 2005, SMRCD184 (originally 1968).

63. *Ibid.*

64. Kitts, *Ray Davies*, p. 153.

65. *Ibid.* p. 20.

66. Yvonne Roberts, 'The charm of Ian Dury: Not a blinkin' thickie and doing very well', *Sunday Times*, 21 May 1978, p. 42.

67. Available on Kilburn and the High Roads, *Handsome*, Castle Records, 2004, CMRCD995 (originally 1975).

68. Available on Ian Dury, *New Boots and Panties*, Edsel Records, 2007, EDSX 3001 (originally 1977).

69. Available on disc 2 of Ian Dury, *New Boots and Panties* [2-disc edn], Edsel/Demon, 2004, MEDCD751.

70. Descriptions of Dury's stage performance culled from various sources: Richard Balls, *Sex & Drugs & Rock'n'Roll: The Life of Ian Dury*, London: Omnibus, 2001, pp. 140, 177; Brian Case, 'On the Tahn. Ian Dury & the Blockheads: Hammersmith Odeon', *New Musical Express*, 20 May 1978, p. 45 (text and photos); *Ian Dury – On My Life* (BBC1, 25 September 1999); *Sight and Sound in Concert*, filmed for the BBC, 10 December 1977, available on a DVD included with a recent CD edition of Dury's classic album *New Boots and Panties*.

71. Balls, *Sex & Drugs*, p. 10.

72. Max Wall, *England's Glory*, Stiff Records, 1977, BUY 12.

73. Wall, *Fool on the Hill*, pp. 227–28.

74. Personal email from Mick Gallagher, 25/07/2005.

75. Case, 'On the Tahn', p. 45.

76. Hugh Fielder, 'Ian Dury and the Blockheads/Whirlwind/Matumbi: Hammersmith Odeon', *Sounds*, 20 May 1978, p. 47.

77. Case, 'On the Tahn', p. 45.

78. Julien Temple (dir.), *The Filth and the Fury*, GB: 1999.

79. *Ibid.*

80. See Andrew Billen, 'Far from the Madness crowd', *The Times* (*Times2*), 21 October 2008, p. 8; Tom Gatti, 'Suggs. Guest list: The world as listed by the Madness frontman', *The Times* (*Playlist*), 16 May 2009, pp. 8–9.

81. 'Baggy Trousers' (single originally released 1980) and 'House of Fun' (single originally released 1982) available on Madness, *Complete Madness*, Union Square Records, 2009, USMCD016.

82. Julien Temple (dir.), *The Liberty of Norton Folgate*, GB: 2009.
83. Victoria Newton, 'The good, the bad & the queen @ Wilton's Music Hall, London', *The Sun*, 14 December 2006.
84. Nicholas Barber, 'A very focused Blur', *The Independent*, 13 August 1995, p. 19. Blur, *Modern Life Is Rubbish*, Food Records, 1993, CDP7894422.
85. 'Parklife', available on Blur, *Parklife*, Food Records, 1994, FOODCD10; 'Country House' available on Blur, *The Great Escape*, Food Records, 1995, FOODCD14.
86. Robert Sandall, 'One man's therapy for lack of Madness', *Sunday Times*, 22 October 1995.

Bibliography

Books

Adler, Larry, *It Ain't Necessarily So*, Glasgow: Fontana/Collins, 1985.

Agate, James, *Immoment Toys*, London: Jonathan Cape, 1945.

Alexander, John, *Tearing Tickets Twice Nightly*, London: Arcady, 2002.

Apollonio, Umbro (ed.), *Futurist Manifestos*, London: Thames & Hudson, 1973.

Artaud, Antonin, *The Theatre and its Double*, London: John Calder, 1977.

Askey, Arthur, *Before Your Very Eyes*, London: Woburn, 1975.

Auslander, Philip, *Liveness: Performance in a Mediatized Culture*, London and New York: Routledge, 1999.

Baker, Richard Anthony, *British Music Hall: An Illustrated History*, Stroud: Sutton, 2005.

Balls, Richard, *Sex & Drugs & Rock 'n' Roll: The Life of Ian Dury*, London: Omnibus, 2001.

Barfe, Louis, *Turned Out Nice Again: The Story of British Light Entertainment*, London: Atlantic, 2008.

Barr, Charles (ed.), *All Our Yesterdays: 90 Years of British Cinema*, London: BFI, 1986.

Bevan, Ian, *Top of the Bill: The Story of the London Palladium*, London: Frederick Muller, 1952.

Billington, Michael, *How Tickled I Am*, London: Elm Tree, 1977.

Booth, Michael R. and Joel H. Kaplan (eds.), *The Edwardian Theatre*, Cambridge: Cambridge University Press, 1996.

Braun, Edward (ed.), *Meyerhold on Theatre*, London: Methuen, 1969.

Bret, David, *George Formby: A Troubled Genius*, London: Robson, 2001.

Bret, David, *The Real Gracie Fields: The Authorised Biography*, London: JR Books, 2010.

Briggs, Asa, *The History of Broadcasting in the United Kingdom, Volume I: The Birth of Broadcasting*, London: Oxford University Press, 1961.

Briggs, Asa, *The History of Broadcasting in the United Kingdom, Volume II: The Golden Age of Wireless*, London: Oxford University Press, 1965.

Bruce, Frank, Archie Foley and George Gillespie (eds.), *Those Variety Days: Memories of Scottish Variety Theatre*, Edinburgh: Scottish Music Hall Society, 1997.

Bruce, Frank and Archie Foley (eds.), *More Variety Days: Fairs, Fit-ups, Music Hall, Variety Theatre, Clubs, Cruises and Cabaret*, Edinburgh: Tod, 2000.

Bullar, Guy R. and Len Evans (eds.), *The Performer: Who's Who in Variety*, London: Performer, 1950.

Bygraves, Max, *I Wanna Tell You a Story*, London: Star/WH Allen, 1976.

Cheshire, D. F. *Music Hall in Britain*, Newton Abbot: David & Charles, 1974.

Collins, Joe, *A Touch of Collins*, London: Headline, 1987.

Cook, William, *Morecambe & Wise Untold*, London: HarperCollins, 2007.

Copeland, Lewis and Faye, *10,000 Jokes, Toasts and Stories*, Garden City, NY: Garden City Books, 1939.

Cryer, Barry, *You Won't Believe This But...*, London: Virgin, 1996.

Davies, Hunter, *The Grades: The First Family of British Entertainment*, London: Weidenfeld & Nicolson, 1981.

Delfont, Lord, *Curtain Up! The Story of the Royal Variety Performance*, London: Robson, 1989.

Desmond, Florence, *By Herself*, London: Harrap, 1953.

Disher, Maurice Willson, *Winkles and Champagne: Comedies and Tragedies of the Music Hall*, London: Batsford, 1938.

Double, Oliver, *Stand-Up! On Being a Comedian*, London: Methuen, 1997.

Double, Oliver, *Getting the Joke: The Inner Workings of Stand-up Comedy*, London: Methuen, 2005.

East, John, *Max Miller: The Cheeky Chappie*, London: Robson, 1993.

Fawkes, Richard, *Fighting for a Laugh: Entertaining the British and American Armed Forces 1939–46*, London: Macdonald and Jane's, 1978.

Fields, Gracie, *Sing as We Go*, London: Frederick Muller, 1960.

Forsyth, Bruce, *Bruce: The Autobiography*, London: Sidgwick & Jackson, 2001.

Goorney, Howard and Ewan MacColl (eds.), *Agit-prop to Theatre Workshop: Political Playscripts 1930–50*, Manchester: Manchester University Press, 1986.

Gottfried, Martin, *Nobody's Fool: The Lives of Danny Kaye*, New York: Simon & Schuster, 1994.

Grade, Michael, *It Seemed Like a Good Idea at the Time*, London, Basingstoke and Oxford: Macmillan, 1999.

Green, Benny (ed.), *The Last Empires: A Music Hall Companion*, London: Pavilion/Michael Joseph, 1986.

Harding, James, *George Robey & the Music Hall*, London: Hodder & Stoughton, 1990.

Holland, Charlie, *Strange Feats & Clever Turns*, London: Holland & Palmer, 1998.

Howard, Diana, *London Theatres and Music Halls 1850–1950*, London: Library Association, 1970, pp. 135–37.

Howerd, Frankie, *On the Way I Lost It*, London: Star, 1977.

Hudd, Roy, *Roy Hudd's Book of Music-Hall, Variety and Showbiz Anecdotes*, London: Robson, 1993.

Hudd, Roy (with Philip Hindin), *Roy Hudd's Cavalcade of Variety Acts: A Who Was Who of Light Entertainment 1945–60*, London: Robson, 1998.

Hudd, Roy, *A Fart in a Colander*, London: Michael O'Mara, 2009.

Jelavich, Peter, *Berlin Cabaret*, Cambridge, MA and London: Harvard University Press, 1996.

Jewel, Jimmy, *Three Times Lucky*, London: Enigma, 1982.

Kavanagh, Ted, *Tommy Handley*, London: Hodder & Stoughton, 1949.

Kitts, Thomas M., *Ray Davies: Not Like Everybody Else*, New York: Routledge, 2008.

Koestler, Arthur, *The Act of Creation* (rev. Danube edn), London: Pan, 1970.

Lane, Lupino, *How to Become a Comedian*, London: Frederick Muller, 1945.

Lynn, Dame Vera, *Some Sunny Day*, London: HarperCollins, 2009.

Ewan MacColl, *Journeyman: An Autobiography*, London: Sidgwick & Jackson, 1990.

Mackintosh, Iain, *Architecture, Actor and Audience*, London and New York: Routledge, 1993.

MacQueen-Pope, W., *The Melodies Linger On: The Story of Music Hall*, London, WH Allen, 1950.

Mander, Raymond and Joe Mitchenson, *British Music Hall: A Story in Pictures*, London: Studio Vista, 1965.

McCann, Graham, *Morecambe & Wise*, London: Fourth Estate, 1999.

McDevitt, Chas, *Skiffle: The Definitive Inside Story*, London: Robson, 1997.

McGrath, John, *A Good Night Out*, London and New York: Methuen, 1981.

Mellor, G. J. *The Northern Music Hall*, Newcastle upon Tyne: Frank Graham, 1970.

Merryn, Anthony (ed.), *The Stage Year Book 1966*, London: Carson & Comerford.

Merryn, Anthony (ed.), *The Stage Year Book 1969*, London: Carson & Comerford.

Midwinter, Eric, *Make 'Em Laugh: Famous Comedians and their Worlds*, London: George Allen & Unwin, 1979.

Monkhouse, Bob, *Crying with Laughter*, London: Arrow, 1994.

Monkhouse, Bob, *Over the Limit: My Secret Diaries 1993–8*, London: Century, 1998.

Morecambe, Eric, Ernie Wise and Dennis Holman, *Eric and Ernie: The Autobiography of Morecambe & Wise*, London: Star/WH Allen, 1974.

Napier, Valantyne, *Act as Known: Australian Speciality Acts on the World Vaudeville/Variety Circuits from 1900 to 1960*, Brunswick, Victoria: Globe Press, 1986.

Napier, Valantyne, *Glossary of Terms Used in Variety, Vaudeville, Revue & Pantomime*, Westbury, Wiltshire: Badger, 1996.

New Encyclopaedia Britannica, Micropaedia, vol. 8 (15th edn), Chicago and London: Encyclopaedia Britannica, 1992.

Norman, Philip, *Buddy: The Biography*, London and Basingstoke: Macmillan, 1996, p. 221.

O'Connor, Des, *Bananas Can't Fly!*, London: Headline, 2001.

O'Gorman, Brian, *Laughter in the Roar*, Westbury, Wiltshire: Badger, 1998.

Orben, Robert, *The Encyclopedia of Patter*, New York: Louis Tannen, 1946.

Orben, Robert, *One-Liners*, New York: D Robbins & Company, 1951.

Pilton, Patrick, *Every Night at the London Palladium*, London: Robson, 1976.

Ray, Ted, *Raising the Laughs*, London: Werner Laurie, 1952.

Reid, Beryl, *So Much Love*, London: Arrow, 1984.

Rhodes, Joan, *Coming on Strong*, Darlington: Serendipity, 2007.

Ripley, A. Crooks *Vaudeville Pattern*, London: Brownlee, 1947.

Ronalde, Ronnie, *Around the World on a Whistle*, Ormeau, Australia: Blackbird, 1998.

Rose, Clarkson, *Red Plush and Greasepaint*, London: Museum Press, 1964.

Schechter, Joel (ed.), *Popular Theatre: A Sourcebook*, London and New York: Routledge, 2003.

Secombe, Harry, *Twice Brightly*, London: Robson, 1974.

Secombe, Harry, *Arias and Raspberries*, London: Robson, 1989.

Secombe, Harry, *Strawberries and Cheam*, London: Robson, 1996.

Singer, Kurt, *The Danny Kaye Saga*, London: John Spencer/Badger, 1959.

Stanislavski, Constantin, *An Actor Prepares*, London: Methuen, 1980.

Stage Year Book 1950, London: Carson & Comerford.

Stage Year Book 1951, London: Carson & Comerford.

Stage Year Book 1953, London: Carson & Comerford.

Stage Year Book 1955, London: Carson & Comerford.

Stage Year Book 1956, London: Carson & Comerford.

Stage Year Book 1957, London: Carson & Comerford.

Stage Year Book 1958, London: Carson & Comerford.

Stage Year Book 1959, London: Carson & Comerford.

Stage Year Book 1960, London: Carson & Comerford.

Stage Year Book 1960, London: Carson & Comerford.

Stage Year Book 1961, London: Carson & Comerford.

Stage Year Book 1962, London: Carson & Comerford.

Stage Year Book 1963, London: Carson & Comerford.

Stanley, Harry and Sandy Powell, '*Can You Hear Me, Mother?*' *Sandy Powell's Lifetime of Music-Hall*, London: Jupiter, 1975.

Stein, Charles W. (ed.), *American Vaudeville As Seen by its Contemporaries*, New York: Knopf, 1984.

Steinmeyer, Jim, *Hiding the Elephant: How Magicians Invented the Impossible*, London: Arrow, 2005.

Sullivan, Denise, *Rip it Up! Rock & Roll Rulebreakers*, San Francisco: Backbeat, 2001.

Titterton, W. R., *From Theatre to Music Hall*, London: Stephen Swift, 1912.

Tolmie, A. W. (ed.), *The Stage Year Book 1949*, London: Carson & Comerford.

Took, Barry, *Star Turns: The Life and Times of Benny Hill & Frankie Howerd*, London: Weidenfeld & Nicolson, 1992.

Trav S. D., *No Applause Just Throw Money: The Book that Made Vaudeville Famous*, New York: Faber, 2005.

Wall, Max, *The Fool on the Hill*, London: Quartet, 1975.

Wilmut, Roger, *Kindly Leave the Stage: The Story of Variety 1919–1960*, London: Methuen, 1985.

Wisdom, Norman (with William Hall), *My Turn*, London: Random House, 2002.

Woodward, Chris, *The London Palladium: The Story of the Theatre and Its Stars*, Huddersfield: Northern Heritage/Jeremy Mills, 2009.

Articles

Anthony Baker, Richard, 'Variety's Iron Lady – Cissie Williams', *The Stage*, 21 January 2005 (www.thestage.co.uk/features/feature.php/6188, 2/7/2009).

Anthony Baker, Richard, 'Cleopatra's nightmare', *Music Hall Studies*, 4 (winter 2009/10), pp. 140–46.

Barber, Nicholas, 'A very focused Blur', *The Independent*, 13 August 1995, p. 19.

Barlow, Reg, 'Mr Sellers and Variety', *The Stage*, 20 August 1959, p. 4.

Barker, Clive, 'The "image" in show business', *Theatre Quarterly*, 8(29) (spring 1978), pp. 7–11.

Barker, Clive, 'What training – For what theatre?', *New Theatre Quarterly*, 11(42) (May 1995), pp. 99–108.

Betjeman, John, 'Architecture for entertainment', *Daily Telegraph*, 16 November 1959, p. 13.

Billen, Andrew, 'Far from the Madness crowd', *The Times* (*Times2*), 21 October 2008, p. 8.

Bishop, W. J., 'Thrills between films: Circus in a cinema', *The Era*, 13 January 1937, p. 5.

Bishop, W. J., 'George Black', *The Stage*, 8 March 1945, p. 3.

Booth, J. B., 'Fifty years: The old music hall – a national product, *The Times*, 18 March 1932, p. 15.

Britten, D. E. 'Harry Roy at the "Bush" ', *The Era*, 3 March 1937, p. 5.

Brown, Ivor, 'Theatre and life', *The Observer*, 29 August 1943, p. 2.

Carroll, Sydney W., 'Nudity is crudity: Away with all flesh', *The Era*, 6 May 1937, p. 1.

Case, Brian, 'On the Tahn. Ian Dury & The Blockheads: Hammersmith Odeon', *New Musical Express*, 20 May 1978, p. 45.

Connor, John, 'Laughs in store', *City Limits*, 4–11 May 1989, pp. 16–17.

Craig, Edward Gordon, 'Madame Bernhardt and variety', *The Mask*, 3(7–9) (January 1911), p. 145.

Curtis, Nick, 'The freak show that's seducing the A-list', *Evening Standard*, 21 September 2005, p. 32.

Davis, Clifford, 'The biggest BBC hoax is out ...', *Daily Mirror*, 15 December 1952, p. 1.

Dell, Chris, 'The Dehl Trio', *Call Boy*, 47(1) (spring 2010), pp. 14–15.

Dickson, E. Jane, 'The best of British', *Radio Times*, 30 May–5 June 2009, pp. 14–18.

Ervine, St John, 'At the Play: Music Hall', *The Observer*, 19 February 1939, p. 14.

Fielder, Hugh, 'Ian Dury and the Blockheads/Whirlwind/Matumbi: Hammersmith Odeon', *Sounds*, 20 May 1978, p. 47.

Foster, Harry, 'Free trade in foreign artists: Harry Foster explains the case for the agents', *The Era*, 16 October 1931, p. 3.

Fryer, Jane, 'THE OLD ONES ARE THE BEST ... at least that's what Paul Daniels keeps telling me!; They're even more ancient than their gags. So why do these geriatric jokers still play to sell-out crowds?, *Daily Mail*, 6 September 2008, p. 60.

Gatti, Tom, 'Suggs. Guest list: The world as listed by the Madness frontman', *The Times* (*Playlist*), 16 May 2009, pp. 8–9.

Gold, Tanya, 'It wasn't singer Susan Boyle who was ugly on *Britain's Got Talent* so much as our reaction to her', *The Guardian* (*G2* Section), 16 April 2009, p. 5.

Goodgame, Beswick, 'Swinging it at Finsbury Park', *The Era*, 13 January 1937, p. 5.

Goodgame, Beswick, 'Larry Adler's "Tune Inn" at Holborn', *The Era*, 14 May 1937, p. 8.

Gray, B., 'Variety material', *The Stage*, 29 June 1939, p. 4.

Helmore, Edward, 'Obituary: Peg Leg Bates', *The Independent*, 11 December 1998, p. 7.

Herbert, Ian, 'Old-time variety returns to Blackpool, with a new face', *The Independent*, 18 February 2006, p. 9.

Hogan, Michael, '*Britain's Got Talent*; the variety show with no variety; Weekend on Television', *Daily Telegraph*, 7 June 2010, p. 30.

Holmwood, Leigh, 'Saturday: A dream come true: Unknown Scottish singleton Susan Boyle became one of the most talked-about people in the world this week after a brief TV appearance. How?', *The Guardian*, 18 April 2009, p. 24.

Holmwood, Leigh, 'National: *Britain's Got Talent*: ITV in the spotlight after "exhausted" Susan Boyle enters private clinic: Psychiatrist queries stress load put on reality TV stars: Talent show runner-up needs to rest, says brother', *The Guardian*, 2 June 2009, p. 11.

Hoskins, Norman, 'The terror of Cranbourn Mansions', *Call Boy*, 46(3) (autumn 2009), pp. 6–7.

Johnson, Andrew, 'Variety the spice of life; Let's give a big hand to … trad acts with a sexy twist: Though the costumes are still gaudy, the corny gags and old-hat magic have vanished as entertainment from the old school returns', *Independent on Sunday*, 16 May 2010, p. 24.

Jones, Liane, 'The impressionist's got form, but Britain's really got talent', *Independent on Sunday*, 17 June 2007.

Jury, Louise, 'Ladies! Gentlemen! "The Good Old Days" return. A new National Theatre of Variety marks the rebirth of a classic form of entertainment', *The Independent*, 21 March 2005, p. 7.

Kimber, Bobbie, 'Impersonation', *The Stage*, 5 December 1946, p. 5.

Lack, Jessica, 'Exhibitions: Variety: Bexhill-on-Sea', *The Guardian* (the *Guide*), 29 October 2005, p. 37.

Lame, Amy, 'A whole new song and dance', *The Times* (*The Knowledge*), 15 October 2005, p. 20.

Lawson, Mark, 'National: *Britain's Got Talent*: Winners and losers: The price of overnight fame – from Amy Winehouse to Susan Boyle', *The Guardian*, 2 June 2009, p. 11.

Lee, Veronica, 'Let's not do the time warp: MORE THEATRE: Best of British Variety Tour Embassy Theatre, Skegness', *The Observer* (*Review* section), 10 August 2008, p. 16.

Lewsen, Charles, 'Twelfth night: Liverpool Playhouse', *The Times*, 12 November 1971, p. 10.

Marriott, R. B., 'Farewell to Max Miller', *The Stage*, 16 May 1963, p. 6.

McKinty, A. W., 'Wyn takes a step', *The Stage*, 16 January 1958, p. 6.

Newley, Patrick, 'Nothing less than poetry in motion', *The Stage*, 21 July 1994, p. 19.

Newley, Patrick, 'King of the bill', *The Stage*, 11 October 2001, p. 12.

Newley, Patrick, 'Obituaries: Terri Carol', *The Stage*, 14 February 2002, p. 13.

Newley, Patrick, 'Getting vocal about variety', *The Stage*, 19 February 2004, p. 51.

Newton, Victoria, 'The good, the bad & the queen @ Wilton's Music Hall, London', *The Sun*, 14 December 2006.

Rickets, W. J., 'Nudity and obscenity: The remedy', *The Era*, 14 May 1937, p. 7.

Roberts, Yvonne, 'The charm of Ian Dury: Not a blinkin' thickie and doing very well', *Sunday Times*, 21 May 1978, p. 42.

Russell, Fred, 'Home truths', *The Performer*, 22 January 1942, p. 5.

Sandall, Robert, 'One man's therapy for lack of Madness', *Sunday Times*, 22 October 1995.

Shrapnel, Norman, 'The Met's final night', *The Guardian*, 13 April 1963, p. 4.

Taylor, D. J., 'Social mobility's a dance that goes round in circles. Best not Go Compare', *The Independent on Sunday*, 17 October 2010, p. 98.

Taylor, Jerome, 'Struggling ITV clears schedules for talent show; *Britain's Got Talent* grabs 50 per cent of Saturday peak-time viewing audience', *The Independent*, 26 May 2009, p. 10.

Wade, Ross, 'TV is killing itself – By murdering variety', *The Stage*, 10 October 1957, p. 6.

Walbrook, H. M., 'Alhambra memories', *The Stage*, 20 July 1933, p. 11.

Woolf, Frank, 'Limit reached in foreign acts? New problem', *The Era*, 17 February 1937, p. 5.

Woolf, Frank, 'Variety's invasion of the cinemas: Great increase in running time', *The Era*, 18 March 1937, p. 5.

Woolf, Frank, 'Comic strip tease: Hullaboloney at Victoria', *The Era*, 8 April 1947, p. 5.

'Fred W. Millis in Bristol: Palace of varieties', *The Era*, 12 August 1899, p. 19.

'Variety theatres', *Manchester Guardian*, 30 January 1906, p. 8.

'The theatres: The theatre of varieties', *The Times*, 24 January 1910, p. 4.

'Royalty in the music hall: The "Command" Performance at the Palace', *Manchester Guardian*, 2 July 1912, p. 9.

Closing of the Tivoli', *The Times*, 26 January 1914, p. 6.

'Variety gossip – Licensing: The Middlesex', *The Stage*, 7 November 1918, p. 8.

'Death of Mr George Formby: A comedian of the old school', *The Times*, 9 February 1921, p. 8.

'Variety gossip', *The Stage*, 13 September 1923, p. 13.

'Mr C. B. Cochran's affairs: A discharge granted', *The Times*, 23 April 1925, p. 5.

'Revival of the variety performance: The popular single "turn"', *The Times*, 4 June 1926, p. 12.

'The end of "The Empire": Home of English ballet', *The Times*, 21 January 1927, p. 17.

'Band conductor put in prison – Unpaid income tax – nobody to accept last-minute payment', *Manchester Guardian*, 20 June 1927, p. 10.

'Variety theatres: The Alhambra', *The Times*, 15 August 1928, p. 10.

'The Palladium: Variety's come-back', *The Era*, 5 September 1928, p. 13.

'Variety Theatres. The Reopening of the Palladium', *The Times*, 5 September 1928, p. 10.

'The music-hall rally', *Manchester Guardian*, 5 September 1928, p. 8.

'The variety stage', *The Stage*, 6 September 1928, p. 11.

'Palladium: Dick Henderson', *The Observer*, 9 September 1928, p. 14.

'Variety theatres: Mr Herb Williams at the Coliseum', *The Times*, 4 December 1928, p. 14.

'The vaudeville campaign', *The Era*, 29 January 1930, p. 9.

'The Alhambra and variety', *The Era*, 12 February 1930, p. 11.

'Variety theatres: The Coliseum', *The Times*, 5 August 1930, p. 8.

'Music-hall thrill: Motor-cyclist's fall when looping loop', *Manchester Guardian*, 26 February 1931, p. 9.

'How the cinemas have helped variety', *The Era*, 16 October 1931, p. 3.

'The Hippodrome', *Manchester Guardian*, 23 August 1932, p. 11.

'Wireless ban developments – Miss Gracie Fields decides to obey prohibitive clause' – Mr Norman Long sticks to the BBC', *Manchester Guardian*, 29 December 1932, p. 7.

'The royal performance', *The Stage*, 25 May 1933, p. 4

'What the variety stage wants – Miss Gracie Fields explains – personality', *The Observer*, 30 July 1933, p. 17

'Variety gossip', *The Stage*, 22 March 1934, p. 12

'The variety stage: Streatham Hill', *The Stage*, 5 July 1934, p. 3

'Search for talent. Lack of new material: public and private auditions', *The Times*, 14 August 1934, p. xvii.

'Miss Gracie Fields: Last night at the London Palladium', *Manchester Guardian*, 22 July 1936, p. 10.

'The art of the music hall – A manager's secrets – £500 a week for a star', *The Observer*, 2 August 1936, p. 3.

'Leicester', *The Stage*, 19 December 1936, p. 6.

'VAF and foreign acts: Protest meeting to be called', *The Era*, 3 February 1937, p. 3.

'Variety at cinema prices: Changes in Manchester district', *The Era*, 17 February 1937, p. 13.

'Holborn Empire', *The Times*, 2 March 1937, p. 14.

'Too many foreign acts: Disclosures at VAF meeting', *The Era*, 10 March 1937, p. 3.

'More cinemas over to variety', *The Era*, 25 March 1937, p. 1.

'The variety stage', *The Stage*, 6 May 1937, p. 3.

'The Palladium: Mr Harry Richman in popular songs', *The Times*, 6 July 1937, p. 14.

'Manchester stage and screen: Robey at the New Hippodrome', *Manchester Guardian*, 13 July 1937, p. 13.

'Holborn Empire: The Boys from Manchester', *The Times*, 10 August 1937, p. 8.

'Personality: Protective steps', *The Stage*, 14 October 1937, p. 10.

'Gramophone Records for children: Favourites old and new', *The Times*, 17 December 1937, p. 21.

'The "times" and the halls', *The Performer*, 6 January 1938, p. 9.

'Biggest variety boom for years. Will there be a famine?', *The Era*, 21 July 1938, p. 1.

'Copyright in personality: VAF and Brussels Convention', *The Era*, 21 July 1938, p. 1.

'Henry Hall and variety', *Manchester Guardian*, 30 August 1938, p. 11.

'The music-hall: Modern influences', *The Times*, 26 October 1938, p. 12.

'As "The Performer" see it: Bill matter', *The Performer*, 10 November 1938, p. 2.

'George Black', *The Performer*, 10 November 1938, p. 19.

'Holborn Empire', *The Times*, 21 February 1939, p. 12.

'Holborn Empire', *The Times*, 11 April 1939, p. 8.

'Lively variety at the Hippodrome', *Manchester Guardian*, 22 August 1939, p. 11.

'Absent friends – Do they matter?', *Daily Mirror*, 29 July 1940, p. 4.

'Variety gossip', *The Stage*, 8 August 1940, p. 3.

'The Palace: Billy Cotton and variety', *Manchester Guardian*, 29 October 1940, p. 6

'Phoenix', *The Stage*, 30 October 1941, p. 4.

'The Coliseum: London police witness "Garrison Theatre"', *The Times*, 4 November 1941, p. 6.

'As "The Performer" sees it', *The Performer*, 22 January 1942, p. 2.

'General Theatre Corporation. Substantial improvement', *Manchester Guardian*, 16 December 1942, p. 2.

'The Princes "magic carpet"', *The Stage*, 3 June 1943, p. 4.

'Death of Mr George Black', *The Performer*, 8 March 1945, p. 5.

'Whitehall Theatre: Peek-a-boo again', *The Times*, 18 July 1945, p. 6.

'Prince of Wales Theatre: A variety programme', *The Times*, 14 August 1945, p. 2.

'Lewisham Hippodrome', *Lewisham Borough News*, 9 April 1946, p. 5.

'Manchester stage and screen: The Hippodrome', *Manchester Guardian*, 16 April 1946, p. 3.

'Hippodrome', *Manchester Guardian*, 4 June 1946, p. 3.

'Finsbury Park', *The Stage*, 19 September 1946, p. 3.

'Round the halls', *The Stage*, 6 February 1947, p. 5.

'Our London correspondence', *Manchester Guardian*, 11 June 1947, p. 4.

'Variety gossip', *The Stage*, 12 June 1947, p. 3.

'Variety gossip', *The Stage*, 24 July 1947, p. 3.

'Round the halls: Chelsea Palace', *The Stage*, 31 July, 1947, p. 5.

'Who's who in royal variety: Pen pictures of the artists', *The Stage*, 6 November 1947, p. 1.

'The Palladium: Mr Danny Kaye', *The Times*, 4 February 1948, p. 2.

'London Palladium', *The Performer*, 5 February 1948, p. 9.

'Round the halls', *The Stage*, 5 February 1948, p. 3.

'Variations in variety', *The Stage*, 25 March 1948, p. 5.

'The variety stage', *The Stage*, 12 August 1948, p. 3.

'Round the halls', *The Stage*, 26 August 1948, p. 5.

'London Palladium: Miss Gracie Fields', *The Times*, 5 October 1948, p. 7.

'Finsbury Park Empire', *The Performer*, 7 October 1948, p. 11.

'London Palladium', *The Performer*, 7 October 1948, p. 11.

'Round the halls', *The Stage*, 10 March 1949, p. 5.

'Profile: Danny Kaye', *The Observer*, 15 May 1949, p. 2.

'The niceness of Mr Kaye: "better me than Hitler–"', *Manchester Guardian*, 13 June 1949, p. 3.

'The Metropolitan', *The Stage*, 6 April 1950, p. 4.

'The importance of being yourself: The humour of Max Bygraves', *The Stage*, 10 August 1950, p. 1.

'Round the halls', *The Stage*, 8 February 1951, p. 5.

'Impresario in music-hall', *The Times*, 23 August 1951, p. 2.

'Four West End appearances', *The Performer*, 7 February 1952, p. 3.

'Televariety', *The Performer*, 7 February 1952, p. 10

'The incomparable Max Miller', *The Stage*, 21 February 1952, p. 1, p. 5

'Variety stage', *The Stage*, 19 September 1952, p. 3.

'Variety stage', *The Stage*, 13 November 1952, p. 3.

'Round the variety halls', *The Stage*, 2 April 1953, p. 5.

'Shepherd's Bush Empire closure', *The Stage*, 24 September 1953, p. 3.

'Round the halls: The Palladium', *The Stage*, 11 March 1954, p. 5.

'Victoria Palace: Off the record', *The Times*, 3 November 1954, p. 6.

'More theatres to close', *The Stage*, 18 November 1954, p. 1.

'Overture', *The Performer*, 25 November 1954, p. 2.

'Bury the words music hall – Says an agent', *The Stage*, 13 January 1955, p. 3.

'Hackney Empire not to close', *The Stage*, 20 January 1955, p. 1.

'Tax menace analysed: Memorandum prepared for Chancellor', *The Stage*, 20 January 1955, pp. 1, 11.

'Six British acts in next Palladium bill', *The Stage*, 31 March 1955, p. 3.

'Two British youngsters triumph', *The Stage*, 14 April 1955, p. 7.

'Transformation of Wood Green Empire', *The Stage*, 14 July 1955, p. 11.

'East Ham Granada: Single, double', *The Stage*, 15 September 1955, p. 5.

'Another music hall to close', *Manchester Guardian*, 19 January 1956, p. 5.

'ATV take lease on Hackney Empire', *The Stage*, 2 February 1956, p. 9.

'Walham Green Granville to close again', *The Stage*, 16 August 1956, p. 12.

'Max Bygraves: Salesmanship at the Palace Theatre', *Manchester Guardian*, 2 October 1956, p. 5.

'Prince of Wales Theatre: A contrast in styles', *The Times*, 9 October 1956, p. 3.

'Scottish Flavour: Let's drive these variety pessimists out of town!', *The Stage*, 6 December 1956, p. 4.

'Metropolitan: Skiffle show', *The Stage*, 24 January 1957, p. 5.

'Chiswick Empire: Ronnie's fans', *The Stage*, 28 March 1957, p. 4.

'Bob Ganjou's new act', *The Stage*, 28 March 1957, p. 4.

'Meet Merian', *The Stage*, 27 June 1957, p. 4.

'London Hippodrome: Shirley Bassey in variety', *The Times*, 23 July 1957, p. 5.

'Half a century of service', *The Performer*, 26 September 1957, p. 1.

'Scottish flavour: Why this "Iron Curtain" of show-business at Solway–Tyne border?', *The Stage*, 24 October 1957, p. 5.

'What we think: Horror comics', *The Stage*, 28 November 1957, p. 3.

'What we think: National Trust for variety theatres?', *The Stage*, 20 February 1958, p. 3.

'Chiswick Empire', *The Stage*, 6 March 1958, p. 4.

'Metropolitan', *The Stage*, 17 April, 1958, p. 4.

'Chiswick Empire', *The Stage*, 21 August 1958, p. 4.

'Finsbury Park Empire', *The Stage*, 4 September 1958, p. 4.

'Chiswick Empire', *The Stage*, 27 November 1958, p. 7.

'40 years on, and happy as sand-dancers: W. & K.'s resounding tinkle', *Manchester Guardian*, 26 June 1959, p. 7.

'Welcome return of Senor Wences', *The Stage*, 4 May 1961, p. 7.

'Evening shadows in the music-hall, *The Times*, 3 July 1961, p. 17.

'No Glasgow Empire re-development yet', *The Stage*, 14 September 1961, p. 1.

'Farewell to the Met', *The Stage*, 3 January 1963, p. 4.

'Glasgow Empire's farewell show', *The Stage*, 7 February 1963, p. 3.

'Glasgow Empire future', *The Stage*, 7 March 1963, p. 3.

'The curtain falls on a famous music hall: End of the Glasgow Empire', *The Stage*, 28 March 1963, p. 5.

'The Met's final night', *The Guardian*, 13 April 1963, p. 4.

'Review: Autumn spectacular at the Palace Theatre, Manchester', *The Guardian*, 19 October 1963, p. 6.

'Max Wall in *Krapp's Last Tape*', *The Times*, 8 November 1975, p. 9.

'Obituary: Ganjou', *The Stage*, 20 January 1977, p. 9.

'Obituaries: Serge Ganjou', *The Stage*, 26 November 1998, p. 33.

Interviews

Morris Aza, Golders Green, 19 April 2010.

Teddie Beverley, by telephone, 3 September 2008.

Teddie Beverley, by telephone, 16 September 2008.

Wyn Calvin, by telephone, 22 January 2010.

Barry Cryer, by telephone, 16 October 2009.

Barry Cryer, by telephone, 20 January 2010.

Michael Grade, by telephone, 28 April 2011.

Roy Hudd, Concert Artistes' Association, London, 12 March 2010.

Ken Joy, by telephone, 15 October 2010.

Warren Lakin, by telephone, 7 September 2010.

Dame Vera Lynn, Ditchling, East Sussex, 12 April 2011.

Chas McDevitt, by telephone, 25 January 2010.

Roland Muldoon, Barbican Centre, 10 September 2010.

Peter Prentice, by telephone, 28 October 2010.

Joan Rhodes, Belsize Park, 30 March 2010.

Ronnie Ronalde, by telephone, 28 August 2009.

Jack Seaton, by telephone, 2 February 2010.
Arthur Smith, Canterbury city centre, 23 May 2009.
Don Smoothey, Ham, 9 October 2009.

Live shows

Britain's Got Talent, Wembley Arena, 21 June 2009, 1.30 p.m.
New Variety Lives, Barbican, 9 September 2010, 8 p.m.

Film

Brunel, Adrian (dir.), *Elstree Calling*, UK: British International Pictures, 1930.
Mitchell, Oswald and Challis Sanderson (dirs.), *Stars on Parade*, UK: Butcher's Film Service, 1936.
Mitchell, Oswald (dir.), *The Dummy Talks*, GB: British National Films, 1943.
Palmer, Greg (dir.), *Vaudeville*, Thirteen/WNET, KCTS/9 Television and Palmer/Fenster 1997.
Maclean Rogers (dir.), *Variety Jubilee*, GB: Butcher's Film Service, 1943.
Herbert Smith (dir.), *British Lion Variety no. 17*, GB: British Lion, 1936.
Herbert Smith (dir.), *Soft Lights and Sweet Music*, GB, British Lion, 1936.
Herbert Smith (dir.), *Calling All Stars*, GB, British Lion, 1937.
Julien Temple (dir.), *The Filth and the Fury*, GB: 1999.
Julien Temple (dir.), *The Liberty of Norton Folgate*, GB: 2009.
Arthur Woods (dir.), *Radio Parade of 1935*, GB: British International Pictures, 1934.

DVD

Elvis: The Ed Sullivan Shows, Image Entertainment/Sony BMG, 2006, cat. no. 88697 00669 9.
The Golden Years of British Comedy, Universal, 2005, DVD 8235253–11.
Sunday Night at the London Palladium, Network, 2010, cat. no. 7952806.

Vinyl

Max Wall, *England's Glory*, Stiff Records, 1977, BUY 12.
Various artists, *Fifty Years of Radio Comedy,* BBC Records, 1972, MONO REC 138M.
Various artists, *Great Radio Comedians*, BBC Records, 1973, MONO REC151M.
Various artists, *Music Hall to Variety: Volume Three, Second House,* EMI/World Records, no date, SH150.
Various artists, *They Played the Empire*, Decca, 1982, RFLD 23 MONO.

Audio cassette

Alexei Sayle at the Theatre Royal, Nottingham, October 1983 (bootleg cassette recording).
Various artists, *Stars of Variety*, Music Collection International, 1994, cat. no. GAGDMC002.

CD

Beverley Sisters, *The Biggest Hits*, Rex Recordings, 2007, REXX 113.
Blur, *Modern Life Is Rubbish*, Food Records, 1993, CDP7894422.
Blur, *Parklife*, Food Records, 1994, FOODCD10.
Blur, *The Great Escape*, Food Records, 1995, FOODCD14.
Lenny Bruce, *The Lenny Bruce Originals Volume 2*, Fantasy Records, 1991, CDFA 526.
Ian Dury, *New Boots and Panties* [2-disc edition], Edsel/Demon, 2004, MEDCD751.
Ian Dury, *New Boots and Panties*, Edsel Records, 2007, EDSX 3001.
Gracie Fields, *Sing As We Go*, EMI/Cedar, 1990, CPD 7 943222.
George Formby, *'V' for Victory*, Redrock Records, 1995, RKD23 PPL.
George Formby, *England's Famed Clown Prince of Song*, JSP Records, 2004, JSP 1901.
Kilburn and the High Roads, *Handsome*, Castle Records, 2004, CMRCD995.
Kinks, *You Really Got Me*, Select Records, 2000, SELCD560.
Kinks, *The Kinks Are the Village Green Preservation Society*, Sanctuary Records, 2005, SMRCD184.
Madness, *Complete Madness*, Union Square Records, 2009, USMCD016.
Max Miller, *There'll Never Be Another*, Pulse/Castle Communications, 1998, PLS CD 268.
Max Miller, *Max Miller*, EMI Comedy, 2000, 7243 5 28599 2 4.
Harry Roy, *The Cream of Harry Roy*, Flapper/Pavilion Records, 1991, PAST CD 9741.
Robb Wilton, *Robb Wilton's War*, Flapper/Pavilion Records, 2001, PAST CD 7854.
Various artists, *The Best of British Comedy*, Disky, 2002, CB 795122.
Various artists, *Great Radio Stars Volume Two*, Pavilion Records, 1991, PAST CD 9728.
Various artists, *A Night at the Music Hall*, JSP Records, 2007, JSP 1903.
Various artists, *Those Wonderful Comedians*, Memoir Records, 2001, CDMOIR 556.
Various artists, *Variety – "Live!"*, Windyridge Records, 2005, WINDYVAR14.

Television

Culture Show, the BBC2, 19 August 2008.

Heroes of Comedy, Channel 4, 31 January 1992.
Ian Dury – On My Life, BBC1, 25 September 1999.
Story of Light Entertainment (Part 1: Double acts), BBC2, 22 July 2006.
Story of Variety with Michael Grade (Part 1, 'After the war'), BBC4, 28 February 2011.
Story of Variety with Michael Grade (Part 2, 'Onto the box'), BBC4, 7 March 2011.
Turns, BBC2, 14 August 1982.
Turns, BBC1, 30 August 1984.
Turns, BBC1, 10 July 1989.
Turns, BBC1, 24 July 1989.
Turns, BBC1, 31 July 1989.
Turns, BBC1, 7 August 1989.
Turns, BBC1, 14 August 1989.

Radio

The Good Old Days? Radio 3, 29 November 2009.

Internet

Louis Barfe, 'London Belongs to Television' (at: www.transdiffusion.org/emc/studioone/london.php; 9/3/10).
'About the Show' (at: www.bbc.co.uk/whenwillibefamous/about/about_show.shtml; 18/4/11).
'About Us' (at: www.mediumrare.tv/mrare.html; 8/10/10).
'BERYL ORDE AND EDDIE POLA video newsreel film' (at: www.britishpathe.com/record.php?id=28184; 27/8/10).
'Clayton "PegLeg" Bates – Tap' (at: www.youtube.com/watch?v=9EFLYETrWpc; 25/8/10).
'DANNY KAYE 6 (ROYAL COMMAND PERFORMANCE) video newsreel film' (at: www.britishpathe.com/record.php?id=81650, 20/7/10).
'DANNY KAYE 7 (ROYAL COMMAND PERFORMANCE) video newsreel film' (at: www.britishpathe.com/record.php?id=81651; 23/7/10)
'DANNY KAYE 8 (ROYAL COMMAND PERFORMANCE) video newsreel film' (at: www.britishpathe.com/record.php?id=81652; 23/7/10).
'THE DEHL TRIO (issue title – STREAMLANED) video newsreel film', www.britishpathe.com/record.php?id=36608, 30/7/2010
'(ELECTRIC WOMAN) video newsreel film', www.britishpathe.com/record.php?id=16639, 24/8/10
'FAMOUS COMEDY JUGGLER video newsreel film' (at: www.britishpathe.com/record.php?id=10826; 26/8/10).
'FRED ROPER AND HIS WONDER MIDGETS video newsreel film' (at: www.britishpathe.com/record.php?id=27646; 27/8/10).

'FREDDIE BAMBERGER' (1654.25), 1936 (at: www.britishpathe.com/record.php?id =28678; 6/7/09).

'JASPER MASKELYNE video newsreel film' (at: www.britishpathe.com/record.php?id=10853; 25/8/10).

'Joan Rhodes Carbaret Act' (at: http://video.google.com/videoplay?docid=-2787370493823940699#; 25/8/10).

'LONDON CLUBS AND CABARETS – TROCADERO RESTAURANT video newsreel film' (at: www.britishpathe.com/record.php?id=9390; 27/8/10).

'PEG LEG BATES COMPILATION vintage african american historical' (at: www.youtube.com/watch?v=2icYxQazgI0; 25/8/10).

'PICCADILLY THEATRE OF VARIETIES video newsreel film' (at: www.britishpathe.com/record.php?id=28682; 27/07/10).

'RADIO PARADE reel 6 video newsreel film' (at: www.britishpathe.com/record.php?id=76255; 27/8/10).

'REVELER (JUGGLER) (aka REBLA) video newsreel film' (at: www.britishpathe.com/record.php?id=36937; 26/8/10).

'Think a Drink Hoffman' (at: www.youtube.com/watch?v=okGBeX-BTD8; 24/8/10).

'TONIGHT IN BRITAIN – reel 1 video newsreel film' (at: www.britishpathe.com/record.php?id=74960; 27/7/10).

'TONIGHT IN BRITAIN – reel 2' (1323.04), 1953' (at: www.britishpathe.com/record.php?id=74961; 6/7/09).

'Variety' (at: www.bfi.org.uk/whatson/bfi_southbank/exhibitions/mezzanine_and_beyond/previous_atrium_displays/variety; 18/4/2011).

'Variety Acts at the De La Warr Pavilion' (at: www.thisisliveart.co.uk/projects/variety/variety.html; 9/3/10).

'Vaudeville Act: Lowe, Hite and Stanley' (at: www.youtube.com/watch?v=SA6wYvVnq4g; 25/8/10).

'WHAT THE PUBLIC WANTS! REEL 3 OF 4' (1911.15), 1933 (at: www.britishpathe.com/record.php?id=77255; 6/7/09).

'Wilson, Keppel & Betty Ride Again' (at: www.youtube.com/watch?v=OMZJf5x6QKs; 27/8/10).

'Wilson Keppel & Betty (Patsy) 1940s' (at: www.youtube.com/watch?v=Bj7bOxpXf-o; 27/8/10).

Ephemera

Programme for the Oxford, week ending 24 July 1897 (from the private collection of Max Tyler).

Programme for the New Cross Empire, week commencing 21 November 1904 (from the private collection of Max Tyler).

Programme for the London Pavilion, week commencing 25 July 1932.

Programme for the London Palladium, week commencing 19 September 1932.

Programme for the Finsbury Park Empire, week commencing 11 January 1937.

Programme from the Empress, Brixton, week commencing 17 August 1942.

Programme for *Variety Comes Back to the London Palladium*, October 1943.

Programme for the London Casino, dated 5 April to 1 May 1948.

Programme for Finsbury Park Empire, week commencing 19 April 1954.

Programme for Finsbury Park Empire, week commencing 7 June 1954.

Programme for Finsbury Park Empire, week commencing 5 July 1954.

Programme for Lewisham Hippodrome, week commencing 8 April 1946.

Programme for the Regal Theatre, Hull, week commencing 3 March 1958.

Britain's Got Talent Live Tour 2009 Programme.

Transcript of the Lawson Trout record cards, made by the British Music Hall Society.

What I know about Women!!! By 'Monsewer' Eddie Gray (blank book given out as a novelty calling card).

Index